THE NOVEL IN MOTLEY

LADY HAMILTON AS 'SENSIBILITY'

FROM THE ENGRAVING BY CAROLINE WATSON, ENGRAVER TO
HER MAJESTY QUEEN CHARLOTTE. AFTER ROMNEY

THE NOVEL IN MOTLEY

A HISTORY OF THE BURLESQUE
NOVEL IN ENGLISH

BY

ARCHIBALD BOLLING SHEPPERSON

1967
OCTAGON BOOKS, INC.
New York

Reprinted 1967

by special arrangement with Harvard University Press

OCTAGON BOOKS, INC.
175 FIFTH AVENUE
NEW YORK, N. Y. 10010

LIBRARY OF CONGRESS CATALOG CARD NUMBER: 67–18785

Printed in U.S.A. by
NOBLE OFFSET PRINTERS, INC.
NEW YORK 3, N. Y.

TO

MARY ORRELL AMBLER

AND

GAY BOLLING SHEPPERSON

WHO GLADLY LEARN AND GLADLY TEACH

FOREWORD

THE duty of acknowledgment becomes a pleasure when it can be directed to friends.

My thanks are due first of all to Dr. James Southall Wilson, founder and former editor of the *Virginia Quarterly Review* and Edgar Allan Poe Professor of English at the University of Virginia. He proposed this work, christened it, and read and patiently criticized it during the various stages of its long period of incubation. Much of what merit it may have is due to his shrewd critical judgment and exquisite literary taste. I am under hardly less obligation in this work to Dr. John Calvin Metcalf, Linden Kent Memorial Professor of English and Dean of the Department of Graduate Studies at the University of Virginia. He has read and ably criticized it and has generously contributed to it from his truly wonderful store of knowledge; he introduced me to the period it mainly covers in a stimulating course and was chiefly instrumental in procuring for me the means to carry on research. Among other friends who have helped by criticism and in various other ways are: Dr. Atcheson L. Hench, Professor of English at the University of Virginia; Dr. Majl Ewing, Assistant Professor of English at the University of California at Los Angeles; Dr. Malcolm MacLeod, former Instructor in English at the University of Virginia; and Dr. R. Cecil Garlick, Instructor in the Department of Romanic Languages at the University of

Virginia. Finally, a grateful word in memory of three
dear "female Quixotes," the late Misses Ella, Constance, and Rose Page of "Keswick," Cobham, Virginia who provided physical and spiritual sanctuary
in a home of unmatchable charm during many
months of labor.

My thanks are also due to the University of Virginia for awarding to me for a year the Bennett Wood
Green Fellowship, and to the library staffs of the
University of Virginia Library, the Library of Congress, the British Museum, and the Bodleian. More
indebtedness than can be acknowledged by footnotes
or bibliography is felt to three vigorous and scholarly
books by Governor Wilbur L. Cross of Connecticut:
The Development of the English Novel, *The History of
Henry Fielding*, and *The Life and Times of Laurence
Sterne*. I wish to acknowledge here also the meticulous and trenchant criticism that has been given the
book by Dr. G. Howard Maynadier, Assistant Professor of English, Emeritus, at Harvard University,
who read the manuscript and made many valuable
suggestions for its improvement.

A. B. S.

University of Virginia
August 29, 1936.

CONTENTS

THE NOVEL IN MOTLEY

I. THE BEGINNINGS OF PARODY AND BURLESQUE

THAT type of literary satire embraced by the terms 'parody' and 'burlesque' has in general been ignored by modern critics as an unruly step-child, not entitled to a place within the family circle of respectable literature. Mistakenly adjudged as unmitigated foolishness, as 'mere imitative ridicule,' it has been treated, when it has been noticed at all, with the half-patronizing, half-contemptuous attitude which serious-minded persons always assume toward those who wear the cap and bells. This attitude is perhaps due partly to the deplorable parodies that were written during the last forty years of the nineteenth century, — unfortunately the period when parody writing was most widely practised and the one in which its present reputation was made. "All parodies are bad," wrote Brander Matthews in *The Galaxy* for May, 1874, "but there are exceptions." The exceptions at the time he wrote were very few indeed.

In the eighteenth and early nineteenth centuries, however, when satire was a spontaneous form of expression, parody and burlesque occupied a place in literature that was far from insignificant. The quality of the literary satire that appeared in the form of fiction, and as a criticism of fiction, was especially high. During its first century, the novel received

from the serious critics only the most fitful and grudging attention. The periodicals noticed the majority
of novels with brief descriptive reviews into which was
thrown a word of praise or blame according to the reviewer's opinion as to whether the work in question
would do good or harm; for Richardson's view of the
novel as a moral instrument was still the dominant
one. In the absence of formal criticism, it is not surprising to find that parody and burlesque should have
proved powerful agents in controlling the excesses of
this youthful literary form. The popularity of the
novels of sensibility and the romances of terror is evidence that the readers as well as the writers of novels
were in need of such agents. Thus the burlesque
novel was created as a necessary balance wheel to the
serious novel; and for a century it served its purpose
well. It is not too much to say that by far the most
effective criticism of the fiction that appeared before
Waverley was in the form of burlesque and parody-
burlesque novels.

The word 'burlesque' as applied to literature has
been used indiscriminately to include caricature, travesty, and parody — themselves words of which the
meanings are not widely differentiated. 'Burlesque'
has been applied in a general sense when the work referred to was only partly humorous in intention or
when the elements of caricature and parody, or parody and travesty, were confusingly mingled. It seems
necessary, therefore, to attribute to 'burlesque' as
exact a meaning as possible and to define the terms
'burlesque novel' and 'parody-burlesque novel.'

'Burlesque' came into the English language from the French, but it was originally derived from the Italian *burlesco* (formed from another Italian word, *burla*, meaning 'a joke, fun, a playful trick'), and was first used in the early sixteenth century in the works of the comic poet Francesco Berni. The type of writing which it described — the broad, the coarse, the grotesquely humorous — is as old as any kind of writing; but the popularity and influence of Berni caused his word to be adopted in Italy and elsewhere and also gave a new impulse to burlesque writing. The French poet Sarassin introduced it among the court poets of Louis XIV, where it was made the fashion by Paul Scarron. The latter's works, having become well known in England at the time of the Restoration, inspired there a host of imitators, among whom were John Phillips, Charles Cotton, and Samuel Butler, author of *Hudibras*. Burlesque continued to be a favorite method of satire in England throughout the first half of the eighteenth century and thus was a weapon ready filed for the hand of Fielding, who was to attack with it the absurdities of the first English novel.

'Parody,' derived from παρῳδία, originally meaning 'a song sung beside,' early acquired among the Greeks the connotation of 'comic parallel' and was usually applied to literature. Hipponax of Ephesus, the earliest parodist known by name and sometimes called the Father of Parody, wrote in the sixth century B.C. a parody of the *Iliad*. His satires against two Chian sculptors, Bupalus and Athenis, are said to have driven them to suicide. Homer, Aeschylus, Sophocles,

Euripides, Ovid, and Vergil were the classic authors most frequently parodied. From mediaeval times numerous parodies of the lives of the saints, of the Mass, and of other religious ceremonies survive. The popular mediaeval beast epics, while consisting mainly of social satire, frequently parodied the form and style of serious works. In the Renaissance, political and social satirists used parody in the mock romance and the picaresque tale; and some of the Elizabethan dramatists, notably Shakespeare in *Love's Labour's Lost* and *A Midsummer Night's Dream*, and Beaumont and Fletcher in *The Knight of the Burning Pestle*, wrote parodies of contemporaries. In seventeenth-century England burlesque and parody, always mingled in fact, became confused in name. Dryden, Swift, Pope, and lesser writers combined to give to satire, which may include both parody and burlesque, such prominence and dignity as it had never before attained in England. Satire was transfused into all forms of literature, and it is not surprising that prose fiction, then rapidly advancing toward its evolution into the modern novel, should have frequently been the target and almost as frequently the instrument of satirical writing.

It is with novels written against other novels, rather than with novels of social, political, or philosophical burlesque, that we propose to deal. 'Burlesque' seems the most fitting term to use. It carries the suggestion of grotesqueness and extravagance, and includes the idea of parody, which is actually one of the devices, one of the forms of burlesque writing.

It is conceivable that a burlesque work might be written without the aid of parody; but every parody belongs to the general class of burlesque literature. Burlesque is the more independent of the two and is not obliged to follow, so strictly as parody must, the lines of its original; it ridicules not so much the form as the spirit or aim of another work. Lastly, burlesque usually attacks a group of works by different authors, or by the same author, which have a common character; parody, on the contrary, attacks one work only.

Even with these distinctions allowed there is still some overlapping. Consequently, two terms have been employed for the two principal types of the humorous novel that form the subject of this study. *Burlesque novel* is applied to that form of fiction which incorporates the salient features of some type of novel, by one author or by several different authors, and holds them up to ridicule or criticism by presenting them in an absurd, grotesque manner, incongruous with the serious intention of the original works. It must be borne in mind, however, that the burlesque novel is less broad, less grotesque, and less extravagant as a rule than general, or non-imitative, burlesque, such as that of Scarron or Butler. A *parody-burlesque* differs in only two respects: it is written against a particular work rather than a type, and it employs parody as the principal means of burlesque.

The relationship of the burlesque and parody-burlesque novels to the novel proper is twofold. In their imitative capacity they are essentially parasites, with humor as their main reason for existing. Like all works of humor they are also critical; the more successful ones indirectly rather than directly. It will be seen that burlesque novels have appeared with greatest frequency when some type of fiction has erred into extravagance. Likewise, parody-burlesques have appeared when some individual novel, such as Richardson's *Pamela* or Bulwer-Lytton's *Eugene Aram*, has presented an absurd view of life or a corrupt, specious system of morality. It will be seen too that in their corrective capacity as agents of morality and criticism these two closely related types of the humorous novel have exerted considerable influence on English fiction.

II. RICHARDSON AND FIELD-
ING: *SHAMELA* AND
SHAMELIA

AROUND the forge of the blacksmith's shop in the little village of Slough, about halfway between London and Windsor, on a late winter's afternoon of the year 1741, is assembled a group of twenty or thirty villagers. There is a small sprinkling of men and a child or two, but most of them are women. They are listening with absorbed and gaping attention to the words of a man seated in the centre. It is the blacksmith, and he is reading from a decent calf-bound volume, the twin of which is lying closed beside him on a work-table. The hard breathing and tense expressions of his audience tell of fascinated interest which it has never been his pleasure to call forth before, not even when he read them that thrilling tale about a shipwrecked sailor, so stirring to his own imagination. This story is altogether different; its scene is an English country house which might be any one of a dozen by which they are surrounded. Its heroine — for the central figure is a woman — is, curiously enough, a simple servant girl. But she is pretty and vivacious; and withal demure, religious, and honest, which is to say, virtuous, and that is to say, chaste. Except that she is such a scholar, and except that her name is Pamela, she might be young

Mary Martin, who has just got a place as waiting maid at Squire Enslow's, and whose mother is standing over there against the door with her hands wrapped up in her apron.

The blacksmith reads on in a halting, monotonous tone. His words tell how the young woman, Pamela, has just put up for the night at a little inn in Lincolnshire. At length she has escaped the importunities of her lovesick young master, and is returning, this time really returning, unscathed to the home of her anxious parents, the humble Gaffer and Gammer Andrews. But the end is not yet reached, as the still expectant faces of the audience show. With tantalizing deliberateness the story moves on to its delightful conclusion. Pamela is recalled by her repentant but still ardent lover; Pamela is married to him; Pamela is made a lady; Pamela is happy; everybody is happy, and there is general rejoicing. The face of Mrs. Martin relaxes into an audible prayer of thanks which proves a signal for even greater outbursts. Never before has a mere book furnished such suspense, such relief, such occasion for unrestrained enthusiasm. Words are poor things when one is genuinely moved. Led by their mentor, the band of listeners, now become a joyful mob, rushes through the door, down the street and into the parish church. Soon the twilight air of the peaceful street is rent by the clangor of a bell. And this is how the village of Slough paid its tribute to the first genius of the English novel.

The whole world paid tribute, paid it generously and vociferously. Pamela, the sweet and virtuous

Pamela, was the word on everybody's lips; and admiration for the book, the character, and the author was felt and expressed by the high and the low, the ignorant and the learned, the good and the wicked. Pope declared the book would do more good than twenty sermons; Lord Chesterfield commended the soundness of its moral teaching; Lady Mary Wortley Montagu grudgingly allowed the fascination of the 'fat little printer.' A London divine even recommended the novel from his pulpit. The storm of Richardson's success soon swept across the channel. Diderot acclaimed his masterpiece in a tearful eulogy; Crébillon acknowledged that without *Pamela* the Parisians would not know what to read or to talk about; the German translator declared that Richardson was on a par with Homer. The little moralist's head was completely turned, and no wonder, for within a few months after the appearance of his tear-compelling novel, he was to be even further gratified by the sincere flattery of imitation.

The lax copyright laws of the eighteenth century made not only imitation but even plagiarism feasible, and the horde of hungry Grub Street authors was only too eager to snatch the crumbs that fell from Richardson's plentiful feast. The first two volumes of *Pamela* had reached their fourth edition in May, 1741; in the next month appeared a spurious, anonymous volume entitled *Pamela's Conduct in High Life*, which provoked, in December of the same year, the third and fourth volumes of *Pamela*, "by the author of the two first." In November a French translation had been published as *Paméla, ou la Vertu Récompensée*,[1] and simultaneously, in England, *Pamela, a Comedy*, by James Dance [alias Love], in which David Garrick made his first appearance on the stage. Throughout the century in France, Holland, Germany, and Italy there appeared translations, abridgments, imitations, dramatizations, and adaptations in numbers too great to mention. The year 1803 saw the publication of Le Suire's *La Paméla Française*; and in far-away Italy, at so late a date as 1810, the virtue of the celebrated English maiden was being exalted through the medium of a musical farce, *Pamela nubile*, by G. Rossi.

The phenomenal success of Richardson's novel is too evident to be denied and too well known to need further substantiation here. His strong and immediate appeal to the reading public was due partly to novelty. Hitherto the two most popular types of fiction had been the disjointed picaresque tale and the long, digressive, pseudo-moralistic romances of Mlle. de Scudéry and her French and English imitators. In the seventeen-twenties Defoe had revived a drooping interest in the novel of adventures by bringing his heroes into closer accord with the experience of his public. But even so the settings of his stories were remote. Colonel Jacque and Captain Singleton went far afield; Robinson Crusoe inhabited a tropical island; and Moll Flanders, while she moved in the familiar

---

[1] Not to be confused with *Paméla, ou la Vertu Récompensée*. Comédie en cinq actes, en vers. Par le citoyen François de Neufchateau. Paris, 1794-95.

atmosphere of the London streets, was too exceptional and unappealing to provide that sense of interchangeable experience for which the eighteenth-century readers all unconsciously were longing. But Richardson, with his educated servant girl heroine, his domestic setting, and above all his average attitude toward ordinary human relationships, struck the fortunate chord. Pamela, Mr. B ——, Parson Williams, and Mrs. Jewkes are made of the same stuff as their author and his readers. The scenes and situations are those into which the most inexperienced of his admirers could transplant himself without an effort; and the sedative moral maxims which flowed with such oily smoothness from his pen, were tempered no less perfectly, because guilelessly, to the average taste. He cajoled; he flattered; he reassured. Never was there so beautiful an example of popularity achieved by the sheer force of being commonplace.

All should have been serene, but was not. In the very next year after the two modest volumes of *Pamela; or, Virtue Rewarded* had commenced their insinuating way into the public heart appeared *Pamela Censured*, in which the author dared aver that Richardson, despite his avowed intention to the contrary, was really a corruptor and not a reformer of the public morals. And before the outraged moralist could recover from this stroke he was confronted by another little volume, this time a mere pamphlet, innocuously called *The Virgin in Eden; or, the State of Innocency*; but to Richardson it must have seemed rather a serpent in Eden with a sting in its tail, for it had appended to it an impudent essay in which "Pamela's Letters" were "proved to be immodest Romances painted in the Images of Virtue."

Its author, Charles Povey, Gent., was clearly a religious fanatic with an unforgivably literal mind. "The Work," he states in reference to *Pamela*, "hath obtained a glorious Character in the Eye of Some; they recommend it to their Families equal to *The Whole Duty of Man*, to instill Religion into the Minds of both Sexes." But "I had not gone through two Sheets, before I perceiv'd myself, as it were, convey'd within the Circles of Lewdness; nay, even in the Bed-chambers frequented by Women as charming as Nuns, in company with wild Rakes. This is a true Resemblance of modest *Pamela*, and her wanton Master. What can these Representations be call'd, but Romances to corrupt the Morals of the Age? *Pamela* is dress'd in Airs, that cannot but raise vain Desires in Men as chaste as Joseph when tempted by his Mistress. All the images are so very natural that Way, that were they to be acted in a Play, there would not want an Audience of wicked Men and Women to excite their Passions to wicked Actions." And Richardson had openly declared that he had no interest in his novels except as instruments of moral teaching!

But the polemical Mr. Povey had not finished yet. "As I am a Christian, and beleive that I must account for every Act of Life, I dare not repeat some Expressions often mention'd in *Pamela's* Letters. To read them Virtue cannot but blush. What is more indecent than the Passages in the Summer-house, in

Mrs. Jarvis's Apartment, and at Night in *Pamela's* Chamber when she was undress'd, and her Master in the Room with the Servant-Maid's Cloaths on, and her Apron over his Face; as also that immodest Passage of their both being in naked Bed together? These Scenes are Paradoxes to me, to be printed and called *Virtue Rewarded.* Good God! Can amorous Embraces delineated in these Images, tend to inculcate Religion in the Minds of Youth, when the Blood is hot, and runs quick in every Vein? Are these Lights to direct the Soul to a crucify'd Jesus? Are they pictures to extinguish Vice, and restrain the Wickedness of the Times? . . ."

Perhaps this carping critic, so obviously misled by his own evil imagination, would not have been so annoying had not his voice been so insistent. But, unbelievable as it must have seemed to Richardson and his chorus of female admirers, the disagreeable book succeeded to a second edition in the same year.

And this was only the beginning of a deluge. Almost immediately an anonymous author directed another vicious thrust with *Anti-Pamela; or, Feign'd Innocence Detected*, published "as a necessary Caution to all young Gentlemen." Its heroine, Syrena Tricksey, is everything that Pamela pretended not to be. Naturally inclined to vice, she is encouraged by her mother. She is trained above her station and has all her hopes set on a wealthy husband or lover. Like Pamela she secures a position in a well-to-do family; but she makes the mistake of yielding to Vardine, the first gallant who hails her at the window. The mistake is realized, not after she yields, but when she discovers that he is penniless. Her reproachful mother aids her in securing another position as companion to an old lady. In this household she becomes the mistress of both the father and the son. Then her artful mother suggests a stratagem for securing the son as a husband; she must pretend that he has raped her and demand marriage. This scheme is almost successful, but the marriage is prevented by the discovery of the mother's plotting letter. Lover succeeds lover, and Syrena has finally degenerated into a common prostitute, when the story ends abruptly with a promise of more.

Syrena Tricksey is a strong indictment of Richardson's heroine. Her story is chiefly told in letters to her mother, which are signed "your dutiful" or "your obedient" daughter — just as Pamela's had been. The closet scene from *Pamela* is frankly parodied, and several descriptions of amorous engagements between Syrena and her lovers are modelled on similar passages in the prototype. Syrena has an innocent face and a mouth full of morals. On one occasion she "cannot forbear reflecting, how shocking it is when those who should point out the Paths of Virtue, give a wrong Bent to a young and uninform'd Mind, and turn the pliant Disposition to Desires unworthy of it." To her fourth lover, Lord R ——, she yields at their first meeting. He presents her with ten guineas "as a Token of his Affection." "'On these terms,' said she, 'I take it from my dear Lord; but were every Piece a Thousand I would reject them with

Scorn if offer'd as the Purchase of my Virtue — I am
no Prostitute,' continued she, 'and if I thought you
look'd on me as such, and having accomplished your
Desires would never see me more, I would this Instant undeceive you, by running your Sword through
my too fond, too easily charm'd Heart.' Lord R ——
smiled within himself to hear her talk in this roman-
tick Stile."

And some of Richardson's readers must have
smiled too and some of them rejoiced over this well
aimed blow at his moralistic heroine.

The next attack was also anonymous and indirect.
Antipamela; ou, memoires de M. D ——,[2] purported
to be the autobiography of a *femme d'amour*, who gave
it to the public for the commendable purpose of showing "how wrong Advice and Training can corrupt an
innocent Maiden." The heroine, when she has
reached the proper age, is given by her unscrupulous
mother to be the mistress of a man named Kiel. He
is rich, but he is hideously deformed. The young girl
rebels and flees with a charming nobleman, whom she
soon deserts for a still more alluring lover. From him
she is carried off by the persistent Kiel, who, under
the cover of anonymity and darkness convinces her
that his attractions are far greater than she had supposed. She marries him and he dies conveniently
soon. His riches then enable her to marry the man of
her choice. *Antipamela* is decidedly pornographic

[2] The title page says, "Traduit de L'anglois a Londres, MDCCXLII";
there is no trace, however, of such a book having been published in
France. It is assumed that the book, although written in French, was
originally published in London.

underneath its transparent moral veil; its only real connection with *Pamela* is that *Pamela* obviously inspired it.

There are many other such contemporary works in which Richardson is attacked — directly, as in Povey's *The Virgin in Eden*, and indirectly, as in the two 'anti-Pamelas' just discussed. Among them are: *The True Anti-Pamela; or, Memoirs of Mr. James Parry*, 1742; *The Fair Adulteress*, 1744; *The Life of Miss Fanny Brown; or, Pamela the Second (a Clergyman's Daughter)*, by John Piper, Esq., 1760; and, at an undetermined date before 1775, *Memoirs of the Life of Lady H———, The Celebrated Pamela*. All of these, in part at least, are imitations of *Pamela*; all of them draw on it for characters and situations; but each of them expresses disapproval of the work in part or as a whole. While this disapproval is not expressed in burlesque form, except for occasional parody of a passage or a scene, it is the same sort of disapproval as was expressed by the burlesquers, both early and late. Moreover, these works, partly imitative of *Pamela* but partly critical of it, help to establish an important fact — one that has received too little emphasis. [3] They show that Richardson was not accepted with the unanimous and unthinking enthusiasm with which he is usually accredited; that, even at the height of his enormous popularity, he was the subject of much unfavorable criticism — criticism which justly accused his novel of provoking immoral thoughts in the minds of his readers and of stimulat-

[3] See, however, B. W. Downs's *Richardson* (London, 1928), chapter iii.

ing imitations not so nicely glossed over with didacticism as his own work had been. They show also
that Fielding, although he was the first and the most
noteworthy, was not the only contemporary to pierce
through Richardson's specious philosophy of mate-
rialism.

There was recently republished, after a century and
three quarters of neglect in the lumberyard of abandoned literature, a brilliant pamphlet, about fifty
pages in length, which appeared in 1741, just after the
third edition of *Pamela*. The name of this first burlesque of the first English novel was *Shamela* [4] and its
title is an epitome of the method of its burlesque, for
the change of name is accompanied by a correspond-
ing change of character — the object being to show
that the actions and events as recorded by Richardson are shams and falsehoods. Too intelligent and too
honest to be duped by the naïve sophisms of the tech-
nically virtuous serving maid, the pseudonymous
author of *Shamela* possessed the courage and the
genius to give the world a logical and humorous, if
none too delicate, *exposé*. In doing so he showed him-

---

[4] The full title is: *An Apology for the Life of Mrs. Shamela Andrews.
In which, the many notorious Falshoods and Misrepresentations of a Book
called Pamela, are exposed and refuted; and all the matchless arts of that
young Politician, set in a true and just Light. Together with a full Account
of all that passed between her and Parson Arthur Williams; whose character
is presented in a Manner something different from that which he bears in
Pamela. The whole being exact Copies of authentic Papers delivered to the
Editor. Necessary to be had in all Families. By Mr. Conny Keyber, London: Printed for A. Dodd at the Peacock, without Temple Bar.* MDCCXLI.
The first edition was published in April and a second in November of the
same year. There was an edition published in Dublin in 1741 also. The
first reprint, edited by R. Brimley Johnson, was in 1926.

self to be a past master of burlesque method; moreover, he was a robust moralist, genuinely detesting hypocrisy and vice. But he nevertheless exerted enough restraint to prevent his denunciation from becoming too bitter, and enough detachment to forestall the accusation of personal animosity. He had too the judgment to write frankly and humorously about sex; and lastly, he had enough wit to make his readers laugh even while they were being preached to.

The man who in his day combined all these qualities, and who is almost certainly the author of *Shamela*, was Henry Fielding.[5]

He was admirably fitted for the task. Humor, particularly satirical humor, was with him an attitude of mind. Even when he is dealing with his most serious situations and characters, one can fancy a lurking smile upon his face, a smile prompted by innate amusement at the absurdity of human pretensions. Affectation, he declared, whether in life or literature, was an infinite source of amusement; and the corrective for affectation and insincerity was laughter. Fielding, the detached intellectual, produced laughter by means of satire — satire which was elevated into pure comedy in *Joseph Andrews* and *Tom Jones*, but which was the basis and inspiration for all his literary work. It is natural and fitting, therefore, that such a man should have been among the first to detect the insincerity of the conspicuously successful

---

[5] This is the verdict of W. L. Cross in *The History of Henry Fielding*; it has been corroborated by R. Brimley Johnson in his introduction to *Shamela* and by Aurelien Digeon in *The Novels of Henry Fielding*.

Pamela, and to attack, by burlesquing it, the Philistine morality of its characters and its author. Burlesque was not only Fielding's natural medium of expression; it was the one in which lay, at this time, his greatest claim to popularity.[6] What wonder then, when he saw his avowed enemies, hypocrisy and vanity, stalking so fearlessly abroad in the persons of Pamela and her unctuous creator, he should seize that weapon all ready to his hand, and sally forth to have a tilt with them?

The dedication of *Shamela* to 'Lord Fanny' is a thrust at Conyers Middleton, whose recently published *Life of Cicero* was dedicated to the effeminate Lord Hervey. This is followed by two congratulatory epistles in mockery of those that had been published in the second edition of *Pamela*. These letters, supposed to be addressed to the 'editor,' one from him-

---

[6] His first dramatic effort, the adaptation called *Don Quixote in England*, had been followed by similar pieces: *Love in Several Masques*, *The Temple Beau*, and *The Author's Farce*. April, 1730, saw the first performance of the inimitable *Tom Thumb the Great*, which, says W. L. Cross, "gives the first signs of Fielding's marvelous gift for parody," and achieved, next to *The Beggar's Opera*, the greatest dramatic success of the century. From 1730 to 1740 he had produced a multitude of poems, dramas, and pamphlets which satirized the theatre, fashionable society, and the corrupt administration of Robert Walpole. If we included his articles in *The Champion*, *The Grub Street Journal*, and similar periodicals, almost a hundred examples might be given. Moreover, his taste in reading leaned heavily in the direction of burlesque. He not only knew but had deliberately imitated the *Margites* ascribed to Homer, the *Satiricon* of Petronius, and *The Frogs* of Aristophanes; he had translated several of Molière's plays; and he had read and been strongly influenced by Scarron's *le Roman comique* and *Virgile travesti*, and by Samuel Butler's *Hudibras*. Lucian and Juvenal, Rabelais, Cervantes, and Swift were among his favorite authors. He was steeped in the literature of satire and burlesque.

self and one from John Puff, Esq., ridiculously over-
rate the book; they predict that it will be translated
into all languages and known to all nations and ages,
and the editor modestly adds that he is preparing several other letters and even verses for the second edition. The practical effect was to make Richardson
withdraw the commendatory letters from all editions
of *Pamela* that afterwards appeared.

Fielding's framework is also a take-off on Richardson's. A certain Parson Tickletext writes to his friend
Parson Oliver recommending *Pamela* as a book that
is being praised in every pulpit and every coffee-
house, a book which "resembling Life, outglows it,"
in which "modest Beauty seeks to hide itself, by
casting off the Pride of Ornament, and displays itself
without any Covering," and which "presents Images
to the Reader, which the coldest Zealot cannot read
without Emotion." Parson Oliver, after having read
the book, replied that he is shocked at this "Epidemi-
cal Phrensy" raging in the town and among the
clergy. He knows the true story of Pamela, for he lives
in the very same neighborhood that she does. He
has in his possession the actual letters which passed
between Pamela and the other persons concerned
in her history. The true name of this wench was
Shamela. Her father had been a drummer in a
Scotch regiment and stood in no good repute at the
Old Bailey. Her mother had sold oranges at the
playhouse, and it was even uncertain whether she had
ever been married. Parson Oliver encloses with his
letter the 'actual' correspondence between Shamela

and her friends; (it is mercifully far less voluminous than that recorded by Richardson). At the end of the book is printed another letter from Parson Tickletext to Parson Oliver, in which the former acknowledges that he has been misled and declares that he now believes the story of Shamela to be the true one. He has made some inquiries on his own account and has learned that Shamela is actually in town. Since her marriage to her master, she has deceived him with her former lover, Parson Williams, has been turned off, and is now being prosecuted by her outraged husband in the 'spiritual' court.

The letters forming the main body of the burlesque are an outline of the important scenes and incidents in *Pamela*. But the author has been able to alter completely the spirit and meaning without changing more than a few of the facts. Shamela is a pert, illiterate miss with no respect for her mother, who, it develops, merits no more than is given her. Since the death of 'that old Put,' her mistress, the young squire has taken a fancy to Shamela and has several times attempted to kiss her. She has pretended to be shy but has let him succeed nevertheless. On one occasion the sport has been spoiled by the entrance of Mrs. Jervis. "*How tiresome,*" she reflects in the first letter to her mother, "*is such Interruption!*"

In reply her mother warns her that she has a difficult part to act, and reminds her of her former slip with Parson Williams. Shamela saucily answers that when her mother reproaches her with indiscretion the pot is calling the kettle black, and that anyway she is going to repent of her sin with the parson and read some good books, since he has told her that that will make amends. In her next, Mrs. Andrews wonders how a daughter of hers could so have misunderstood her. All that she meant was that Shamela should take pains to be rewarded before she took any final step, — and not give something for nothing as she had in the former instance. She encloses a copy of Mr. Whitefield's sermons.

Richardson's famous bedroom scene offered easy game to the burlesquer. In *Pamela* Mr. B —— has hidden himself in the closet of the room in which Pamela and Mrs. Jervis are sleeping. Pamela, almost completely unclothed, is saved from being ruined only by the intervention of Mrs. Jervis, and by falling into a series of fits which lasted for three hours. She is represented as being in a state of fright and dismay; and, before she became unconscious, defended herself with commendable vigor. Richardson gives a graphic account of it all, dwelling on details with the obvious relish of a naturally lascivious mind freed from a show of propriety by the consciousness of his moral purpose.

In *Shamela* the facts are almost the same:

"Thursday Night, Twelve o'clock.

"Mrs. Jervis and I are just in Bed, and the Door is unlocked; if my Master should come — Odsbods! I hear him just coming in at the Door. You see I write in the present Tense, as Parson Williams says. Well, he is in Bed between us, we are both shamming a Sleep. He steals his Hand into my Bosom, which I, as if in my Sleep, press close to me with mine, and then pretend to awake. — I no sooner see him, but I scream out to Mrs. Jervis, she feigns likewise but just come to herself; we both begin, she to becall and I to bescratch very liberally."

Shamela then tells how she pretended to fall into a swoon but is really scarcely able to keep from laughing aloud as she passively aids the bashful Booby all she can. But Booby, alarmed at her apparently lifeless condition, instead of carrying on when she pretends to come to, apologizes for what he has already done, and retires. *"O what a silly Fellow is a bashful young Lover!"* is Shamela's moral deduction from this episode.

The keynote to the burlesque of the character of Pamela is the change of her name to Shamela, and it must be confessed that Shamela is the more convincing character. In her letters to her mother the reader is made to feel that he is at last getting at the truth of a matter about which he has had suspicions all along; that is to say, Pamela's virtuous intention in her relations with Mr. B ———. It is true that a confession of guilt is always more convincing than a profession of innocence; and the letters of Richardson's Pamela are little more than an attempt to justify her conduct in a set of exceedingly questionable circumstances. Nevertheless, there is in *Shamela* an air of frankness and sincerity, and a dependence on the logical, normal interpretation of motives that is not to be found in the preachments of the self-justifying Pamela. Animalistic Shamela, although she owes her very existence to her sedate and virtuous sister, is the more lifelike, and, despite her coarseness, the more appealing character.

The change of Squire B —— into Squire Booby is also significant of a change of character. Richardson makes us detest the lover of Pamela for his artful and relentless campaign against her virtue and forces us into toleration of him when he succumbs to her determined resistance and marries her. He is made out to be an almost irresistible force that exhausts itself against an immovable body. But in Shamela the force is anything but irresistible and the body only too willing to be moved, and so we have the ludicrous spectacle of a man employing strategy to obtain that which is his for the mere asking; and when we do not despise him for being a fool we laugh at him for his elaborate unpracticality. Thus the situation of *Pamela* is as ludicrously reversed in *Shamela* as it later is in *Joseph Andrews*.

Parson Williams, although his name remains the same, undergoes as complete a metamorphosis as the other two. He is no longer the dignified young cleric with a well controlled passion for his patron's serving-maid, but a rollicking, ale-drinking, tobacco-puffing young country clergyman, who is not at all backward about poaching on his master's preserves, whether it be on the hunting-field or in the servants' quarters. He has had his will with Shamela a year before the story commences, and means to go on having it, welcoming her marriage with Squire Booby as a means by which his own character will be protected and his revenue increased. He quiets his conscience with his theories that the spiritual and the physical are things apart, that a man can err in being righteous over-much, and that repentance and sermon-reading will make up for any sin. He is a sort of Blifil inside and a Tom Jones outside.

The minor characters of the burlesque are but slightly developed, and ruthless liberties are taken with the original story. Lady Davers and her genteel friends, for example, are declared to have been mere "inventions of the Biographer," and never to have existed at all; which is only another way of saying that Richardson's pictures of high life are too unreal to deserve attack.

Burlesque literature can be judged by laxer stand-ards than are usually applied, but even so, *Shamela*, while never vulgar, is brutal and coarse. It also has a sketchy, hurried air, as if it had been dashed off im-mediately after its author had finished reading Rich-ardson's novel, before his anger had had a chance to cool. But scorn and indignation are subordinated to laughter. As Mr. Digeon says,[7] the spirit of the whole thing is epitomized in a remark of Shamela's: "And so we talked for an hour and a half, about my Vartue," and later, "O what a charming Word that is, rest his Soul who first invented it." For Richard-son's morbid obsession with the theme, Shamela's creator offers as an antidote a whole-hearted, brusque, and at times uncouth frankness, which, while it may purge the system a little too violently, does at any rate a thorough job.

[7] *The Novels of Henry Fielding.*

Richardson was convinced that Fielding was the author of *Shamela*, and never forgave him. Nor is it any cause for wonder that Richardson, as much the dupe of his own specious moralizing as the most gullible of his readers, totally lacking in a sense of fun or humor, and fired with the zeal of a self-appointed reformer, should detest the man who accused him of insincerity, unnaturalness, and vice.

Joseph Andrews, published almost a year after *Shamela*, in February, 1742, was begun in a somewhat less boisterous spirit of raillery, with Richardson's novel again the object of the ridicule. In his introductory chapter Fielding comments on the value that biographies of great and worthy persons have in disseminating the seeds of virtue among the youth of both sexes. He cites as examples the lives of Jack the Giant-killer, Guy of Warwick, Argalus, Parthenia, and of the Seven Champions of Christendom:

> But I pass by these and many others to mention two books lately published, which represent an admirable pattern of the amiable in either sex. The former of these, which deals in male virtue, was written by the great person himself, who lived the life he hath recorded, and is thought by many to have lived such a life only in order to write it. The other is communicated to us by an historian who hath borrowed his lights, as the common method is, from authentic papers and records. The reader, I believe, already conjectures, I mean the lives of Mr. Colley Cibber and Mrs. Pamela Andrews.

It is thus that Fielding announces his intention of striking a blow at two of the men of his generation who most aroused his antagonism, using as a two-edged sword the character of Joseph Andrews. Here he presented the identical type of man that Colley Cibber had described himself as being, but, with delightful irony, added the one virtue that Cibber, for fear of being ridiculed, had not dared to claim — that of chastity. A thrust with the same weapon served for Richardson. Pamela's virtue was the most widely discussed topic of the day. But that which was so desirable in a woman, was, in a man, to the eighteenth century mind, absurd. Hence one of the most effective ways of ridiculing Pamela, and through her Richardson, was to set the virtue of her brother Joseph on a par with her own.

Joseph Andrews begins as a fairly close parody-burlesque of *Pamela*, but the burlesque element dwindles into occasional satirical thrusts in the main part of the novel, although it comes in again fairly strong at the end. The first ten chapters tell of Joseph's struggle to maintain his chastity against the importunities of Lady Booby. He is the servant; she is the mistress. He is the brother of Pamela; she is the aunt-in-law of Squire Booby. The situation is exactly the same as that around which Richardson's entire novel is built — with the sexes of the two principal characters reversed. But in chapter xi, Joseph flees from the scene of temptation (as his sister had not done!), and begins his wanderings through the countryside; the charming Fanny Goodwill is introduced as a motive for his virtuous conduct, and he ceases to be ridiculous and begins to have the reader's sympathy.

Joseph Andrews is in the main a realistic novel. From the time that Joseph begins to take on an entity of his own, independent of Pamela, real life rather than Richardson's novel becomes the moving force of the work. Fielding realized that a continued parody-burlesque on the order of *Shamela* must become monotonous, and that so long a novel must stand on its own merits, rather than on the defects of some other novel. But it is his method, and not his purpose, that changes. In a larger arena he continues to combat his two arch enemies, vanity and hypocrisy, so well impersonated in the two men already mentioned. But now as he destroys, he rebuilds; for realism has this advantage over satire, that it sets up something else in place of that which is torn down. Fielding's realization of this was a natural advance in the growth of his genius, in his progress from the youthful ebullience of his farces and satirical pamphlets to the ripe wisdom of his novels. Reaction in the hands of genius may be as strong a force as direct action; and the history of the novel, like the history of a people, may be thought of as nothing more than an account of force and counter-force. The novels of Richardson were a positive reaction against the extravagant romances of his time; but in their corrective rôle they themselves were guilty of absurdity. This absurdity, quickly apprehended by Fielding, was curbed by his capable hand. At first his instrument was satire; later it was realism.

But who was to raise the weapon against Fielding? Who would dare attack with ridicule that man who had proved himself so adroit a master of the art? Richardson had neither the talent nor the inclination, but was content to remain sulking in his literary harem, seeking solace from his female flatterers. An occasional spiteful letter to a friend was all the positive satisfaction he permitted himself. The truth is there was little opportunity for attack; the crevices in Fielding's armor were too well reënforced. Although *Tom Jones* came in for a share of abuse, this was chiefly criticism in the direct form. *An Examen of the History of the Foundling*, cast in letters from the author to a friend, is described by *The Monthly Review* as an abusive attack, ungentlemanly, ill-founded, and badly written. Still other pamphleteers baldly accused Fielding of immorality, of obscenity, and of offence against good taste. Only in one instance did the criticism take the form of fiction, and that can scarcely be called burlesque.

In 1745, the celebrated vagabond-scamp, Bampfylde-Moore Carew, had published his autobiography; not, it is true, written by himself but by a sort of 'ghost writer,' called in the eighteenth century an historiographer. Carew was a notorious leader of the gypsies and eventually became their king. His memoirs are thought to be authentic; and, since he lived in the neighborhood of Bath and is known to have been seen once at the home of Ralph Allen, it is possible that he and Fielding were acquainted. It seems that Carew was much offended on reading the chapter in *Tom Jones* about the gypsies. Although his own volume had already appeared, he took occasion, when it was republished in 1749, vigorously to attack Fielding and his book. There is first of all a long dedication in ironic vein "to the Worshipful Justice Fielding," containing many quotations from *Tom Jones* to illustrate accusations of lowness, coarseness, moral corruption, self-conceit, and hypocrisy. It closes with "a Parallel drawn after the manner of PLUTARCH, between Mr. BAMPFYLDE–MOORE CAREW and Mr. THOMAS JONES." Throughout the book, but chiefly in the first part, there are slurs at Tom Jones's character, comparisons being made between him and the villainous autobiographer himself, always to the latter's advantage. At the end there is a short summary of "the actual Facts in the Life of the Foundling"; these are amusingly distorted so as to make him out a villain. There is also some parody of Fielding's style; for example, a passage describing the death of the king of the mendicants begins: "Reader, if thou hast ever seen that picture of Seneca, bleeding to death in his bath, with his friends and disciples standing around him; then thou mayst form some idea of this assembly." As W. L. Cross remarks,[8] it is very amusing to observe the greatest rascal in all England thus picking flaws in the conduct of Tom Jones. It is of interest to note that the comparisons to *Tom Jones* were expunged from the 1779 edition of Carew's book as "unworthy, unnecessary, animated by personal spite, interrupting the narrative, and adding to the expense of the book."

It was in *Amelia* that Fielding laid himself most

[8] *The History of Henry Fielding.*

open to attack, but there is little criticism of it in burlesque form. In his first edition of the novel he had
had the temerity to inflict his heroine with a broken
nose, and his literary opponents never allowed the
public to forget about it. Moreover, since one of the
chief allegations against his second novel had been the
lowness of the life portrayed, the scribblers, the chief
of whom was Bonnell Thornton, combined the circumstances of Amelia's noselessness, as they were
pleased to term it, Booth's dissipations, and the
poverty-stricken condition of the principal characters
to make Fielding out a portrayer of the low and vulgar. *Amelia* became one of the battle-grounds in
what Fielding, as editor of *The Covent-Garden Journal*,
termed a "Paper War between the Forces under Sir
Alexander Drawcansir and the Army of Grub-street."
This war contains only a few episodes that are of interest here.[9] It seems that in one of his humorous
articles in the *Journal*, Fielding, under the name of
Sir Alexander Drawcansir, had referred to "Peeragrin
Puckle" and "Rodorick Random" as small com-
manders in the army of Grub-street, who, when they
learned that the opposing army was headed by a
younger brother of General Thomas Jones, had fled
incontinently from the scene of action. Smollett,
offended at the sally, retaliated a week later with a
sixpenny pamphlet entitled *A Faithful Narrative of
the Base and Inhuman Arts that were lately practiced
upon the Brain of Habbakkuk Hilding, Justice, Dealer,
and Chapman*, which he signed "Drawcansir Alex-

[9] For a full account, see W. L. Cross's *The History of Henry Fielding*.

ander." The pamphlet represents 'Hilding' as a disgusting reprobate, drunken, snuff-besmeared, and foaming at the mouth. He is pictured riding down the Strand on a jackass at the head of a bedraggled army of ragamuffins, numbering in their disorderly ranks the noseless Amelia, arm in arm with Booth; Tom Jones; a sheep-stealer disguised as the Man of the Hill; and 'a notorious felon and imposter' called Partridge. Their leader has been bribed to attack Peregrine Pickle; but when that doughty hero appears at the head of a band of Smollett's characters, they all take flight, except a few, who are arrested and sent to a 'house of correction.' To this attack Fielding made no reply.

In the same month appeared the first issue of a periodical created solely for the purpose of ridiculing Fielding. It was called *Have at You All; or, The Drury-Lane Journal*. Its editor, who styled himself Madam Roxana Termagant, was Bonnell Thornton. The paper had twelve issues. Every item of every number was aimed at Fielding under one of his various *noms de combat*, — Sir Alexander Drawcansir, Mr. Justice Scribble, Pasquin, etc., etc. At the end of No. 1 was placed the following mock advertisement of a volume which never appeared:

This day is published,
(In four Volumes Duodecimo, with the
help of Dedication, Introductory Chapters, long Digressions, short Repetitions,
polite Expletives of Conversation, genteel
Dialogues, a wide Margin, and large
Letter, Price but 12 s.)

SHAMELIA, a Novel.

Printed for the MAJOR GENERAL
Where may be had
The Works of HERCULES VINEGAR, Esq;
JOHN TROTPLAID, Esq;

_____

THE TRUE PATRIOT

N. B. These are proper to be bound with the
lucubrations of Sir ALEXANDER DRAWCANSIR.

Likewise,
Several d-mn'd Farces.
A Bundle of Political Pamphlets, by the same
hand, pick and chuse for a Penny.

The Complete JUSTICE OF THE PEACE.

It is a pity *Shamelia* was never written; poetic justice
would have been admirably fulfilled if the author of
Shamela had had to defend himself against this boom-
erang cast by his own hand.

A part of it *was* written, although it was not called
'Shamelia.' In No. V of *The Drury Lane Journal* for
February 13, was printed a burlesque, four or five
pages in length, designated as "A New CHAPTER in
AMELIA, *more witty than the rest, if the Reader has but
sense enough to find out the Humour.*" It recounts how
Amelia, surrounded by her numerous offspring, is
awaiting Booth's return, in the company of the erudite Mrs. Atkinson, who, having taken a drop too
much cherry brandy, is snoring by the fire. The
children continually shriek, "Mammy! — Where's
Pappy?" Amelia comforts them with some "Merry
stories about murder." When at length a loud knock-

ing is heard she quiets her agitation with several swallows of beer, but "as it was, she had no power to wag, but sat upright in her chair with both arms expanded, stiff and motionless as if she had been tied to a stake, or put into the ducking-stool." Booth, very drunk, staggers in, accompanied by Sergeant Atkinson. The Sergeant has to keep Booth at arm's length and hold his nose into the bargain. Amelia gulps some more beer, and oblivious of her husband's condition, clasps him to her "till her delicate nose scented something about him not savoury."

Booth's own nose has been reduced to a pulp and this enlists Amelia's *particular* sympathy. Mrs. Atkinson gives a horse-laugh on seeing his "flattened proboscis":

"'Monstr' horrend' inform' ingens, cui lumen ademptum! Hoc magis esse velim, quam pravo vivere naso Spectandum nigris oculis, nigroque capillo!'

"'Ha done with your Nasos and your Negroes (quoth Amelia in a pet) and don't ye laugh at other people's haps.' — 'Why, Madam, (replied Mrs. Atkinson, a little dumfounded) sure a body may talk Greek, mayn't one, without' — here a hiccup opportunely cut the thread of her sentence. 'God bless you, poor woman!' (Cried Amelia and lifted up her hands.) 'God bless you; I have no more need of God's blessing than you — Madam!'"

The burlesque continues for several more pages, less humorously and more obscenely. It concludes with the statement that the piece might have been spun out two more pages, if the breaks had been put in; but the editor wanted his readers to have three-pennyworth for their threepence.

It can readily be seen that Bonnell Thornton in attacking Fielding for vulgarity was guilty of greater
offence than was Fielding himself. The curious objection of eighteenth-century readers to having their fiction deal with scenes of poverty and squalor is here
illustrated. In fact, the most frequent criticism of
Fielding's novels and plays was that they portrayed
'low' life.

After Fielding's death there were found among his
books only two works of modern fiction; one of these
was Francis Coventry's *Pompey the Little; or, the Life
and Adventures of a Lap-dog.*[10] Published in 1751, it is
a satirical work which can still be enjoyed by the modern reader. The author takes the rôle of mock biographer and with much wit and good nature recounts
the birth, parentage, amours, and adventures of his
picaresque canine hero. He causes him to serve a
variety of masters in high and low life, to wander in
Italy, to visit London, Bath, and Cambridge, and
finally to die at the advanced age of fourteen years.
The main intent is satire on society, but contemporary literature is not neglected. Coventry states in
the introduction that he has been encouraged by reflecting that this is a life-writing age, "where no Character is thought too inconsiderable to engage the
publick Notice, or too abandoned to be set up as a
Pattern of Imitation. The lowest and most contemptible Vagrants, Parish-Girls, Chamber-Maids, Pick-
Pockets, and Highwaymen, find Historians to record

[10] Introduction to *Pompey the Little*. The Golden Cockerel Press, 1926.
(Reprint of the second edition.)

their Praises, and Readers to wonder at their Exploits: Star-gazers, superannuated Strumpets, quarreling Lovers, all think themselves authorized to appeal to the Publick, and to *write Apologies* for their Lives. Even the Prisons and Stews are ransacked to find Materials for Novels and Romances." He is confident, since the majority of books are written by the saddest and about the saddest dogs of the time, that his is superior from the point of view of subject-matter, if not of elegance and grace. Lord Clarendon, Conyers Middleton, and Henry Fielding are taken to task by name, and many others are satirized by implication. By far the most amusing part of the novel, and the only part that entitles it to mention as burlesque, is the 'Essay on Nothing.' It must be written, says the author, because that self-styled king of biographers, Fielding, has decreed it. He then rambles on in an aimless but delightful parody of Fielding's introductory prefaces; it is entirely without malevolence, for the second edition carried a laudatory dedication to Fielding as the greatest of English novelists.

III. THE OFFSPRING OF TRISTRAM SHANDY

THE birth of *Tristram Shandy*, the novel, was almost as sensational as the birth of the character. First of all there was a near miscarriage that night at Stillington Hall when Stephen Croft rescued the manuscript from the flames, where Sterne, annoyed because one of his auditors fell asleep, had petulantly cast it. But the book's greatest difficulty, like its hero's, was in securing a midwife. *Tristam* had been begot in January of '59; late fall saw him long overdue and that necessary official still to seek. Dodsley of London had declined the honor. But on January 1, 1760, after a period of gestation three months longer than the normal, he saw the light of day at York, under the reluctant sponsorship of John Hinxman. Once born, he proved to be an abnormally precocious infant with a propensity for heroics. The witnesses to his provincial birth had been enthusiastic but too few in number. Nothing would do but to get himself born all over again in London. This time Dodsley willingly consented to play the rôle of Dr. Slop, and on April 3, *Tristram*, with Garrick as godfather, achieved his public and official entrance into the great world. Meantime he had matured as rapidly as his far-famed kinsman Gargantua; but not even Gargantua, nor indeed Hercules, could boast of such feats as were to be performed in his cradle by this hare-brained offspring of a York prebendary and the Comic Muse. For this hero, in the modern sense certainly more human than divine, was destined to bewilder the world, his progenitor, and himself, by fathering at the age of four months, half a dozen children of his own, and by the end of his first year almost twenty more. It is true that most of them were deformed and all illegitimate; but there can be no doubt that *Tristram* was their parent.

Sterne was at first delighted. "There is a shilling pamphlet wrote against *Tristram*," he exclaimed in a letter to Stephen Croft, early in 1760. "I wish they would write a hundred such." Two years later, when his wish had been only half fulfilled, he was ready to cry "Enough!" So in the first chapter of the sixth book of *Tristram Shandy*: "Did you ever think the world itself, Sir, had contained such a number of Jack Asses, — How they view'd and review'd us as we passed over the rivulet at the bottom of that little valley! — and when we climbed over that hill and were just getting out of sight — good God! what a braying did they all set up together!

"— Prithee, shepherd! who keeps all those Jack Asses? —"

The reviews, imitations, burlesques, and parodies of the Grub Street "Jack Asses" almost certainly aided the success of *Tristram Shandy* more than they hindered it. Often unforgivably bawdy, because stupidly so, they nevertheless contain some wit at Sterne's expense, though not often to his detriment, and occasionally evince merit independent of the element of parody that is the basis for many of them. Frequently it is impossible, almost always it is difficult, to determine when the authors of these skits are burlesquing Sterne and when they are merely imitating him, for Sterne himself often wrote burlesque — in the broader sense of the term — and his imitators, even the most literal of them, necessarily wrote the same kind of burlesque, even when they had no thought of parody. When the element of parody or parody-burlesque was obviously present in a particular work, the fact has been stated in discussing it. In doubtful cases, an attempt has been made to offer a description which would leave the reader free to draw his own conclusion. Some straight imitations and a few direct criticisms have been mentioned for various reasons which will be apparent.

On April 19, 1760, was published a shilling pamphlet, — *Explanatory Remarks upon the Life and Opinions of Tristram Shandy; wherein The* MORALS *and* POLITICS *of this* PIECE *are clearly laid open,* by "Jeremiah Kunastrokius, M. D." [1] Like so many others that followed, it was printed in the same letter and size as *Tristram Shandy* so that the two works might be bound together. Its author, who pretends to be the son of the physician mentioned insultingly by Sterne in his first volume, states that his purpose is to furnish explanation for those readers in Mesopotamia, the moon, and 'other illiterate planets,' who

---

[1] The same author was probably responsible for *The Life and Opinions of Jeremiah Kunastrokius*, which appeared later in the same year.

do not understand *Tristram Shandy* because of the too great wit of its author. All the most improper incidents are selected, described, and proved by elaborate reasoning, in excellent parody of Mr. Shandy's manner, to be perfectly innocent. But the author's ironical intent is evidenced unmistakably by his interpretation of one of Uncle Toby's most famous remarks:

"— My sister, I dare say, added he, does not care to let a man come so near her****."

One would be inclined to imagine, that a man of my friend *Tristram's* strict morals had concluded the sentence before the asterisms and that they were a meer error of the press, though they had run through two editions, if he had not immediately added:

"— My sister, mayhap, quoth uncle *Toby*, does not chuse to let a man come so near her****," make this dash, — 'tis an aposiopesis. — Take the dash away, and write *backside* — 'tis bawdy. Scratch backside out, and put cover'd way in, — 'tis a metaphor; — and I dare say, as fortifications ran so much in my uncle Toby's head, that if he had been left to have added one word to the sentence, — that word was it.

Notwithstanding my strict reliance upon *Tristram's* veracity, and my great opinion of his uncle Toby's purity of expression, I cannot be induced to believe that his uncle Toby said *backside*, *bawdy* or *not bawdy*, or was metaphorically inclined to express himself in a *covered way*. Naked truth, I believe, he thought the best — four *asterisms* are but four *asterisms* — and ever since asterisms have been in use, we have been taught that their number should be supplied by a like number of letters to make out the sense.

Curious, indefatigable, unblushing readers, consider what letters will properly supply the place, without infringing upon the sense. — Mind I have already exploded uncle

Toby's "backside" and "covered way." What do you think of head? There are but four letters in that word. — *Arm* and *leg* have but three letters, and be hanged to them. *Thigh* comes near it, but there is a letter too many. — I have it — the *third*, the *twentieth*, the *thirteenth* and the *nineteenth* letters of the English alphabet certainly compose the word,[2] though it is not to be found in any Lexicon extant — I hope.

Later on we are told that Uncle Toby's hobby-horse was unquestionably ****, and his favorite argument the *argumentum ad rem*.

Explanatory Remarks is a burlesque, very well done in parts, on the style, and form, or rather formlessness, of *Tristram Shandy*. But it is even more a good-natured — a suspiciously good-natured — attack on Sterne's morals and on his inaccuracies and incomprehensibilities in political matters. *The Critical Review* believed "that the author [of *Tristram*] himself is here giving breath to the trumpet of fame; and, under the form of explanatory notes, pointing the finger at some of those latent strokes of wit . . . which may perchance have escaped the eye of the less discerning reader. The same turn of humor appears in this as in the former production." It does indeed, and the hand that wrote it is a friendly one. Surely, for a man who culled the best passages from his letters to his wife and included them in letters to his 'sentimental' mistress, such a trick would not have been inconsistent. Scarcely anything was.

[2] The modern 'curious, indefatigable, unblushing,' reader will do well to recall that the English alphabet of the time had only twenty-five letters, *i* and *j* being counted as one letter.

The wittiest and most helpful of the 'attacks' that appeared at this time[3] was *The Clockmaker's Outcry against the* AUTHOR *of The Life and Opinions of* TRISTRAM SHANDY. A company of London clock-makers are reading the book at a meeting of their club when their ire is aroused at the clock-winding episode. One of them in a formal oration before the others makes a mock condemnation, the style of which is a parody of Sterne's. The pamphlet is little more than an excuse to quote some of Sterne's wittiest and bawdiest passages and to make humorous com-ments upon them. The author quotes, and then adds, "O filthy, as well as what follows"; he quotes again, and then, "Here the cloven hoof appears." Another quotation, and, "*Before consummation!* O thou caitiff, as bawdy as ignorant!" In what follows he takes the opportunity of displaying an even more de-tailed knowledge of sexual matters than Sterne. "There is so frequent mention of begetting, and such promises of mighty discoveries to be made," he says in an aside, "considering the writer's philosophically-affected indifference to things sacred, it is strange he has not called his work the *Genesis* and *Revelations* of TRISTRAM."

At the end the orator becomes spokesman for the indignant members of his profession. Orders for clocks, he says, are being countermanded because of the immodest connotation of the word 'clock.' In-stead of the usual salutation, street-walkers now say,

---

[3] It was advertised in *The London Chronicle* for May 8–10, 1760. A corrected second edition was advertised in the May 15–17 issue.

"Sir, will you have your clock wound-up?" Watch-winding has become the signal between lovers.

Alas, reputable, hoary clocks, that have flourished for ages, are ordered to be taken down by virtuous matrons, and be disposed of as obscene lumber, exciting to acts of carnality . . . All this hath been occasioned by that type of Antichrist, that foe to everything that is good. His infernal scheme is to overturn church and state: for clocks and watches being brought into contempt and disuse, nobody will know how the time goes, nor which is the hour of prayer, the hour of levee, the hour of mounting guard, etc., etc., etc. consequently an universal confusion in church, senate, playhouse, etc., must ensue and we be prepared for the reign of that dreadful being so long foretold; and of which SHANDY is the undoubted forerunner. — Ah, woful for the sons and daughters of man!

> Time's out of rule; no Clock is now *wound-up*:
> TRISTRAM the *lewd* has *knock'd* Clock-making up.

Throughout the rest of May and in June and July the presses of London steadily rained imitations, serious and mock criticism, skits, letters, poems, and plays on the subject of *Tristram Shandy*. Its author was accused directly and by implication of immorality, salaciousness, irreverence, plagiarism, frivolity, and dulness. Guilty as he was of almost all these charges except the last, his accusers were usually more guilty; and the dulness which they wrongfully attributed to Sterne made their own crimes even more heinous. The bawdiness of Tristram was the cause of even greater bawdiness in others. "God forgive me," wrote Sterne to Miss Macartney, "for the volumes of Ribaldry I've been the cause of."

Besides lending his name to a horse-race, a salad, and a game of cards, Tristram gave inadvertent assistance to a succession of struggling authors who hesitated not at all to use his valuable name and the names of many of his family and associates, and even of his creator Sterne, without asking leave. *Tristram Shandy in a Reverie*, *Tristram Shandy at Ranelagh*, *Tristram Shandy's Jests*, *The Life and Opinions of Miss Sukey Shandy*, *The Life and Opinions of Jeremiah Kunastrokius*, *The Life and Amours of Hafen Slawkenbergius*, *Tristram Shandy's Description of the General Elections*, and many other worthless but annoying imitations, not to mention the several forgeries of the later volumes of *Tristram Shandy* published under Sterne's name, all appeared before April, 1766. The epithets hurled at them by the critical magazines — 'contemptible,' 'obscene,' 'absurd,' 'bawdy,' 'obscure,' 'dull' — were well deserved.

About the middle of July, 1760, was published a deadly serious attack on Sterne, which, nevertheless, contained much unintentional humor: *A Genuine Letter from a Methodist Preacher in the Country to Laurence Sterne, M. A. Prebendary of York.*[4] The chief grounds of complaint are that the author of a book like *Tristram Shandy* should have the audacity to publish a volume of sermons. "O Sterne! thou art scabby, and such is the leprosy of thy mind that it is not to be cured like the leprosy of the body, by dip-

---

[4] This letter was soon afterwards published in a garbled form as being by "the Reverend George Whitefield, B. A.," but was declared by *The Monthly Review* to be a forgery.

ping nine times in the river Jordan." The *Sermons*
"have been penned by the hand of the Antichrist"
and *Yorick* is a name that Shakespeare or the Devil
must "have put into thy head, and which thou hast
prophanely prefixed to two volumes of sermons."
Sterne is "wicked," "a libertine"; he "must have
rebirth," and "Jesus the man-midwife" will officiate.
He writes "to please whoremasters and adulterers";
let him "chew the cud of piety" which is "very different from Dr. Slop's wafer." He should turn Methodist, but no! the writer "can prove that you and all
your brethren of the Church of England are all rank
Methodists." Drawing inspiration from his own oratory he advances to an impassioned peroration:

You say that Tristram Shandy's misfortunes began nine
months before he was born, and I really believe that
your perverseness and prophane turn began nine months
before you were born.

Pray then for the new birth; there will be no occasion for
winding up a clock, regeneration does not depend on wheels
and springs ... Sterne, you have a hobby-horse and
that hobby-horse may lead you to destruction, except you
listen to some man of God ... Listen, therefore to the
advice that I give you, and don't despise it, because it
is given by a poor Methodist preacher. I know you are a
scholar, but should you be puffed up with the pride of
human learning, and criticize the words I utter, should you
look upon the words of sobriety as folly and enthusiasm,
God forgive you!

Yorick's Meditations, which came out late in June
or early in July, received and deserved more praise
than any of the derivatives of *Tristram* that had ap-

peared. The unknown author is a skilful imitator of the spirit as well as the style of Sterne's work, and is also a keen satirist and burlesquer. "The more I meditate upon nothing," he begins, "the more I am convinced of its importance. This same nothing has been of great service to many an author. I could mention one that has lately filled two whole volumes with nothing; the book's vastly dear; but what does it contain? why just nothing, and that proves the author's abilities. Any blockhead could write if he had something to say for himself; but he that can write upon nothing must surely be a superlative genius."

Between his meditations "Upon Midwives" and "Upon the Homunculus" occurs a digression on modesty, the chief point of which is to defend Yorick against the imputation of indecency. "Know, vile wretches, I despise your base misrepresentations; all the works of Yorick are as chaste as his sermons . . . 'tis you yourselves, whose impure imaginations make the obscenity you reprehend." He predicts that *Tristram Shandy* will become a book for the parlor window; and that the sermons, bound in red morocco and gilt, will remain triumphant upon the same shelves with the Bible, the Prayer-Book, and *Pilgrim's Progress*.

During the "Meditation on Hobby-horses," the author is interrupted by Uncle Toby, who comes riding in on his own hobby-horse, gets down, reads the meditation, and complains that so serious a subject should be treated lightly. When he had left, "I deliberated whether I had best follow his advice, or resume my meditation; and having concluded for the latter, rubbed my forehead two or three times, and stretched my head, an expedient pretty frequent with authors of this age, when they find themselves at a loss for a thought. . . . But after I had knocked several times for wit, and found nobody at home, I resolved to conclude my meditation, since my hobbyhorse grew restive and would carry me no farther."

A very general complaint against *Tristram Shandy* had been of the difficulty of understanding it, several critics having maintained that its incomprehensibility was the cause of its popularity. 'Yorick' discusses this in his meditation on "Obscurity in Writing":

From wandering in the mazes of digression, we descend naturally into the Bathos of the obscure and unintelligible. O, venerable obscurity! how many authors owe their fame to thee, from the mystic Jacob Behman down to the jocose Tristram Shandy. The more unintelligible an author is that pleases, the greater must be his genius no doubt. The meanest may please when he makes himself understood; but he must surely be a superlative genius who pleases, whilst his readers do not understand a word he writes. Obscurity! thy influence is equal in the jocose, the serious, and the sublime — the jest most pleases when it is most deep. **** would make a stoic laugh . . . You must know, Sir, that men have but two ends in speaking or writing, viz. to make others understand their meaning, or else to keep their meaning concealed. I have generally the latter in view when I write. Obscurity was always my idol, and surely great must be its excellence, since one of its great enemies has been obliged to acknowledge, that 'tis a characteristic of a silly man and a silly book to be seen through. It follows then of course, that obscurity is the characteristic of a wise man and a shrewd book. To what did all the sages of antiquity, who so long governed mankind by their superiority of intellects, owe their success? To obscurity. In what does the whole merit of a riddle consist? In obscurity. To what do the stars owe all their brightness? To the obscurity of the firmament. And in fine, what must the reknown of the most famous heroes end in? Obscurity.

In the meditation "Upon a Close-stool" he reflects how often the works of learned and indefatigable authors have visited such a place. Perhaps his own may some day end there. But no! he cannot endure the horrid thought — *The Meditations of Yorick* shall never be condemned:

> 'Ad ficum et piperum et quicquid chartis
> Amicitur ineptis.'

The book is chiefly an imitation of *Tristram Shandy*, but it contains frequent passages of parody. "This alone," said *The Critical Review*, "of all the numerous publications, palmed on the world for Mr. Sterne's, has catched the comic powers of the ingenious writer."

Late in December the author of *Yorick's Meditations* published *A Supplement to the Life and Opinions of Tristram Shandy*. It is but a poor attempt at another burlesque of *Tristram*, with digressions, irrelevancies, conversations with the reader and the critic, Latin quotations, unfulfilled promises to explain later, and above all hints of indecencies. The author gets Tristram born with a very vulgar description — but he does not know what to do with him afterwards.

The third and fourth volumes of *Tristram Shandy* made a belated appearance in January, 1761. This gave occasion for the publication, in March, of a rather elaborate work which, although it is chiefly an imitation of Sterne, also contains some burlesque and parody. *The Life and Opinions of Bertram Montfichet, Esq.* is a copy of the style, content, characters, and format of *Tristram Shandy,* even to the Greek motto on the title page of the second volume. The author, writing in the person of Montfichet (fixed mountain), commences with a long, laudatory dedication to Tristram Shandy, in which he acknowledges his indebtedness. The principal characters are Mr. and Mrs. Montfichet (Mr. and Mrs. Shandy), Uncle Dick (Uncle Toby), Bertram (Tristram), and three learned physicians, Black- , Blue- , and Red-beard. There is also a character, Yorrick, who, standing on a tub placed on a table, preaches a burlesque sermon on the text of Gay's epitaph:

> Life is a jest, and all things show it;
> I thought so once, and now I know it.

The occasion is a feast prepared by Uncle Dick, and the account of it is a parody of Smollett's "feast of the ancients" in *Peregrine Pickle.* The book closes with the author's boast that he has outdone Sterne, because at the end of his second volume Bertram has just been begotten. It is a dull book with a few bright spots. The author's promise to give the public two more volumes, if they were demanded, was never fulfilled.

The scribblers were silent for six months and then in late October came *A Funeral Discourse, occasioned by the much lamented Death of Mr. Yorick, Prebendary of York and Author of the much admired Life and Opinions of Tristram Shandy*, which was "preached before a very mixed Society of Jemmies, Jessamines, Methodists and Christians, at a Nocturnal Meeting in Petticoat Lane, and now published at the unanimous Request of the Hearers by Christopher Flagellan, A. M. and enriched with the Notes of Various Commentators." The orator's text is "Alas, poor Yorick!" and his purpose is to prove that Sterne is intellectually, though not spiritually, dead. His death was caused by the failure of the third and fourth volumes of *Tristram Shandy*, the failure being due to Dodsley, who forced Sterne to write while he was still the fashion. There is some good burlesque when the orator 'lapses' into the style of *Tristram Shandy*, apologizes for the lapse, and gets out of it again.

Sometime during 1761 was published *Explanatory Remarks upon the Fourth and Fifth Volumes of Tristram Shandy*, a continuation of the first set. The author was unfortunately unable to sustain the high quality of his earlier burlesque imitation.

The Life, Travels, and Adventures of CHRISTOPHER WAGSTAFFE, GENTLEMAN, *Grandfather to* TRISTRAM SHANDY was declared to have been "originally published in the latter end of the last century" and intended "as the full and final answer to every thing that has been, or shall be, written in the out-of-the-way way." The dedication is explanatory:

To Tristram Shandy, Gentleman,
QUEER SIR:

The following history of the Life, Travels, and Adventures of Mr. WAGSTAFFE, naturally throws itself under your protection. I hope you are not one of those purse-proud fellows that shun an *old acquaintance* in distress, to whom they have formerly been under *some obligations*. If he does not make so considerable a figure in the polite world as you have done, this ought in justice to be ascribed not so much to his want of merit as to the unsettled taste, and capricious judgement of this age and nation. However, let his reception be at present what it will, he is sanguine enough to believe that an impartial and judicious posterity will hold him almost in the same degree of esteem and veneration with yourself. This, among other well-grounded notions, is likewise the opinion of,

QUEER SIR,
Your sometimes admirer,
frequently imitator,
but more frequently burlesquer,
and many times neither,

THE EDITOR.

With mock seriousness, the 'editor' points in his preface to the many similarities between his book and Sterne's; and, since he claims that his work is merely the republication of a volume nearly a hundred years old, proves that Tristram Shandy is very much indebted to Christopher Wagstaffe. One chapter contains a set of rules which every author and editor ought to learn by heart: a book is a thing of no determined magnitude; a chapter is a part of a book, and sometimes, by the art of incoherence, may be a book itself; a short train, or a half a dozen lines of asterisks, signifies that an author's meaning is not to be understood, or denotes something bawdy or blasphemous, left out to be wickedly and absurdly supplied by the reader's imagination. Chapter xxiii proves that every man in England from the king to the cobbler is a "SON OF A B-T-H." Chapter ii of the second volume has a dedication to "all silly folk," who are declared to be the most powerful party in favor of modern authors. Near the end the editor calls his work a "vile, ridiculous imitation of *Tristram Shandy*"; he then reviews his own book and in the review prints, as if by mistake, a letter to a friend in which he tells of the rapidity and ease with which the book was written; he has written anything that has come into his head and if his readers are displeased, why, not one man in a hundred can say why he likes *Tristram Shandy*.

A Sentimental Journey was published late in February, 1768, and Sterne died less than a month later. These two events gave a favorable opportunity to the unscrupulous garreteers, and imitations appeared with slightly decreasing frequency throughout the rest of the century and the first two decades of the next. On the whole, it was better imitated than *Tristram Shandy* had been; but strangely enough, there were but few attempts to burlesque it, although its excessive sentiment and sensibility made it far more vulnerable than its predecessor. As with the derivatives of *Tristram Shandy*, it is sometimes impossible to distinguish between what is straightforward imitation and what is burlesque. Hall-Stevenson's *Yorick's Sentimental Journey*, 1769; Richard Griffith's *Posthumous Works of a Late Celebrated Genius*, 1770; *Sentimental Lucubrations*, by 'Peter Pennyless,' 1770; *Sentimental Tales*, 1771; *The Rambles of Mr. Frankly*, by Mrs. E. Bonhote, 1772; *The Adventures of a Hackney Coach*, 1781; *Yorick's Sentimental Journey Continued*, 1788; *The Letters of Maria*, 1790; *A Sentimental Journey through Italy, Switzerland and France*, by 'Mr. Shandy,' 1793; and *Maria; or, a Shandean Journey of a Young Lady*, by 'My Uncle Oddy,' 1823; all of these may be described as uninspired imitations or 'continuations' which contain little if any humor, burlesque or otherwise.

Of the better imitations the first was *A Sentimental Journey*, "by a Lady," published in *The Lady's Magazine* in installments from 1770 to 1774. It is a very uneven work. At times the style is in excellent imitation of Sterne's; at others, it is so extremely sentimental that we suspect the 'Lady' of being a sly and intermittent burlesquer. For example, the following passage, which recalls Trim's grief at the death of Lefevre in *Tristram Shandy*:

I gave her all the assistance in my power. A tear, which compassion had extorted from my eyes, was on the point of falling — I pulled out my handkerchief to wipe it off — But no, says I, putting my handkerchief again into my pocket; it is a libation to distress, and it fell on her neck — As I stood contemplating it — I could not help saying to myself — a diamond in that situation would not shine with half the luster. A second fell near to the first; and heightened the beauty of its sister.

In 1781, the playwright, Leonard Macnally, author of a recently successful two-act farce called *Retalliation*, had produced at Covent Garden *Tristram Shandy*, "a sentimental, shandean bagatelle, in two acts." It was fairly successful on the stage, was published in 1783, and had a second edition the same year. Macnally showed good judgment in using the language of Sterne as far as was feasible and in crowding his play with incidents from the novel. He published, also in 1781, under the pseudonym of 'Plunder,' an excellent imitation of *A Sentimental Journey* called *Sentimental Excursions to Windsor and Other Places*, described on its title page as "a shandean bagatelle, under various heads and tales." Some of the 'heads and tales' are: The Star and Garter, Origin of Hoops, The Waggon Rut, Traveling Picquet, The Poor Seaman, The Old Maid and the Old Soldier, Chit Chat, Story of County O'Dunn and the Queen of Portugal, *Un Petit Souper*, etc. The book had appeared in detached pieces in *The Public Ledger*. The author says that since Sterne had imitated Rabelais, Cervantes, and Montaigne, there is no reason that he should not imitate Sterne. Parentheses, pointing hands, dashes, etc. are effectively employed; the introduction is at the middle of the volume. Sterne's blank page is filled in with Sterne's unexecuted chapter on button holes — and buttons — written in a style which is perhaps an amiable burlesque of Sterne. The book is extremely *risqué*, but is lively and witty. The "Star and Garter" episode alone would entitle it to a better Jate than it has had.

Two short-lived magazines sprung up as further evidences of Sterne's popularity. One was the unsuccessful *Sentimental and Masonic Magazine*, which was founded by a young Irish student in 1792 and which expired after a few issues. The other lasted from 1773 to 1775. It was *The Sentimental Magazine; or, General Assemblage of Science, Taste, and Entertainment*, "calculated to amuse the mind, to improve the understanding, and to amend the heart." Although it contains, perhaps, no conscious burlesque of Sterne, there is certainly unconscious burlesque in the ludicrously sentimental passages to be found in almost every contribution. The advertisement commends the age for embracing sentiment, to which the former age was a stranger. It states that the magazine was to contain, in each installment: a sentimental journey through life; a letter from a town gentleman to a country gentleman, which might be sentimental, satirical, or critical; a sentimental fable in French, with a prize of a silver medal offered for the best translation; and a sentimental history, which, "at the same Time that it forces Tears of Sensibility from the Eye, shall inspire the Heart with the Love of Virtue." In the number for January, 1774, appears a "sentimental biography" of Sterne. A complete file of this tearful magazine exists in the private library of George Washington at Mount Vernon.

The imitations of Sterne did not end with the century. Intermittently, down to 1826, comic works appeared which in their titles, subtitles, or prefaces paid tribute by mentioning Sterne, Mr. Shandy, Uncle

Toby, Trim, or Yorick. In none of them does there seem to be any conscious effort to burlesque Sterne. Perhaps the latest burlesque of him that has appeared is *A Sentimental Journey*, "by a Sterne Shade." This short skit was reprinted in Walter Hamilton's *Parodies of the Works of English and American Authors*, 1888, without mention of the original date of publication. It depicts a traveller standing at the foot of Ludgate Hill trying to decide whether to go to the Lord Mayor's show. He is detained by his sentimental interest in the things around him: an ass drawing a barrow along Farringdon-street, a poor dead mackerel in a basket. He hears a small voice repeating, "I can't get on! I can't get on!," turns, and discovers a caged squirrel on a treadmill. But when he tries to set the squirrel free, it bites his fingers. At the end of the three chapters he is still standing exactly where we found him, and has not yet decided whether to go to the Lord Mayor's show.

These burlesques and imitations which have been examined bear about the same relationship to the history of the burlesque novel as the works of Sterne do to the history of the regular novel. They are exceptional, extreme, eccentric. To equal Sterne, by imitating him, was next to impossible; to excel him, even with the licence of parody and burlesque, was quite as difficult. It is the business of the burlesquer to imitate the idiosyncrasies of his author and carry them to the extreme. But at the extremes of eccentricity, of bawdiness, of sentiment, and of wit, the lesser writers always discovered that Sterne had arrived first, had arrived with mercurial agility and magic ease. This appearance of ease was deceptive and led many an unwary imitator and critic to underestimate and even totally to misunderstand this truly great and original genius.

Early in the childhood of Tristram Shandy, in September, 1760, Goldsmith had made him the subject of one of *The Citizen of the World* papers, which appeared in *The Public Ledger*. "It has been observed, and I believe with some truth, that it is very difficult for a dunce to obtain the reputation of a wit; yet by the assistance of the figure bawdry, this may be easily effected, and a bawdy blockhead often passes for a fellow of smart parts and pretensions." And later: "But bawdry is often helped on by another figure, called pertness; and few indeed are found to excel in one that are not possessed of the other." The point to these remarks is in the title of the essay: "The Absurd Taste for Obscene and Pert Novels, such as Tristram Shandy, Ridiculed." Goldsmith's point of view was shared so far by Horace Walpole and Dr. Johnson; but Goldsmith went even further. He was present to hear Dr. Johnson remark: "Any man who has a name, or who has the power of pleasing, will be very generally invited in London. The man Sterne, I am told, has had engagements for three months." But when, with Boswellian temerity, Goldsmith appended, "And a very dull fellow," Dr. Johnson, who was always as honest as Dr. Johnson could be, crushed him with "Why, no, Sir."

A persistent minority of critics has always maintained, like Goldsmith, that Sterne's effects are
achieved by the cheap devices of eccentric typog-
raphy, plagiarism, and indecency. We have tried to
show that these were precisely the methods, and frequently the only methods, employed by his burlesquers and imitators. Except in a few instances, most
of which have been noted, the burlesques missed fire
and the imitations were uninspired. Is not that
strong proof that Sterne's success depended, and depends, on something more than mere 'bawdry' and
'pertness'?

IV. THE MOCK ROMANCES; OR, DON QUIXOTE IN PETTICOATS

WHEN *Don Quixote*, first and greatest of the burlesque novels, was published in 1605, the romance of chivalry was in its last decaying stage. It had served its usefulness and outlived its period and would certainly have come to an end, though to a less glorious one, if Cervantes himself had perished in the battle of Lepanto thirty years before. Chivalry had gone with mediaevalism and even in England and Spain the Renaissance was a fact; full half a century back literature had begun its apelike imitation of the new manner of living and thinking. The real Don Quixote was Cervantes, tilting at the windmills of a dead but unforgotten literature; and therein lies the irony of many a burlesquer's jest. Literary satire, like other forms of humor, demands a sympathetic audience, which, in order to be able to laugh, must possess a potential if not an actual sense of the absurdity of the thing attacked. Thus burlesque and parody appear most often and most effectively when readers are already beginning to be surfeited with the type of literature that is being satirized. The appearance of *Don Quixote* was not merely a signal for the death of the mediaeval chivalric romance; it was also an evidence that the end was at hand. We shall see that this was generally true of the long line of burlesque novels of which it was the parent. Some of these have already been discussed; still others will be dealt with in later chapters.

The influence of *Don Quixote* in English literature was to manifest itself first in Beaumont and Fletcher's play *The Knight of the Burning Pestle*, produced about 1610; the boyish hero is an apothecary's son named Ralph, who creates much diversion for himself and others in the rôle of a knight errant. For almost a century, with a few exceptions to be noted later, there are to be found no imitations of the famous Spanish masterpiece in English literature. When the Quixotic character does reappear, in Steele's *The Tender Husband*, 1705, it is under the sponsorship of Molière, who, along with other French writers, had borrowed Cervantes' weapon to ridicule the 'historical' romances of Mlle. de Scudéry and her imitators.

These interminable romances, popular in France in the first part of the seventeenth century, were introduced into England even before the Restoration and took root and flourished there for more than a century. Thousands of pages long, vapid, diffuse, and artificial, they were written by the small group known as *les précieux*, who were attempting to keep alive the manners and ethics of another day, the system of courtly love. They were historical in the names of places and characters but in little else, and were actually written about contemporary events and characters. The central figure is a hero in the grand style, mighty and valorous, noble in mind and feeling, a relentless enemy, a generous foe, a faithful friend, and at the same time an irresistible but delicately sensitive lover. The heroine, although of the same high rank, is separated from him by 'insurmountable' obstacles, which are eventually overcome. The main outline of the plot is obscured under a heavy tangle of episodes and digressions, of adventures within adventures, and still other adventures within those. All of the principal characters have confidants to whom they recount the histories of their lives and from whom they receive the same favor. When not thus engaged, they carry on dialogues filled with moral sentiments, ethical disquisitions, and discussions of their highly specialized and artificial system of making love. The behavior of the characters, with their rantings and faintings, their fits of sensibility and their extraordinary repressions, is so highly unnatural and unconvincing that it is remarkable that these chimerical romances found a single reader. The fact is that they found thousands.

But almost from the first they began to receive the ridicule that they deserved. The contemporary satirist, Charles Sorel, took his cue from *Don Quixote* and burlesqued them in *le Berger extravagant*, 1639; his hero Lysis attempting to live the life of an ancient Gallic shepherd in seventeenth-century Paris. Saint-Évremond and Scarron, the latter with *le Roman comique*, written before 1651, followed close upon his heels. In 1659 Molière wrote and produced *les Précieuses ridicules*, which remains the most famous burlesque upon this school of romancers. The heroine

of this charming play is Madelon, intended as a caricature of Mlle. de Scudéry herself. She is a young
bourgeoise who has come under the influence of the
romantic fiction of her day. With her friend, she tries
to imitate in her own life the conduct which she finds
in the romances — with ludicrous results. Unmistakably descended from the famous knight of La
Mancha, she herself is the ancestress of a long line of
similar heroines who were to recur in English burlesque fiction for the next two centuries.

Molière continued his anti-romantic writing in *les
Femmes savantes*, *le Misanthrope*, and in still other
plays. In 1666 came Furetière's *le Roman bourgeois*;
in 1678 Subligny's *Mock-Clélia* depicted a romantic
maiden who imagined herself to be the heroine of a
Scudéry romance and fled from men who had no intention of pursuing her.

It is notable that the romances were translated into
English some years before the Restoration had introduced a vogue for everything that was French.
Translations of Mlle. de Scudéry's *le Grand Cyrus* and
Clélie, of La Calprenède's *Cléopâtre* and *Cassandre*,
and of Gomberville's *Polexandre* were all published
between 1647 and 1656. There is abundant evidence
of their popularity both then and later. Dorothy Os-
borne refers to them in her letters to Sir William
Temple; Samuel Pepys, after having reproached his
wife for telling stories out of *le Grand Cyrus*, later
succumbs himself and buys "Cassandra and some
other French books" — for his wife. It is notorious
that many dramatic writers drew their plots and

much of their style from these same romances. On Mlle. de Scudéry's *Almahide* alone are based plays by Lee, Settle, Crowne, and Dryden. Lady Lurewell, in Farquhar's drama, *The Constant Couple*, 1700, says that her first downfall from virtue was due to wrong notions imbibed from reading *Cassandre*. Seventeenth-century letter-writing for a time became heroic in style, the letters dedicatory to the plays being directly imitative of those in the romances. It was even the fad to write imitations. Roger Boyle's *Parthenissa*, 1654, his *English Adventures*, 1676, and Crowne's *Pandion and Amphegenia*, 1665, are examples.

England was no slower to imitate the satires than she had been the originals. In 1676 appeared a novel called *Zelinda*, by "T. D.,"[1] which was asserted to be a translation from the French of M. de Scudéry,[2] but which is really a parody of an heroic romance. During the next quarter of a century there followed a number of plays influenced by Molière's in ridicule of the *précieux*. Among them are Richard Flecknoe's *The Damoiselles à la Mode*, printed in 1667; Mrs. Aphra Behn's *The False Count*, acted 1682; and Shadwell's *Bury Fair*, acted 1689. In 1699 there appeared a work by an unknown author, an imitation of Furetière's *le Roman bourgeois*, called *The Adventures of Covent Garden*. Like Smollett's novel, it is the story of a picaresque hero named Peregrine and his

---

[1] Jusserand thinks T. Duffet. See *The English Novel in the Time of Shakespeare*.

[2] The romances of Madeleine de Scudéry were published under her brother's name. "T. D." probably supposed that they were written by him. Mrs. Lennox makes the same error in *The Female Quixote*.

adored Emilia; it is an anti-romance containing much satirical discussion of the heroic dramas of Dryden and others. Farquhar, in *The Beaux' Stratagem*, 1707, parodies the hero of the French romances in the character of Aimwell, who, when he declares his love, rants and rages like Oroondates.

Steele's *The Tender Husband*, 1705, deserves particular description because of its similarity to certain later burlesque novels. Biddy Tipkin, the heroine, is the daughter of a rich banker. ". . . By being kept from the world, she has made a world of her own. She has spent all her solitude in reading romances, her head is full of shepherds, knights, flowery meads, groves, and streams." Pounce, who thus characterizes Biddy, has promised Clerimont, a penniless young officer, that he will help him gain possession of Biddy and her ten thousand pounds. He tells Clerimont that if he talks to Biddy like a man of this world, he will accomplish nothing. Clerimont replies: "Oh, let me alone — I have been a great traveler in fairy land myself, I know Oroondates: Cassandra, Astraea and Clelia are my intimate acquaintance." Clerimont wins Biddy's love with his talk of a Scudéry hero, and she is willing to scorn convention and elope with him to avoid being forced on the man of her parents' choice, her boorish cousin, Humphrey Gubbin. Biddy is the first English example of the romantomaniac type of heroine, a type which reappeared frequently in the novels of the next hundred years.[3] Jane Austen's Catherine Morland

[3] There can be no doubt that Steele owed his conception of the char-

of *Northanger Abbey* is one of the last and best depictions.

The French romances continued to be well known in England throughout the first quarter of the eighteenth century and beyond. In *The Spectator* for April 12, 1711, Addison places among the books on the table of Leonora, a fashionable young lady: "'Cassandra,' 'Cleopatra,' 'Astraea' . . . the 'Grand Cyrus,' with a pin stuck in one of the middle leaves . . . 'Clelia,' which opened of it self in the place that describes two lovers in a bower." In the same year Lady Mary Wortley Montagu writes that in her youth the romances had corrupted her judgment "as much as that of Mrs. Biddy Tipkin's." In 1725 there was another English edition of *Cassandre*, and in 1731 of *Cléopâtre*. The sentimental notions derived from them were ridiculed in *The Beggar's Opera* in 1728. In 1730 and 1734 we find the romances indirectly caricatured in Fielding's *Tom Thumb the Great* and in Carey's *Chrononotologos*, both of which are mainly burlesques of the heroic drama *à la* Dryden and his school. Samuel Johnson confessed to Bishop Percy that when he was a boy he was "immoderately fond" of reading romances of chivalry, and attributed to these "extravagant fictions, that unsettled turn of mind which prevented his ever fixing in any profession." In describing to Boswell his wedding journey of 1735, he complained that Mrs. Johnson caprici-

---

acter to Molière. Several speeches in *The Tender Husband* were translated literally from *les Précieuses ridicules*, and others from Molière's *le Sicilien*.

ously rode first fast and then slow for the pleasure of forcing him to suit his pace to hers: "Sir, she had read the old romances, and had got into her head the fantastical notion that a woman of spirit should use her lover like a dog." In *The Rambler*, No. 115, 1751, Johnson introduces the character of a young lady, Imperia, who, "having spent the early part of her life in the perusal of romances, brought with her into the world all the pride of Cleopatra; expected nothing less than vows, altars, and sacrifices; and thought her charms dishonoured, and her power infringed, by the softest opposition to her sentiments, or the smallest transgression of her commands."

The French themselves had not entirely ceased to burlesque the heroic romances. In 1738 there was published at The Hague a burlesque novel by Marivaux entitled *Pharsamon, ou Nouvelles folies romanesques.*[4] It tells of a guardian who encourages his young ward Pharsamond to read the ancient and modern romances so as to become inspired with gentlemanly, noble feelings. Pharsamond takes his reading so seriously that he soon begins to play the romantic hero in earnest. Burlesque adventures ensue. In the end he and three fellow victims are cured by a quack doctor who accidentally discovers a remedy. This long and not very amusing imitation of Cervantes was translated into English by J. Lockman in 1750.

By 1750 the French romances had almost run their

[4] A later French edition was called *Pharsamond, ou le Don Quichotte François.*

course. Their long period of popularity in England can partly be accounted for by the scarcity of other types of fiction. In the seventeen-twenties Defoe, and, later, Richardson, Fielding, and Smollett had been creating the taste for a new type of fiction. By the mid-century, the reading public was willing and eager to laugh at the absurdities of the old. In other words the moment had come in England for a successful parody of the French romances.

Mrs. Charlotte Lennox, author of *The Female Quixote; or, the Adventures of Arabella,* was the daughter of Sir James Ramsey, Lieutenant-Governor of New York. Born in New York in 1720, she was sent at an early age to London, where she lost no time in becoming a professional authoress. She was befriended by Samuel Johnson, who assisted her with various translations and other works, and who, in the year of his death, said to Boswell: "I dined yesterday at Mrs. Garrick's, with Mrs. Carter, Miss Hannah More, and Miss Fanny Burney. Three such women are not to be found: I know not where I could find a fourth, except Mrs. Lennox, who is superior to them all."[5]

Although the modern reader may find *The Female Quixote* too long, and in some respects as tiresome as the romances Mrs. Lennox was burlesquing, it was well received in the author's own day and afterwards. It was, moreover, the first of many English novels to

---

[5] Clara Reeve, although she praised Mrs. Lennox, thought that her satire "came thirty or forty years too late" when "the taste for these Romances was extinct." *The Progress of Romance* (1785), ii, p. 6.

imitate closely the purpose, as well as the style, of *Don Quixote*. First published in 1752, it was reprinted in 1783,[6] again in 1810, and finally in 1820.[7] In 1754 it was translated into German, by an unknown hand, as *Don Quixote im Reifrocke*.

Mrs. Lennox received high approbation from two of her most famous fellow-craftsmen. "The writer has genius"; stated the author of *Pamela* and *Clarissa*, "she is hardly twenty-four and has been unhappy." But Fielding admired her too. "[*The Female Quixote*] is, indeed, a work of true humour; and cannot fail of giving a rational, as well as very pleasing amusement to a sensible reader, who will at once be instructed, and highly diverted."[8] He adds that he prefers it in many respects to "the inimitable Don Quixote." Still later, in his *Journal of a Voyage to Lisbon*, he mentions "the inimitable author of *The Female Quixote*." As a final tribute, the book was found in his library after his death along with *Pompey the Little*: the only two works of modern fiction, not excluding his own, which he had preserved.

The first English novel to satirize a type of literature, it is more readable than many of the better known serious novels of its day. It was destined

6 In the *New Novelist's Magazine*, vol. 12. The next year this magazine printed Alonzo Fernandez de Avellaneda's *A Continuation of the History and Adventures of the Renowned Don Quixote de la Mancha*, translated into English from the French by W. A. Yardley. In his preface Yardley states that there had been two previous translators, a Captain Stevens and a Mr. Baker. He declares that Baker's translation (1745) was a verbatim copy of Stevens's. Stevens's had been reprinted in 1760.

7 By Mrs. A. L. Barbauld in her *British Novelists* series.

8 *The Covent Garden Journal*, March 24, 1752.

to be a model for many of the later burlesque novels.

Arabella, motherless daughter of an English marquis who has retired from the world, is brought up in the utmost seclusion. Nevertheless, she receives a thorough classical education and becomes versed in all the accomplishments of a young lady of fashion. In addition, she is possessed of unusual personal charm. Beauty of face and form, grace, wit, and vivacity are added to all that is attractive and desirable in a young lady of her station.

Since she showed an early fondness for reading, her father has allowed her to roam unfettered through his library. Without his knowledge she has gained access to that part of the library which was her mother's, which contains the works of the French heroic romancers. She reads these voraciously, each one many times over; and, lacking any experience of the world, takes them for exact representations of life.

She has come to believe that she herself is a heroine, that her charms are irresistible, and that every man she meets is bound to fall in love with her. She must be proud and haughty, must receive the passionate avowals of her lovers with cold disdain, and never give them the promise of a favor until they have been her 'servants' for ten or fifteen years. She may command them to live or to die, and they must obey. One stern look from her eyes, she believes, will cause the death of any man. More than this she supposes herself to be in constant danger from scoundrels who are on the alert to rob her of her virtue. She believes, never having been acquainted with anyone but her father, that all young men and women hold themselves subject to the laws of chivalric love; that everyone of consequence has led an adventurous life, of which he will gladly tell the 'history' upon request.

The marquis, unaware of Arabella's romantic madness, invites his nephew, Mr. Glanville, to visit him, with the intention of arranging a marriage between the two cousins. Glanville, prompted by his uncle and by his own inclinations, proposes; but Arabella scolds him harshly for his boldness, not in loving her, but in declaring his passion so soon. She commands him to leave her presence forever. Glanville is mystified at first, but soon discovers the cause of her peculiar conduct. He reveals this to her father, who, enraged, commands that all the books be burnt. But the clever Glanville saves them, reads in them himself, and sets about winning Arabella back to a normal outlook on life. He really loves her and is convinced that she loves him, in spite of her haughty conduct.

Now follows a series of episodes in which Arabella behaves exactly as she believes the heroines of *Clélie*, *le Grand Cyrus*, etc., would have behaved under similar circumstances. These episodes occupy the major part of the two volumes.

In the end, Glanville, who has remained faithful and ardent, is the cause of Arabella's being removed to Bath. It is hoped that contact with the outside world will work a cure. Here she meets a sensible, elderly woman who had been similarly afflicted in her youth. Her sympathetic understanding is gradually bringing Arabella back to normal, but she is unfortunately called away. Finally Arabella, in fleeing from some men who she mistakenly supposes are pursuing her, is almost drowned in a river and falls desperately ill as a consequence. During a long convalescence she is persuaded of the absurdity and immorality of her conduct by a clergyman. She recovers in both mind and body, readily consents to marry Glanville, and all ends happily.

It can readily be seen that the similarity to *Don Quixote* is very great indeed. The general plan is exactly the same, and even some of the incidents, such as the burning of the books, are adapted with little change. Arabella has her Sancho Panza in Lucy, her unromantic but credulous maid. Loyal to her mistress in her most extravagant adventures, Lucy can never really enter into the spirit of them, since she is constantly encountering realities which her prosaic mind cannot transform into romance. Quixote-like, Arabella justifies each of her vagaries by citation of 'authority,' her head being full of quotations from her beloved romances. But in style and in most of the subject matter the two books differ as much as might naturally be expected. Mrs. Lennox is no female Cervantes, although she shows considerable skill and originality in adapting the Spanish masterpiece for eighteenth-century English readers. This is exemplified in the closing incident. It will be recalled that Don Quixote fell into a sleep that lasted for six hours, and that on awaking he declared that a heavenly vision had shown him the error of his ways. Arabella is cured by a clergymen — a heavenly agent, it is true; but his method is a logical argument which proves to her the folly and unreasonableness of her conduct.

In structure the novel is a succession of incidents strung on the thread of Arabella's romantic madness. On one typical occasion she, having noticed that the new under-gardener is dignified and handsome, becomes convinced, on these grounds alone, that he is a nobleman in disguise come to pay tribute to her beauty. She is torn between her desire to communicate with him and her conception of what ought to be the conduct of a romantic heroine:

These thoughts perplexed her so much, that, hoping to find some relief by unburdening her mind to Lucy, she told her all her uneasiness. Ah! she said to her, looking upon Edward, who had just passed them, how unfortunate do I think myself in being the cause of that passion which makes this illustrious unknown wear away his days in so shameful an obscurity! Yes, Lucy, pursued she, that Edward, whom you regard as one of my father's menial servants, is a person of sublime quality, who submits to this disguise only to have the opportunity of seeing me every day. But why do you seem so surprised? Is it possible that you have not suspected him to be what he is. Has he never unwillingly made any discovery of himself? Have you not surprised him in discourse with his faithful squire, who certainly lurks hereabouts to receive his commands, and is haply the confidant of his passion? Has he never entertained you with any conversation about me? Or have you never seen any valuable jewels in his possession, by which you suspected him to be not what he appears?

Truly, madam, replied Lucy, I never took him for anybody else but a simple gardener: but, now you open my eyes methinks I can find I have been strangely mistaken; for he does not look like a man of low degree, and he talks quite in another manner from our servants. I have never heard him indeed speak of your ladyship but once; and that was when he first saw you walking in the garden, he asked our John if you was not the marquis's daughter; and he said you was as beautiful as an angel. As for fine jewels, I never saw any, and I believe he has none; but he has a watch, and that looks as if he was something, madam: nor do I remember to have seen him talk with any stranger that looked like a squire.

But Arabella persists in her belief, and when Edward is discovered a few days later stealing carp from the fish pond, she persuades herself that he has really been trying to drown himself because she has refused to notice him. She seeks occasion to command him to live and be happy, but is prevented by his being dismissed from her father's service.

When she attends the races for the first time, she mistakes them for the Olympic games which she has read about in the novels of Mlle. de Scudéry. The jockeys, she supposes, are gallant knights riding in a tournament, "dressed in some peculiar modern style."

Sir George Bellmour, the clever, wicked (but not *too* wicked) Lovelace of the piece, is in love with Arabella. Since he has read the French romances too, he pretends to fall in with her folly, and on a certain occasion humors her in a request for his 'adventures.' She is prepared for something highly colored and romantic, and Sir George does not disappoint her. He demands fifteen minutes to compose his thoughts, during which the rest of the company must keep silence. Then he begins to relate a series of adventures, with himself as the hero, that would do credit to the imagination of the whole *précieux* group combined. Arabella is completely taken in; Glanville and his sister, understanding the situation, say nothing; but Sir Charles, Arabella's bluff, literal-minded old uncle, thinks that Sir George is an impudent coxcomb, shamelessly boasting of his own incredible exploits. He frequently interrupts the narrator with "Impossible!" "Preposterous!" while Arabella defends him with corroborating incidents recalled from the romances themselves. The situation is amusingly handled, and the parody digression contains the best satire in the book.

Although the novel has its amusing parts, it is too long to be really effective as a burlesque. The same situations are repeated with unpardonable frequency and with little variation. Moreover, Arabella is represented as too charming, witty, and sensible outside of her one folly to be convincing in it. Given the same fantastic background as Don Quixote, and she too might have been a pathetically humorous figure; but in English country houses and watering places, moving in a society of eighteenth-century ladies and gentlemen, she never quite comes to life. To do Mrs. Lennox justice, she was more interested in reforming the morals of her young lady readers than she was in making them laugh. At the time, novel reading was looked upon as a sad occupation for the young, tending to crowd the mind with silly fancies and to suggest wicked conduct to hitherto guileless misses. Mrs. Lennox was therefore writing not so much a humorous criticism of the romances as a serious warning against them. Such an attitude is hopelessly out of tone in a novel that ought to have been pure extravaganza, and it is only at the times when the author puts aside her earnestness that her undertaking succeeds. Like almost all pioneers, she suffers by comparison. Maria Edgeworth, Jane Austen, and Eaton Stannard Barrett all outdid her; but they owed to her many suggestions for their adaptations of *Don Quixote*.

In 1762, five years after his translation of *Don*

Quixote, Smollett published his wholly uninteresting imitation of it — *The Adventures of Sir Launcelot Greaves*. Since this ineffectual knight errant fought against social chimeras and not literary ones, the novel does not concern us here.

The only other one of the 'Quixotic' novels which requires special attention now is *The Spiritual Quixote*, 1772,[9] by the Reverend Richard Graves, which, although it is written mainly against Methodism, contains a lengthy episode of a young woman whose head has been turned by the fiction she has read. The hero, Geoffrey Wildgoose, is young, rich, and well educated, but lacks occupation. He hears of the new religion of Methodism and becomes an ardent convert. He precipitately begins an evangelistic tour on foot through the English countryside with a peasant named Jerry Tugwell as his Sancho Panza. Wildgoose is as mad on the subject of Methodism as was Humphrey Clinker, one year his senior; but at length he is restored to his right mind and returns home after his summer's wandering to lead the peaceful life of a country gentleman.

One of the means of his restoration to sanity is a young girl whom he meets at Gloucester in the home of a Mrs. Sarsenet. Her story forms an episode in the novel.

Julia Townsend is the daughter of a well-to-do country gentleman. Her mother having died, she is allowed by her

[9] *The Monthly Review* reproached the Reverend Mr. Graves for having used this title. In 1754 there had been a translation from the French of 'Rosiel de Silva' entitled *The Spiritual Quixote; or, the Entertaining Adventures of Don Ignatius Loyola.*

father to indulge indiscriminately a natural taste for reading. The books which she found most to her liking were the collection of an old maiden aunt; they "consisted of Dryden's plays, and all the dramatical works of the last age; novels, and romances of every kind." Julia decides to imitate the examples of the heroines about whom she has been reading. She runs away to London, with twenty pounds in her pocket, intending to make a name for herself and return home either wealthy, famous, or the wife of a nobleman. In the London coach a benevolent old gentleman, having learned her story, persuades her to return home the next day. But she oversleeps herself and misses the coach, remaining unprotected in the inn where the friend had secured her lodging. Her ignorance of the city and world in general makes her the easy prey of a procuress, but she escapes with her virtue intact and arrives eventually at the home of Mrs. Sarsenet, thoroughly cured of her attack of romantics.

The similarity between Julia and Arabella is obvious. It is interesting to note that both Mrs. Lennox and Graves found it necessary to account for their heroines' reading matter being out of date: Arabella's books had belonged to her mother and Julia's to an aunt. Both girls were brought up in seclusion, out of touch with the circulating libraries, which had long ago replaced the French romances with the more modern type of fiction.

The 'Quixotic' novels continued to be written down to the time of Scott. In later chapters we shall see how they were used to ridicule and to correct the extravagancies of the sentimental, the revolutionary, the Gothic, and the historical novel. We may briefly mention here, however, several of the type which are not burlesque novels in the sense of being burlesques of other works of fiction, but which employ the method of *Don Quixote* against the 'new' philosophy of Rousseau and his disciples. *The Philosophical Quixote; or, Memoirs of Mr. David Wilkins,* 1782, a burlesque of recent philosophical theories, was a two-volume letter novel — "dull for the general reader, and as dull for the scientists," said *The Monthly Review. The City Quixote,* 1785, a political satire, was also mediocre. *The Amicable Quixote; or, the Enthusiasm of Friendship,* 1788, in four volumes, was somewhat better; the story of a man in pursuit of friendships, it has interesting passages, but succeeds better as a sentimental essay than as a novel. It was translated into French. *William Thornborough, the Benevolent Quixote,* 1791, was received but with mild approval. In 1797 *The History of Sir George Warrington; or, the Political Quixote* was palmed off as "by the author of the Female Quixote." The hero's temporary madness is due to reading Paine's *The Rights of Man.* Lastly *The Infernal Quixote,* 1801, by Charles Lucas, is the story of still another villain who learned lessons in evil-doing from his reading in contemporary philosophy. This novel was also translated into French.

One of the earliest American novels was of the Quixote family. *Modern Chivalry; or, the Adventures of Captain John Farrago and Teague O'Regan his Servant,* by Hugh Henry Brackenridge, was published in four parts, 1792–1797. It is not a burlesque of a novel, its satire being directed against social institutions rather than against other novels.

V. ANTIDOTES TO
SENTIMENTALITY

MADAM, a circulating library in a town is an ever-green tree of diabolical knowledge! It blossoms through the year! And depend on it, Mrs. Malaprop, they that are so fond of handling the leaves, will long for the fruit at last." Mrs. Malaprop's reply, "Fie, fie, Sir Anthony, you surely speak laconically" seems less malapropos when we consider that Sir Anthony's sentiment was being less wittily and more wordily expressed by almost every critic of the time. 'Laconically' or ironically spoken, it represented the opinion of many an agitated moralist of the eighteenth century to whom the circulating library seemed a very baleful influence.

Fifteen years before *The Rivals*, there was produced at the Theatre Royal, on December 5, 1760, a comic skit entitled *Polly Honeycombe: a dramatick Novel*, by George Colman the Elder. Like Mrs. Lennox's Arabella, and like Sheridan's Lydia Languish, Polly Honeycombe has had a reading diet consisting almost entirely of novels — the modern novels of the circulating libraries. Her admired heroines have taught her to be contemptuous of leading a 'comfortable' life with the Mr. Ledger of her parents' choice, so she has given her heart to Mr. Scribble, who offers more romantic possibilities. After she has eloped from her father's house with Scribble and been dragged back, she learns that he is a footman and the nephew of her nurse. "Lord, papa," she exclaims, "what signifies whose nephew he is? He may ne'er be the worse for that. Who knows but he may be a foundling and a gentleman's son, as well as Tom Jones?" Her parents will not allow the match with Scribble, however, and Ledger refuses to marry her because he considers she has been contaminated. The father, in despair, ends the play with the sentiment that "a man might as well turn his daughter loose in Covent-Garden as trust the cultivation of her mind to a circulating library!" The epilogue was written by David Garrick:

> *Enter Polly, laughing: a book in her hand.*
> My poor Papa's in woeful agitation —
> While I, the cause, feel here (*striking her bosom*) no palpi-
>   tation.
> We girls of reading, and superior notions,
> Who from the fountain-head drink love's sweet potions,
> Pity our parents when such passion blinds 'em.
> One hears the good folks rave — one never minds 'em.
> Till these dear books infus'd their soft ingredients,
> Asham'd and fearful, I was all obedience,
> Then my good father did not storm in vain,
> I blush'd and cried, 'I'll ne'er do so again:'
> But now no bugbears can my spirit tame,
> I've conquered fear — and almost conquered shame.
> So much these dear instructors change and win us;
> Without their light we ne'er should show what's in us. . . .

Polly declares that by reading novels women will learn the art of war; thus they will get control of their fathers and husbands and rule the country; she will be their leader — General Honeycombe!

Among the novels which she has read are: *The History of Dick Careless*, *The Adventures of Tom Ramble*, *The History of Sir George Trueman and Emilia*, *The British Amazon*, *Tom Faddle*, *Clarissa*, *Tom Jones*, *Crutched Fryars*, and *Amelia*. But in the preface to the published play, Colman gives a list of one hundred and eighty-two more, extracted from the catalogue of a circulating library. Among the more lurid titles, from which the reader "may, without any great degree of shrewdness, strain the moral" of Colman's performance, are: *Agenor and Ismeaa; or, The War of the Tender Passions; Amours of Philander and Sylvia; or, Love-Letters between a Nobleman and his Sister; Amorous Friars; or, The Intrigues of a Convent; The Devil Upon Crutches in England; or, Night Scenes in London; The Fair Adultress; The Memoirs of Fanny Hill; Prostitutes of Quality; or, Adultery à la Mode.*

By 1780 the principal elements had united to form that type of novel which, along with the Gothic romance, was to occupy English writers and readers to an almost unbelievable extent for the next thirty-five years. With Richardson sentimentalism had come of age; with Sterne it had reached maturity; and soon it was to suffer an early senility in the works of such writers as Henry Mackenzie, Mary Robinson, Elizabeth Hervey, and countless others deservedly forgotten. The tremendous popularity of *Pamela* and its well known successors had not failed to have its effect on the second- and third-rate novelists of the time. Not content with mere imitation, they expanded the most florid and exceptionable portions of the novels that inspired them into long narratives of which the sole object was to thrill the reader with a succession of emotional episodes, tricked out with every device of sentimentality. The circulating libraries fattened and multiplied; and by making these inferior productions accessible to those who could not afford to buy them, they propagated among a new class of readers a taste for the cheapest sort of sentimental trash. The youth of the novel as a literary form and the inexperience of many of its readers were conducive to extremes. It is fortunate that in those days of the English novel's adolescence few more serious excesses should have been indulged in than 'sentiment' and 'sensibility.'

Most of these works can be read now only as literary curiosities. The best known and one of the earliest of the sentimental novels was Henry Mackenzie's *The Man of Feeling*, 1771. Fifty years after it appeared, a Scotch lady who had wept over it in her youth, tells of how she read it aloud to a group of friends, and how instead of weeping they laughed, and how she herself was unable to restrain her mirth. *Tristram Shandy* and *A Sentimental Journey* are the only ones among them that have withstood the revolutions of literary taste; the rest have become ridiculous travesties of their very selves.

A further glance at the titles of some of the novels and fictional essays of the day may prove illuminating. Between 1770 and 1780 appeared *The Assigna-*

tion, a Sentimental Novel; The Tears of Sensibility; The Sentimental Spy; The Embarrassed Lovers; The Delicate Objection; or, Sentimental Scruple; and *Travels for the Heart.* Between 1780 and 1790 appeared: *Distressed Virtue; The Effusions of Love; Female Sensibility; The Sentimental Deceiver; Sentimental Memoirs; The Favourites of Felicity; The Errors of Innocence; The Victim of Fancy; Excessive Sensibility; The Curse of Sentiment; The Illusions of Sentiment.*

Meanwhile the world of criticism had divided itself into those who attacked and those who defended the novel. It is characteristic of the period that the dispute should have been placed on moral, rather than artistic, grounds. Novels were seldom regarded as 'literature' before the time of Scott, and so it became a question of whether, as a means of amusement, they were harmful, harmless, or helpful to the minds of the young ladies who were always pictured as the principal novel audience. Critical discussions, outside of the reviews of particular novels, were rare indeed before 1800; but from the time of Richardson on, the literary journals had reviewed each novel from the point of view of its probable influence on its readers; frequently when the critic could find no other word of praise he would end his description with the grudging allowance that "the work can do no harm." The number of defenders was small, and that of the censors and burlesquers was great; but greater in force and numbers were those who unperturbedly continued to supply the public's demand for horror and tears.

In *Polly Honeycombe*, Colman had written against the circulating libraries as the means by which cheap literature was made available to young girls. In *The Sale of Authors*, 1767, an imitation of Lucian's *Sale of Philosophers*, Archibald Campbell also made the novels of the circulating libraries, and their authors, the subject of satirical jest. Among the authors whom Mercury, the auctioneer, disposes of to the highest bidder, is the 'Reverend Buffoon' (Sterne), who is seen laughing at his own jokes, which nobody understands but himself — jokes which have already appeared in *Tristram Shandy* and those which are about to appear in the ninth volume.

The Placid Man; or, Memoirs of Sir C. Belville, 1770, contains an interesting defence of novel-reading. In opposition to the views of the 'carping critics,' the author, Charles Jenner the Younger, regards novels as "pleasing and innocent amusements." Several years later Samuel Johnson expressed the same general opinion, when, in a conversation about the pernicious effects of *The Beggar's Opera*, he observed: "As to this matter, which has been very much contested, I myself am of opinion, that more influence has been ascribed to The Beggar's Opera, than it in reality ever had; for I do not believe that any man was ever made a rogue by being present at its representation."

But these were minority opinions; even the novelists themselves often held otherwise. A. Bancroft, in *The History of Charles Wentworth*, 1770, tells how the mother of his heroine withheld from her daughters

romantic novels apt to provoke their passions, allowing them only those that taught virtuous conduct. As
an awful example he permits another young lady to be
seduced because she has learnt carnal desire and light
behavior from reading the wrong sort of novels. The
subject of one of the episodes of Mackenzie's *The Man
of Feeling* is Miss Atkins, a common prostitute, who
attributes her first fall from virtue to the fact that
her reading "was principally confined to plays, novels, and those poetical descriptions of the beauty of
virtue and honour, which the circulating libraries
easily afforded." In *The Sylph*, a sentimental novel
of 1779 by Georgiana Cavendish, Duchess of Devonshire, the villain furthers his designs on a young village girl by lending her the 'pernicious volumes' of
Pamela.

Clara Reeve, in *The Progress of Romance*, 1785, expresses firm belief in the influence of novels for good
or evil. Despite the fact that she is the author of one
of the first Gothic novels, the works of fiction which
she is willing to recommend for the improvement of
young minds are few indeed: the only novels are
Richardson's. In *The Microcosm* for May 14, 1787,
appears a mildly satirical essay by George Canning.
With burlesque intent he offers for sale some admirable titles for modern novels: "Clarissa Clear-
starch," "Frederick Freelove," "Generous Incon-
stant," "Grogram Grove," "Gander Green,"
"Louisa; or, the Purling Stream," "Eliza; or, the
Little House on the Hill," and a number of others. In
the end, he turns serious and assails the current novel

for containing "observations without aptness and re-
flections without morality."

By the end of the century the feeling against novels
as improper reading for young girls had reached a
high pitch. The reviewers were almost unanimous in
judging works of fiction on moral grounds alone. *Will
Whimsical's Miscellany*, 1799, a Shandean essay on
various subjects, contains a statement which humorously summarizes the critics' point of view: "The
Girl who has inflamed her passions by 'Novel-
reading,' is a Piece ready charged and primed: the
least *Spark* (if I may be excused the treble pun?) —
will make her *go off*." In "The Good French Governess," published among her *Moral Tales* in 1800,
Maria Edgeworth displayed her usual balanced judgment in defending the *good* books and attacking the
bad. The young charges are advised not to read
"trifling, silly novels," but are encouraged to read
Dr. John Moore's *Zelucco*, which Mr. Gibbon had
called "the best philosophical romance of the age."
In *Ormond*, 1817, she records a remarkable instance
of the influence of novels on character. The hero,
who, in the seventeen-sixties was a youth of twenty,
accidentally stumbles on Fielding's masterpiece,
reads it, and resolves to "shine forth an Irish Tom
Jones." For some months he took to such "vagrant
courses" that Miss Edgeworth's prudish muse "fore-
bore to follow him"; however, he persevered in the
new found pleasure of reading novels and in time
came to *Sir Charles Grandison*. Through this the im-
pressionable young man was won to better ways and

so became again a proper subject for his author's pen.

The best contemporary analysis of the sentimental novel was given by the Scotchman, Hugh Murray. In 1805 he published in Edinburgh *The Morality of Fiction; or, An Inquiry into the Tendency of Fictitious Narratives*. His conception of the typical novel of manners is based, as he says, chiefly on the works of Charlotte Smith:

A young gentleman and lady, paragons of beauty and excellence, meet accidentally with each other. Both are instantly seized with the most violent passion, over which reason possesses no kind of controul. The lover throws himself at the feet of his mistress, or, by expressive gestures, makes a sufficiently evident declaration of his sentiment. She, on her part, is equally enamoured, but is withheld by modesty, or by the necessity of lengthening out the story, from making an immediate confession. This is at last obtained; but if the affair, as in ordinary cases, were to end here, the reader might have reason to complain of the scanty amusement afforded him. Obstacles must therefore be raised; inhuman parents, and detested rivals, must unite in opposing the completion of the lovers' felicity. Embarrassments arising from want of fortune are generally resorted to as the means of placing an insuperable bar to their union. On a sudden, however, these are removed; wealth flows in from unexpected sources; friends are reconciled; rivals are killed or discarded; the two parties are married; upon which the scene closes, there being nothing more to be done or said.

Murray adds that the characters are always perfect but that they are not engaged in active or useful employment, or in public life; they saunter from one place to another in search of amusement and are ex-

clusively occupied with love. Their ideas are of so refined a nature that frequently language fails and
blank spaces are left which the reader must fill in for
himself: "Hence these works, to such as do not find a
key to them in their own minds, appear wholly absurd and unintelligible; and hence, too, an unusual
exultation in those who can decypher the secret characters which are thus hid from vulgar eyes." Finally
the story is filled with improbable incidents, unexpected meetings, and unhoped for deliverances.

Copious illustration can be provided to justify
Murray's strictures. The question of parental control, for example, was agitated by almost every critic.
Beginning with *Clarissa* and *Tom Jones*, works of
fiction had consistently presented young people of
both sexes who disobeyed their elders not only with
impunity but usually to positive advantage. In Colman's list of 1760 appears *Bubbled Knights; or, Successful Contrivances*, "plainly evincing, in two familiar
Instances lately transacted in this Metropolis, the
Folly and Unreasonableness of Parents' laying a Restraint upon their Children's Inclinations in the
Affairs of Love and Marriage." In the same list
Clarissa is described as "comprehending the most
important Concerns of private Life, and particularly
showing the Distresses that may attend the Mis-
conduct of both Parents and Children in relation to
Marriage." Still another on the list is *The Impetuous
Lover; or, The Guiltless Parricide*. In 1793, appeared
*The Penitent Father; or, Injured Innocence Trium-
phant over Parental Tyranny*; in 1796, *Parental*

Duplicity; or, The Power of Artifice. In 1786, *The Novelist's Magazine* published a tale, by a Mr. Cumberland, entitled *Memoirs of a Sentimentalist; or, The Adventures of Sapho and Musidorus.* Sapho has been ordered by her father to marry a man she does not love. To avoid obeying him she plans to flee to a lonely cottage; but Musidorus, a 'superannuated sentimentalist' with whom she carries on a friendly correspondence, persuades her to elope with him to Gretna Green. She protests that she does not love him, but he reassures her by saying that he will gladly give her the protection of his name and that his advanced years will prevent him from ever making the demands of a husband. On the journey, Musidorus falls victim to an attack of the gout, which soon "flies to his stomach" and causes him to be seriously ill. A charming young soldier named Lionel appears from nowhere; Sapho falls in love with him. Her father, who by this time has arrived in pursuit, gives his consent to the match and they are married. Then Mr. Cumberland draws his moral, which is: that sentimental young ladies should never disobey their parents!

This really immoral tendency of the sentimental novel, as we shall see, was attacked by the burlesquers as well as by the serious critics.

Perhaps the favorite object of the burlesque novelists was the excessive sensibility of the heroes and heroines, which enabled them to divine things not perceptible to the ordinary person. Strangers could be distinguished as friends or enemies by a mere glance; friendships were formed between members of the same and opposite sexes after a brief word or gesture. The heroine of *The Castle of Ollada*, 1795, elopes from her father's house with a young peasant whom she has seen only twice and scarcely spoken to. *The Critical Review*, in pointing this out, reprobates all novels that contain such incidents and characters. But an astounding example of sensibility passed unnoticed by all the contemporary critics; it is to be found in *The Shrine of Bertha*, 1796, by Mrs. Mary Elizabeth Robinson.[1] Bertha is an orphan who is totally ignorant of the identity of her parents and of all salient facts pertaining to them. One day, as she is walking past a certain grove, there comes over her "an instinctive and irresistible impulse" that within that grove her mother lies buried. She enters it and discovers a grave, which upon later investigation, proves to be indeed her mother's.

Sensibility carried to extremes could be positively harmful, or so it seemed to the author of *The Excess of Sensibility; or, Charles Fleetwood*, published by *The New Novelist's Magazine* in 1786. This seriously intended *exemplum* warningly depicts a young man so imbued with sensibility that he is unable to tolerate the society of ordinary people. He visits three friends in turn: a man about town, a farmer, and a domesti-

---

[1] Mrs. Robinson published in the same year, *Angelina*, a novel in three volumes, of which *The Critical Review* said: "Were we permitted to consider this novel as a burlesque of romantic absurdity, we should certainly pronounce it a work of considerable merit." Her *Vancenza; or, the Dangers of Credulity* had three editions in 1792, the year of its publication. Her novels were extremely popular; several of them were translated into French.

cated father of a family; but he finds all of them too
crude for his newly refined tastes. On his way home
he stops in silent awe before a grand scene of nature;
but his mood is rudely broken into by a passing
stranger who bursts into a song called "Push about
the jorum." Fleetwood pales with disgust and walks
away, a solitary eccentric who has become the victim
of his own excessively delicate feelings.

Richard Brinsley Sheridan, with an artist's fine
sense of proportion, realized that the most appropriate attitude toward the current variety of sentimentality was satirical humor, of the lightest possible
quality. His caricature of the sentimental heroine in
The Rivals, although it appeared in 1775, too early to
correct the folly of his own generation, has provided
laughter ever since. It will be recalled that Lydia
Languish, like Polly Honeycombe, was a devoted
patron of the circulating libraries and that she too
used her maid to procure the forbidden volumes. She
possessed, as did Julia Townsend, a copy of *The Whole
Duty of Man*; but it adorned her dressing table and
was used "to press a few blonds, ma'am," and to conceal *The Innocent Adultery*, when Mrs. Malaprop entered the room. Just as Clerimont in *The Tender
Husband* was forced to use romantic expedients to win
Biddy Tipkin, so Captain Absolute must pretend that
he is Captain Beverley to countervail Lydia's novel-
induced repugnance to marrying a man chosen by her
aunt.

The first outright burlesque of the sentimental
novel was written by a sixteen-year-old Oxford stu-

dent in 1791. It is unfinished and was unpublished until 1839,[2] but it is interesting partly because it was the first, and partly because its author was Matthew Gregory Lewis, who four years later was to publish the most sensational novel of his time — a novel which was to offend in many of the very particulars that he had earlier burlesqued.

Lewis's youthful burlesque is entitled *The Effusions of Sensibility; or, Letters from Lady Honoria Harrow-heart to Miss Sophonisba Simper*; it is described as "a pathetic novel in the modern taste, being the first literary attempt of a young lady of tender feelings." In Letter I, Lady Honoria tells of her enforced depart-ure from her ancestral home to make a visit of a few weeks to London in the company of her father. For no apparent reason she is convinced that she will never view the "antique towers," "verdant bowers," and "moss-covered fountains" again. She departs by carriage in a passion of sentiment and tears. Her thoughts on the journey are concerned with an amia-ble youth whom she has seen but never spoken to, whose name she does not know, but with whom she is frantically in love. She arrives in London just in time to dress for the Duchess of Dingledon's ball, and although she is in no mood to receive the flattering adulation which she is certain will be accorded her by all the men of rank, "in order not to disgrace her father by refusing the invitation," she arrays herself in a "pale, blue-edged robe, with straw color and

[2] In Mrs. Baron-Wilson's *The Life and Correspondence of Matthew Gregory Lewis*.

slightly silver border, made up in the prettiest taste in the world, all [her] own fancy, and never seen before." When she was introduced to her dancing partner he "spoke with bold assurance and insolent admiration; he even dared at the first introduction to gaze at [her] in the face for at least half a minute, although he could not avoid observing the modest confusion which covered [her] diffident cheek with blushes." She dances to the admiration of all until the jealous Lady Mountain Mapletree throws a fan at her feet and causes her to fall and sprain her great toe. Indignantly she leaves the ball room, somewhat consoled by the murmur of compliments that are paid to her modesty and to her graceful retirement from an awkward situation. As her gallant hands her into the carriage, he says:

"I hope your ladyship will permit me to inquire tomorrow morning how your ladyship's great toe does." This was too marked a speech for me possibly to mistake it for any thing but an open declaration of the most ardent passion. I blushed violently; looked down in confusion, and hesitated for some minutes; till at length recovering myself, I replied, with admirable presence of mind, "Sir, you are very good, and I shall be extremely happy to see you."

Letter II is from Miss Simper in reply, and it reveals her as a caricature of the playful-sympathetic confidante of the type of Anna Howe in *Clarissa*. The burlesque breaks off in the middle of Letter III, Lewis evidently realizing that his satire is too exaggerated to be effective. It is impossible to say whether *The Effusions of Sensibility* is a take-off on Richardson's novels or on the imitations of them; probably it is both. In the ball-room scene there is some suggestion of parody of a scene in *Evelina*. Although there is too little incident and too much mock sentimentalizing, the fragment shows surprising ability in a boy of sixteen. It is true that Jane Austen's *Love and Freindship*, written when she was the same age, is superior in all respects, but it is hardly reasonable to expect as much from the author of *The Monk* as from the author of *Pride and Prejudice*.

The Advantages of Education; or, History of Maria Williams, 1793, "a Tale for Misses and their Mammas," was not so much a burlesque as an antidote to the novel of sensibility. Mrs. Jane West, a female intellectual with a sense of humor writing under the name of 'Prudentia Homespun,' declares in her introduction that the heroine of her novel shall be "simple in her manners, gentle in her disposition, possessed of an improved mind, and a benevolent heart." It is her intention "to explode those notions which novel reading in general produces, by delineating life in false colors. Expectations are formed which can never be realized; the consequence of which is that life is begun in error, and ended in disappointment." Furthermore, marriage is not to be held up as the "great desideratum" of the female sex. *The Advantages of Education* is an Edgeworthian sort of novel a little above the average of the day.

In 1797 the same author produced *A Gossip's Story*, also intended to counteract more than to burlesque the extremely sentimental type of novel. The two heroines are sisters. The younger, Marianne, like her namesake in *Sense and Sensibility*,[3] has been so affected by reading novels that she has become tender-hearted to a fault. Her eyes are frequently observed to 'swim in sensibility.' Her high-flown conception of the duties of friendship causes her to refuse the man she loves because she believes that her friend is also in love with him. The friend has expressly denied this, but Marianne thinks that she too is concealing her feelings for friendship's sake. Finally Marianne is married to her lover and is eventually cured. The elder sister, Louisa, is similar in most respects to Elinor Dashwood; she is sensible, calm, prudent, and serves as a foil for Marianne.

The anonymous author of *Susanna; or, Traits of a Modern Miss*, 1795, took for her central character the young lady who has received all her ideas about life from circulating library novels. A frank imitation of Mrs. Lennox's *The Female Quixote*, the book is lively and humorous, and, despite its too great length of four volumes, is reasonably entertaining to the reader of today. Susanna is a heroine enterprising in folly, who reforms only to lapse again, laughing meantime with the reader at the absurdity of her former pose. Having come to grief in her rôle of a sentimental young lady of fashion, she next imagines herself the persecuted heroine of a haunted castle. When the ghost proves to be merely a thieving servant who has taken advantage of his mistress's romantic folly, Susanna

[3] *Sense and Sensibility* was written in 1797, the year that *A Gossip's Story* appeared, but was later rewritten, and was not published until 1811.

becomes normal for a time, but is soon induced by convenient circumstances and further novel-reading to act as a languishing pastoral maiden, playing 'Amelia' to her lover's 'Celadon.' Her husband's untimely interruption of a tender scene and his con- sequent desertion of her give her the opportunity to assume the rôle of the persecuted but submissive wife. Soon tiring of this, she next becomes, under the tu- telage of the fashionable Lord Morven, a sporting young woman of the ultra-smart married set. With each change of character she affects a different style of dress. The distressed wife wears a Quakerish cos- tume of brown silk and her straightened hair is re- strained by a modest mob-cap; her air is drooping, her step slow and solemn, her eye downcast and mirth- less. But the gay young sportswoman appears in a scarlet habit, half boots, and a black velvet hunting- cap; her stride is mannish; her speech witty and boisterous.

Like her prototype Arabella, she suffers a long ill- ness near the end of the story and becomes normal; but for a time only. "One of those self-taught Methodist missionaries" happens to stop at a neigh- boring city "with a fresh cargo of enthusiasm," and Susanna listens to him at first with astonishment, next with conviction, and finally with zeal. Being fairly rich, she becomes a famous convert and promises to build a chapel in the neighborhood:

Her vanity was flattered by perpetual dedications of hymns and spiritual songs; her picture adorned the closets of the devotees; and her name stood foremost at their prayer meetings. Never before had our heroine been so celebrated; the fame she acquired by sacrificing the pomps and vanities of this wicked world, is incredible. . . . The chapel was actually projected, and a colony of preachers already established; but he who had the merit of her first conversion took the lead, and sat down [sic] in the comfortable birth [sic] of domestic chaplain.

Thus occupied, and in such a fair way to heaven, what more can I have to say of our heroine, who grows every instant too sublime for my pen? She has her rhapsodies, her manifestations, and inspirations; she exhorts the ignorant, who look at her with awe; and she reproves the wise, whilst they smile at these excesses; yet allow, that take it all in all, the *last trait* is the best.

Could the 'self-taught Methodist missionary' have been the eloquent Whitefield, and the neighboring city, Bath? Could the famous convert have been modelled after Selina, Countess of Huntingdon, that intrepid religious Quixote whose Methodist chapel at Bath, one of the half a dozen erected by her unlimited means and zeal, was visited by Lord Chesterfield, Lord Bolingbroke, and the Duchess of Marlborough? It was in this chapel that Wesley, "wondrous clean but as evidently an actor as Garrick," had, before his break with Lady Huntingdon, displeased the fastidious Horace Walpole with his "very ugly enthusiasm." Here too, prudently screened in the curtained recess of 'Nicodemus's corner,' certain bishops of the Church of England had indulged their inimical curiosity. The death of the nobly-born enthusiast occurred four years before the novel *Susanna* was published; but to its readers she was still a living personality, and must have seemed a more than probable prototype for the heroine.

Some of the minor characters of *Susanna* are also parodies of novel heroines. The sentimental Miss Dawson, after a disgraceful quarrel with a rival outside of her box at the opera, "pushed open the door, and stood confessed," before the gaping audience, "in all the elegance of passion." The new vogue for Shakespeare has been taken up by another young lady of the same sort: "I have studied Shakespeare," she exclaims after having just misquoted a passage, "sweet bard of nature! Oh how I adore his works! I live on them! absolutely I could exist days with no other sustenance!" The bourgeois Benfields have rashly named their daughters after novel heroines, and have reason to regret it; for though they were poor, "it was as utterly out of reason to expect Selina Ethelinda would make pyes, or superintend the cooking, as to imagine Adeline Clara Eleonora could darn stockings, or iron her own linen."

Just as in *The Female Quixote*, reality too often encroached upon burlesque. Occasionally too the burlesquer commits a blunder that betrays the sentimentalist that at heart she is. In the first volume, which, by the way, is fairly close parody of *Clarissa*, Susanna is commanded by her father to marry the stodgy Mr. Kirkman. She defiantly refuses, then later consents under compulsion, but a week before the wedding she runs away to the protection of the unwilling Lord Morven, and is at length brought home in disgrace. Her folly had made such ravages on her father that "the *gout*, which had for many days been flying about him, had, in consequence of his extreme anxiety, made a sudden and violent attack on his *stomach*." The doctor declared that he could not live for twenty-four hours, and his "prediction proved but too true; for the next day saw Mr. Bridgeman stretched out, the victim of parental anxiety!"

The author of *Susanna* must be given credit for being the first to burlesque a convention that was as prominent in the sentimental novel as was the haunted castle in the Gothic. Situated in some secluded vale among the hills of Western Britain, perhaps in Usk, perhaps in the enchanted region of Avalon, is a vine-covered cottage. It nestles among the trees of a shady grove, close by a purling stream bordered with flowers that bloom all the year round. Flower-lined too are the paths that wind leisurely through the grove and lead to secret grottoes where dwell the Muses. Within the cottage all is harmony and peace. A few volumes of verse, bound in vellum and written in the antique lettering of the mediaeval age; some musical instruments, a lute, a harp; a landscape traced by the pencil of the fair denizen of the place; these are all that proclaim it to be the abode of any other than the simplest rustic. This shrine of friendship and Platonic love was erected by Sir Philip Sidney for the Countess of Pembroke, and was consecrated for the modest retirement of those who, weary of the strife and hardships of an unfeeling world, sought the peace of solitude and the solace of seclusion. For a hundred years and more it was de-

serted. Millamant and the other Restoration ladies
could satisfy their bucolic proclivities with a stroll in
St. James's Park. A villa at Richmond or at Kew,
perhaps, but Wales! a cottage! (Mincing, my smell-
ing salts! I vow and declare this monster Mirabel has
given me the vapours with his barbarous suggestions.)

This place of retreat was sought again by the senti-
timental heroines of the mid-eighteenth century and
its air of antiquity and desertion made it all the more
charming for them. Sarah Fielding's Ophelia was
among the first to take refuge there and some years
later the establishment was put on a practicable running basis by the German bread-and-butter-cutting
Charlotte. After that it was seldom without one fair
occupant, and usually more; for however eagerly the
sentimental misses might anticipate seclusion, most
of them were human enough to desire, like Maria
Edgeworth's Angelina, "some kindred soul to whom
they might exclaim, 'How charming is solitude!'"

By the time *Susanna* was published in 1795 the
romantic cottage was a well known convention.
Emily St. Aubert had already resided there, *The
Mysteries of Udolpho* having been published in 1794.
In 1786 had come *Love in a Cottage*, by R. Walwyn;
in 1788, *The Cottage of Friendship*, by 'Sylvania
Pastorella'; and a few years before, *Louisa; or, The
Cottage on the Moor*, by Mrs. Helme. *Susanna* contains a burlesque description of the typical cottage, as
does Beckford's *Modern Novel Writing*, published the
next year. Five years later, Maria Edgeworth made
it a feature of her burlesque tale *Angelina; or, L'amie*

inconnue. But despite the burlesques the 'cottage' novels continued to appear uninterruptedly for the next twenty years: *Matilda; or, The Welch Cottage, The Cottage of Merlin Vale, The Mystic Cottager, Alexes; or, The Cottage in the Woods, Lovely Cottager on the Moor, The Cottage Girl, The Cottage Boy,* and *The Cottage of Glenbourne.* Amanda Fitzalan of *The Children of the Abbey* nursed her wounded heart, breakfasted on goat's whey, and quoted Cowper and Akenside in Edwin's cottage in Wales; in one soul-satisfying tale the Gothic and the sentimental heroines were united in *The Cottage of Mystery*!

Susanna had attracted much favorable attention from the reviewers; even more was accorded to two burlesque novels of similar purpose which appeared in the two succeeding years. *The Elegant Enthusiast; or, Modern Novel Writing,* 1796, by 'The Right Hon. Lady Harriet Harlow' and *Azemia,* 1797, by 'Jacqueta Agneta Mariana Jenks,' were correctly judged by *The Monthly Review* to be by the same author, and that author a man. It is now well known that they were from the pen of the wealthy and eccentric William Beckford of Fonthill Abbey.

The suggestion for them must have entered his mind as early as 1790. In that year his step-sister, Mrs. Elizabeth Hervey, published her *Louisa; or, The Reward of an Affectionate Daughter,* a sentimental novel of the Richardsonian order. Although not her first novel, it was a poor one, illustrative of most of the faults of her contemporaries. William Beckford was a good critic, but he was also an affectionate brother;

he compared her novel to Miss Burney's and told her it was better. As for her, she could not help "quaffing with delight the Bowl of Flattery" which he presented. She had never dared to think that he would find so much to please him in the tale, and what pleased her most was that he approved of what she herself deemed the best parts of the book. Beckford's kindly deception was well contrived. Even when his burlesques appeared, the gullible lady "read them quite innocently, and only now and then suspecting that they were meant to laugh at her, saying, 'Why, I vow and protest, here is my grotto, etc. etc.'"

The heroine of *Modern Novel Writing* is Arabella Bloomville; she has a beautiful form, which is "an animated portrait of her mind." She resides in an elegant, retired cottage "at the foot of a verdant declivity overshadowed by woodbine, jessamine, and myrtle, and softly inundated by a sapphire rivulet that wandered through the neighboring woods in serpentine simplicity." The pursuing villain is Lord Mahogany (Lovelace), who is aided by a wicked marchioness (Mrs. Jewkes). Disguised as a drunken maid, he enters Arabella's bedchamber where she lies asleep beside the marchioness; he undresses and crawls into bed. He clasps Arabella's waist and puts his hand into her bosom. Pamela-like (or Shamela-like), she swoons away for half an hour. When she recovers, Lord Mahogany protests that he has not offered her the least indecency. But he clasps her again and she immediately swoons again. When she recovers the second time, Lord Mahogany has departed . . .

Of course Arabella is ignorant of her parentage. One day she enters a room containing a large company of people — among them, the Countess of Fairville. Upon beholding Arabella the Countess swoons, recovers, drinks a cup of coffee, declares that she has seen her first husband under a female form, swoons again, recovers again, and requests Arabella to remove her glove. Then she recognizes her long lost child by a strawberry mark on her arm.

Arabella fell at the feet of her new Mamma and bathed her hand with tears. "Gracious me! For what have I been reserved!" She could say no more. The Countess raised and pressed her to her heart. It was upwards of seven minutes and a half, before either of them could speak, and all present were too much affected to interrupt the silence. At length the Countess gazing tenderly upon Arabella said, "My beloved girl, within these last fifteen months, I have taught myself German." "Aye," cried Doctor Philbert, "the man who can be insensible to the charms of virtue, must be a bad moral character, and viciously inclined." Arabella wept silently upon the neck of her mamma, while Jack Deeply exclaimed, "Well, Poll, what have you got to say to all this?" The bird looked up archly and replied "What's o'clock?"

Harry Lambert, with his "sparkling hazle eyes," his nose "inclined to the Grecian," and his "beautifully spreading whiskers," is the masculine counterpart of the heroine. Like the Man of Feeling, he has been deterred by Arabella's exalted rank from proposing marriage. At length he is elevated to an earldom; this gives him courage. He discovers her on a bank of violets, and in a passionate speech two and one half pages in length, entreats her to make him the happiest of men. They are married the next day, and six months later Arabella presents him with a lovely boy. On his fourth birthday little Tommy falls into a brook and is drowned. His father sees his vest floating near a bridge, finds the body, takes it home, lays it away upstairs, and greets Arabella, who, all unconscious of what has passed, is wondering where the 'little truant' is. Henry tells her, and her grief bringing on a premature childbirth, she presents him with another little boy, much finer than Tommy was. "Fortunately in a few hours Tommy began to breathe again and on the following morning was as merry and playful as ever."

The burlesque contains two ghost scenes and several landscape descriptions à la Radcliffe; there is a benevolent band of Italian banditti who rescue a distressed maiden named Amelia, and then sing "Rule Britannia!" in a chorus. There is a parody of the Man of the Hill episode in *Tom Jones*. One scene is a mock masquerade which is attended by Sir Charles Grandison's grandson accompanied by Sterne's Maria, dressed in straw. Lord Mahogany receives a dish of poisoned fruit from La Contessa Negri. Some one had sent him a letter of warning before he ate the fruit, but he had absent-mindedly postponed reading it until it was too late. Seized with pangs of the poison, he dismounts from his horse, leans against a tree, and composes "an illegitimate sonnet without rhime or reason." Like Lovelace and other sentimental villains, he dies to the reverberations of his own oratory: "The furnace of his skin exhibited a leprous appearance, and his eyes, wild glowing and deep sunk in his head, glaring dismally all around, 'Let me measure the moon,' said he, ''tis full of marrow, faugh! but O this torrent of lobsters — stop them, they curl the Heavens. Bottle up the war in a corn-field, and put my vote in hell. Hold me — the room is in flames and the castle totters, what a serpent is the minister, he has stung mankind — I am a croco-dile.' He now caught hold of the bed cloathes and giving a dreadful shriek, EXPIRED."

A feature which does not appear from the above description is the delightful unexpectedness with which the characters appear and reappear at the mere mention of their names. Near the end the number of characters having become too great for convenient handling, the 'authoress' collects them all at a supper party, causes them to eat from a polluted copper pan, and announces a list of all those "who departed this life in the course of the next twenty-four hours."

Some knowledge of the contents of *Azemia* [4] can be gained from the lines that appear on the title page of the second volume:

Fair views and beauteous prospects I invent,
Pines, poplars, ruins, rocks, and sentiment;
Fond lovers sigh beneath my vines and larches,
While ghosts glide grimly through my glimmering arches.

[4] *Azemia* had a second edition in 1798, and in 1808 there was published a French edition, a translation of the first English edition, under the title *Arnold et la Belle Musulmane*. It was translated by F. Soulès.

The satire on the Gothic and the sentimental novels is repeated from *Modern Novel Writing* with little variation. Much space is given to personal and political satire, the Tories and their leader, Pitt, being derided at every possible opportunity. Among the authors burlesqued are Fanny Burney, Mrs. Radcliffe, Mrs. Mary Robinson, Mrs. Gunning and Miss Gunning, Cumberland, the Misses Lee, 'Peter Pindar,' Mrs. Inchbald, Mrs. Smith, and Anna Seward, the 'Swan of Lichfield.' Mrs. Piozzi appears as Mrs. Albuzzi, a pseudo-erudite lady; the author sneeringly referring to "the universal knowledge of the accomplished *Italian Traveller*, the attractive friend of the *Leviathan of Literature*." Johnson himself is present at a *conversazione* of the bluestockings under the name of Mr. Gallstone; in a polysyllabic harangue he reproves Azemia for reading novels and advises her to read a cookery book instead and learn how to make "the most proportionate puddings, and boil them with the most attention to the adhesive qualities of the oviparous and lacteal ingredients." The poet Cowper is represented as the Reverend Solomon Sheeppen, who had "written several admirable pieces in the very sonorous measure called blank verse, and by these blanks had carried off prizes"; he is also made to take a ride like John Gilpin's. Smollett's Commodore Trunnion is feebly satirized as Captain Wappingshot. Fielding would have smiled at this parody of his description of Sophia:

Let those who have perused the ponderous romances of former ages, endeavor to imagine what must be the attractions of those inimitable fair ones who could secure their conquests for years amidst the rigours of disdain; or, if such have never been your study, imagine what must have been the concentrated beauties of the most celebrated charmer of antiquity; collect 'in thy mind's eye,' all that may have been related of Helen or Polydamna — of Dido — of Thaïs, Laïs, or the Thracian Rhodope — of Lucretia — of the loveliest of the Roman empresses: in more modern times of Fair Rosamond, Diana de Poitiers, Agnes Sorel, or the fair Gabrielle — of the Geraldine of the Earl of Surrey, Petrarch's Laura, or Louise de Kerouaille — the Hampton Court beauties, and 'each bright Churchill of the Galaxy:' — or if all these are insufficient, take something from the Miss Byron, the Clarissa, the Pamela of Richardson: borrow a little from the Sophia of Fielding, and the Narcissa of Smollett; and a feature, a look, an air, from what thou canst call to mind of the favorite heroines of the inferior and more modern schools: and having done so, and composed a figure and face (as little like thy wife, if thou happenest to be a married man, as thy conscience will let thee; as much like thyself, if thou art a woman, as thy humility will permit), thou mayst then, peradventure, furnish thyself with some resemblance of my attractive Mussulwoman, my charming Azemia.

Several months before Azemia learns English, she writes a poem in that language. To justify this phenomenon, Beckford reminds the reader that several other heroines of contemporary novels, "though born in another country, and two or three centuries ago, write the most pathetic and polished poetry, in very pretty modern English"; the example of Emily in *The Mysteries of Udolpho* will be recalled. Azemia writes her poem in parody of Mrs. Radcliffe, upon seeing an ear-wig in a Canterbury bell:

THE FORFICULA AURICULARIS, OR EAR–WIGGE, TO HER LOVE [5]

In what small leaf of verdant fold
Art thou, my wandering love, enroll'd?
Where lurk'st thou, in what lily's bell,
My wanton rover, prithee tell?

Ah! what attracts thy vagrant fancy?
The crimson clove, or velvet pansy?
Where keep'st thou, love, thy flowery state?
In three-lobed leaves, or leaves serrate?

Dost thou now pierce, with forceps keen,
Some raspberry's hirsute globes between?
Hast thou a bower luxurious got
In golden pulp of apricot?

Or dost thou find a lodging spacious
In pea's sweet bloom papilion acreous;
And, snug as priest in ample rectory,
Nestle in honey-flowing nectary?

Say where thy agile form is curling,
In flower that nods o'er streamlet purling;
Where, as in odorous barrack hollow,
Thou fill'st a tuberous corolla!

Hid'st thou in blossom of geranium,
Like pictured nymph in Herculaneum?
Tak'st thou, perchance, thy quarters humble
Beneath the white bean's spotted umbel?

Soft dost thou dream in thick sweet-william,
Or perch on lupine's bright vexillum?

[5] Cf. *The Mysteries of Udolpho*, chapter xxxvi, "The Butterfly to His Love."

Where'er thou art, oh! quickly scud
O'er powder'd bloom, or spicy bud!

Thou com'st! Thy coat of polish'd mail,
Thy biform antlers, crescent tail,
Thy diamond eye so soft and shiny,
Thy many twinkling feet, so tiny —

I see! — and, Wigling, hail the sight:
My soft horns tremble with delight:
Ah! let us now, my love, resort
Where rich Vertumnus keeps his court!

There in the hautboy deeply bury,
Or make our bride-bed in the cherry;
O'er pearly grapes luxurious twine,
And raise young ear-wigs in the nectarine.

Rosella; or, Modern Occurrences, 1799, by Mary
Charlton, received and deserved little attention.[6]
Miss Charlton attempts to ridicule the contemporary
sentimental novel by the conventional method of the
romantomaniac heroine. She adds little that is original or interesting, excepting for the final scene. Rosella, cured of her sentimental folly, is about to be
happily married to Lord Clanallan. Her former elderly friend Selina Ellinger, who has been responsible
for all Rosella's troubles and is still as sentimental as
ever, stalks into the room like the bad fairy at the
feast and announces that Rosella is illegitimate:

"Is this all you would tell me?" asked Rosella.
"God of the universe!" exclaimed the poor lady, "what
have I done? — Oh child of my dearest hopes, give away to

[6] It had only one English edition, but was translated into French as
Rosella, ou les Effets des romans.

your distraction, tear your hair, rend your bosom — anything but this calm, settled despair!"

"I am sorry I cannot comply with every request of your's, Mrs. Ellinger," said Rosella, with great gravity; "but as I am not really in a despairing mood, I have little inclination to act such a tragedy. — I am concerned that you have had so much trouble in seeking me out, merely to mention a circumstance I was well acquainted with."

Mrs. Ellinger gazed at her with an expression of countenance so ludicrously woeful, that Rosella could not forbear smiling.

"Acquainted with it!" exclaimed [Mrs. Ellinger]; "My God! no *dénouement* — no catastrophe!"

In *Men and Manners*, another four-volume production of 1799, Francis Lathom presents a minor character named Eliza Oxmondeley, who is no more than a copy of the romantomaniacs we have already encountered.

In 1816 appeared a novel which, though mainly serious, is obviously derived from the female-Quixotic type of novel. *She Would Be a Heroine*, by Sophia Griffith, is the story of a harum-scarum Irish woman, living in England, who was determined by daring escapades to attract attention to herself as a brave and fearless woman, the equal of any man. She rides to hounds, drives a random team through the streets of London, challenges a nobleman, and fights a duel with him. The death of her husband and soon after of her young son, through her neglect, throw her into a violent illness and a temporary loss of sanity. After her cure she no longer desires to be a heroine. The novel has some lively incidents, but they are insufficient to support the weight of three volumes.

It was the deplorable fate of the American novel to be born of the English in this period of slavery to sentiment, didacticism, and horror. At the first, American novelists showed a regrettable, but not unreasonable subservience to the English. As in England, most of them were women. The novels themselves were of the diluted Richardsonian order, usually consisting of a long series of letters between two young females of tender feelings, whose adventures with seducing villains and tearful heroes were intended to provide occasion for the moral instruction of the reader. The only important variation from this type was the Gothic romances, the best of which were written by Charles Brockden Brown.

There were no burlesque novels written in America before 1808, but several serious novels before that date showed the influence of the English burlesque novel. In Mrs. Sarah Wentworth Morton's *The Power of Sympathy; or, the Triumph of Nature*, 1789, the sentimental Richardsonian hero commits suicide, leaving significantly on a table beside him a copy of *The Sorrows of Werther*. Apparently *Werther* was considered by the novelists of the time to be a very pernicious influence, for in *The Hapless Orphan; or, Innocent Victim of Revenge* there is also a character, a Mr. Ashely, who ends his life with the fateful volume beside him. In this same novel Laura Leason, one of the minor characters, develops into a female Quixote, the first in American literature. As a result of various romantic follies, she is seduced by a young gallant whom she meets at the theatre. This cures her. Later

she marries one of her mother's boarders, a Mr. Gib-
bins, rich but old, who soon after the marriage loses
the use of his limbs from gout. The principal heroine
of the novel, Laura's friend Caroline, dies of a broken
heart because she has been carried off by *two* villains.

"The partiality of some friends to that celebrated
novel, 'The Sorrows of Werter,' gave birth to the following pages," says the anonymous author of *The
Slave of Passion; or, The Fruits of Werter*, 1802. "Such
novels as Pamela, the Fool of Quality, and the Man
of Feeling," he declares later in his preface, "will certainly unfold all the sympathies of nature, must dilute
all the harshness of self, and, like an electrifying
stroke, dash fine feelings through every nerve." The
plot is briefly this: Charles loves Maria, loses his fortune, learns that Maria has married somebody else,
reads *The Sorrows of Werther*, and decides on suicide.
In a letter, his friend Henry persuades him not to
commit suicide. He then discovers that Maria is not
married, recovers a considerable part of his fortune,
and marries Maria. The following edifying passage,
in which the italics are my own, is from his last letter
to Henry:

. . . I am burning in the fire of bliss — Maria is in every
thought — they [sic] recoil from every other subject. I
gaze on the dear author of this commotion with unabating
ardor — my eyes seem ready to devour her — I press her
every moment, *without knowing what I am doing*, to my
breast. My reason seems all fled — passion reigns triumphant — I am lost in a delirium of exquisite transport
— Maria too — but then her extreme delicacy curbs her
love — Adieu! adieu! *I cannot write today.*

Incredible though it may seem, *The Slave of Passion* appears to have been intended and received as a serious novel and not as a burlesque.

The first American burlesque novel was an imitation of *The Female Quixote*, by Mrs. Charlotte Lennox. An interesting coincidence is that Mrs. Lennox was the first novelist born in America, although, as we have seen, she moved permanently to England while still a young girl. Her American imitator was Mrs. Tabitha G. Tenney, whose novel, *Female Quixotism: exhibited in the Romantic Opinions and Extravagant Adventures of Dorcasina Sheldon*, was first published in 1808, with a second edition in 1829. Its preface is addressed "To all Columbian young ladies who read novels and romances," and its purpose is to show the evil effects of such reading. Dorcas Sheldon is encouraged by her father to read novels. He himself is fond of reading them, which displays "a singular taste in a man." Dorcas becomes partly demented from reading sentimental Richardsonian novels, changes her name to Dorcasina, fancies that every man she meets is in love with her, and spurns them all because they do not suit her high-flown notions. She is finally cured, but cured too late; she dies an old maid. *Female Quixotism* has rough and ready humor; it is written in a rapid, forceful style. The horseplay is sometimes too violent, but even so the novel must have come as a welcome relief in those days of sentimental vapidity.

VI. SATIRE FOR THE
NEW PHILOSOPHY

THE last dozen years of the eighteenth century saw the rise and fall of a type of novel of which the method and much of the matter were derived from the writings and the philosophy of Rousseau. The revolutionary novel, or, as it is sometimes called, the novel of purpose, preached a doctrine of radicalism that can be traced through Holbach, Condorcet, Thomas Paine, and others to the author of *le Contrat social*; moreover, in its structural characteristics as a vehicle for distributing ideas it bears an unmistakable resemblance to such novels as Thomas Day's *Sandford and Merton*, 1783, and to Henry Brooke's *The Fool of Quality*, 1765–70, both of which were indebted to Rousseau's *Émile* and *la Nouvelle Héloïse* for their form and for much of their content. The revolutionary novel, from about 1785 until almost the end of the century the most conspicuous type of novel in England, exploited what was known as the 'new philosophy.' Its principal teachings were common ownership of property, absolute personal equality, the ultimate perfectibility of human nature, and, most notoriously, freedom from the restraint of formal marriage.

The inaugurators of the new school of fiction were Charlotte Smith, Elizabeth Inchbald, and Thomas

Holcroft; but William Godwin, who did not come into popular notice until some years after the rest, was universally acknowledged to be the leader. His treatise, *Political Justice*, 1793, and his first novel, *Caleb Williams*,[1] 1794, immediately gained for him an intense, though short-lived, notoriety. He further attracted the notice of the public by beginning about this time, in open disregard of the formality of marriage, to live on terms of "domestic and private affection" with Mary Wollstonecraft. She, by her unconventional conduct and by the radical opinions which she voiced in *A Vindication of the Rights of Women*, 1792, had already become established in the public mind as the type of the female intellectual-revolutionary. Most of the writings against this much attacked group were naturally directed at Godwin and Mrs. Wollstonecraft, as its outstanding representatives.

Public sentiment in England had been opposed to the new philosophy from the start, and the novels which turned it to account received increasingly hostile attention from critics and from novelists outside the radical group. It was in the years from 1799 to 1810, when the revolutionary novel had already declined, that the majority of the burlesques of it appeared, although some few came before that time. The anonymous *Susanna*, 1795, contained a burlesque episode in which the heroine, having enjoyed a taste

---

[1] Its principal character, Falkland, had his noble nature undermined by having imbibed in early youth "the poison of chivalry" from "idle, and groundless romances."

of radical philosophy, learns to conceive of herself as a victim of social injustice. She escapes from her 'persecutors,' and, "with a truly *republican spirit*," sets out for London, where she anticipates experiencing "the joys of 'Liberty and equality.'" But the night is dark and rainy; she takes the wrong direction, and when morning comes she finds herself in Cornwall instead of London, ill from exposure, and without money or friends, an object lesson for radical-minded young ladies. George Walker's *The Vagabond*, 1798, presents, with satirical intent, the character Dr. Alogos, a country gentleman, who, as a result of being converted to Godwinism and Wollstonecraftism, becomes a criminal. Still another philosophical villain is found in Mrs. Jane West's *A Tale of the Times*: a seducer, who by means of sentimental sophistry persuades a young married lady to elope with him.

In November, 1799, appeared *St. Leon, a Tale of the Sixteenth Century*, by William Godwin; in December, appeared *St. Godwin, a Tale of the Sixteenth, Seventeenth, and Eighteenth Centuries*, by 'Count Reginald de St. Leon.'[2] The latter is a very commendable parody-burlesque of the former. Godwin's novel was a wild, improbable narrative, only too obviously designed to reiterate (where it did not retract!) the revolutionary doctrines already set forth in his *Political Justice*, his *Caleb Williams*, and his *Memoirs of the Author of A Vindication of the Rights of Women*. That

---

[2] Edward Du Bois. Cf. *Dictionary of Anonymous and Pseudonymous English Literature*, by Halkett and Laing, edited by Kennedy, Smith, and Johnson (London, 1926). See also *Gentleman's Magazine*, March, 1850, p. 326.

it richly deserved to be parodied, the following synopsis may show:

Count Reginald de St. Leon, heir of a rich and noble family, was born early in the sixteenth century. He was present at an interview between Francis I and Charles V, and took part in the battle of Pavia. He is distinguished for his generous qualities, but his weakness for gambling causes him to lose the bulk of his fortune. This he retrieves by marrying the beautiful and wealthy Marguerite de Damville. He retires with her to the castle of St. Leon and lives happily there until it is time to take his son to Paris to be educated. Here he falls into dissipation again and in an incredibly short time loses his wife's fortune and the remainder of his own. He and his family flee to Switzerland, but after many misfortunes are driven away and are forced to take up their residence in a cottage on Lake Constance.

It is here that there appears one day a mysterious stranger, evidently fleeing from justice. St. Leon gives him protection, but the stranger, already fatally ill, soon dies. On his death bed, he reveals to his protector the secrets of the philosopher's stone and of the elixir of life, on the condition that they shall never be transmitted to another. (The stranger had never made use of the elixir because he had found his life too unhappy to prolong.) St. Leon restores his fortune by means of the philosopher's stone, but the sudden acquisition of wealth excites jealousy and distrust among his neighbors and even in his family. Abandoned by wife and son, he is imprisoned at Constance, escapes to Pavia, but there his house is burned by the populace, who think that he is in league with the devil. In Spain he is imprisoned in the dungeons of the Inquisition, but escapes an auto-da-fé, and, having been restored to youth by the elixir, returns to the repurchased castle of St. Leon for an incognito visit to his daughters. He then begins a tour of benevolence through foreign countries. In

Hungary, his trusted friend Bethlem Gabor throws him into prison. He is rescued by a stranger who proves to be his son. St. Leon reveals himself, but there is little satisfaction in the meeting. In intending good to his son, he does him much harm. The story closes near the end of the eighteenth century, with St. Leon an unhappy wanderer, seeing all that he loves perish, while he lives on forever.

Edward Du Bois, writing under the pseudonym of 'St. Leon' summarizes briefly the contents of Godwin's first volume, (his object, he says, not being to fill up space but to tell a story), and begins his narrative with the appearance of the stranger at Lake Constance. The satire consists almost entirely of quoting from the original statements that are either absurd in themselves or made so by a slight change of circumstance. Sometimes Du Bois adds ironical asides of his own, but usually this is unnecessary. In contrast to the four volumes of *St. Leon*, *St. Godwin* consists of only one, at least a third of which is direct quotation from *St. Leon*.

The following description of Bethlem Gabor is from the parody. The italics and capitals are not Godwin's although his language is given word for word:

"He was more than six feet in stature. His voice was like thunder. His head and chin were clothed with a shaggy hair, in colour a dead black. In the wars he had lost three fingers of one of his hands; the sight of his right eye was extinguished, and the cheek half shot away, while the same explosion had burned his complexion into a colour that was universally dun or black. His nose was scarred, and his lips were thick and large."

Such was the amiable creature I elected for my bosom friend.

"If ever on the face of the earth lived a misanthrope, old Bedlam (for so I used to call him) was the man." "He cursed mankind, he rose up in *fierce defiance of eternal providence*; and your blood curdled within you when he spoke; such was Bethlem Gabor; I COULD NOT HELP ADMIRING HIM!" "In his estimate, the poorest, the most servile of all maxims was that of the author of the Christian religion, to repay injury with favour, and curses with benediction." "I felt myself attached to him."

Near the end of the parody Godwin's advocacy of free love is attacked, but again, chiefly by turning his own words against him:

"From this moment I followed the dictates of my passions, without any impediment — indulging in everything my wishes could suggest." I was a little inconsistent I own, but wasn't Pandora so too? Assuredly she was! But "the heart is free," and I was unable to blame her. "Liberty and no constraint!" was our motto. I hate the man who presumes he has "*the right to monopolize any woman*." Women, like air, were by nature intended as a common advantage to every man who breathes, — and like the air should be permitted, as the poet expresses it, *to go about kissing every one they meet*. These are my sentiments, and I despise the "infamous, thrice-damned villain," that does not subscribe to them. The colonel I have just mentioned did not, and I should have said, that I in consequence felt it my duty to run him through the guts.

Godwin's pomposity and self-importance, shown forth in the character of St. Leon, who is Godwin thinly disguised, are frequently ridiculed. For example:

"This is, I *powerfully feel*, the last adventure I shall ever commit to writing. A few minutes more and I will *lay down my pen*, and resolve, in the most solemn and sacred manner, never to compose another line." Happy had it been for society, if I had made this resolution the minute I left school! "Indeed *all other adventures* must necessarily be *frigid and uninteresting*, compared with those which I have described. Great God! what a fate was mine!" I was fated, gentle reader, to turn philosopher and author.

St. Leon was easy prey; its plot was improbable, its style grossly inflated, and its sentiments and reasoning superficial. If *St. Godwin* had been a little more condensed, and its author less serious-minded, it could stand as a model of parodies. Even so, it occasionally furnishes satire as trenchant as that of *Shamela*, which it closely resembles in method, both being parody-burlesque, rather than burlesque, novels.

The most popular burlesque novel against the radical philosophers was written by Miss Elizabeth Hamilton.[3] Her *Memoirs of Modern Philosophers* was published in 1800 and had three editions within two years. The heroine is a 'female Quixote' named Biddy Botherim, who prefers to be called Bridgetina. She is cross-eyed, has a harsh, shrill voice, and wears ridiculous clothes and false hair. Possessed of no original ideas, she has become a mere parrot for the new philosophy, which she has absorbed from books. Through Mr. Glib, keeper of a circulating library, she makes the acquaintance of a group of 'philosophers' in the neighborhood of her country home. The leader is a Frenchwoman, self-styled the 'Goddess of Rea-

[3] Author of *The Letters of a Hindoo Rajah.*

son,' who sits on a throne in her salon and voices
radical opinions in broken English. Her chief cohort
is Mr. Myope, who is a caricature of William Godwin.
They are all represented as being opposed to neigh-
borly love, marriage, filial duty, God, the Bible, and
to every decent thought and motive. The author lets
us see that their philosophy is assumed for ulterior
purposes; Bridgetina is their principal victim. In the
end she is restored to right thinking, but does not
marry; and the author, aiming a blow at the sentimentalists, ironically takes credit to herself for closing
a novel without a wedding. Much of the satire is
directed against Godwin's *Political Justice*; Rousseau's "Eloisa" is mentioned also, and its philosophical tenets are denounced as 'French' and 'revolutionary.' There is also a sneering reference to *Clarissa*
to show that it encouraged young ladies to be disre-
spectful of their parents.

It is logical enough that this burlesque of the radical philosophy should contain a sub-plot against the
sentimental novel. Julia Delmond, conventional
novel-addict, is seduced by Vallaton, formerly a hair-
dresser, but now become a philosopher from motives
of expediency. In Lovelace fashion, he takes Julia
to a 'house,' debauches her, robs her, and deserts her.
(When the over-indulgent Captain Delmond heard of
his daughter's elopement, "the gout flew to his stomach" and he almost immediately died.) Julia escapes,
but begins to languish away, and achieves a deliber-
ate death with Clarissa-like enjoyment. She repents
her conversion to Godwinism and reëmbraces Chris-

tianity, which she has formerly renounced. Complacent in her certainty of heavenly reward — a sort of
prematurely canonized saint — she issues bulletins of
holiness to all her friends. Her fellow-victim, Bridgetina, receives a long exhortation, of which the closing
words, and the moral of the novel, are: "Go home
to your mother, Biddy; and in the sober duties of life
forget the idle vagaries which our distempered brains
dignified with the name of philosophy."

Among Maria Edgeworth's *Moral Tales*, published
in 1800, there was a miniature burlesque novel
called "Angelina; or, L'amie inconnue." The anti-
heroine, Angelina, having passed through the usual
period of unregulated novel reading, has become particularly fascinated with a new circulating library
novel, "The Woman of Genius." She begins a correspondence with its author, who calls herself "Araminta," and they become bosom friends — by mail.
Angelina elopes from the home of her unsympathetic
guardian, leaving an explanatory note on her toilet
table after the fashion of sentimental heroines. Her
destination is a cottage in Wales, the home of Araminta. Disillusionment begins on her arrival; the
cottage is no idyllic retreat but a dirty, uncomfort-
able hovel; Araminta is absent in Bristol; and
the servant is a rough, ignorant Welsh girl, whose
imperfect pronunciation of English causes an unpleasant complication. The climax comes when
Angelina discovers that her 'unknown friend' is a
brandy-drinking termagant named Hodges, who
speaks an affected sentimental jargon with frequent

lapses into Billingsgate; that the 'Orlando' of the letters is a timid Quaker named Nat Gazabo. The undeceived 'heroine' is rescued from her predicament by the *smiling* and *kindly* Lady Frances *Somerset*, and is reinstated with her guardian, the *cold* and *distant* Lady *Diana Chillingworth*.

Miss Edgeworth's moralistic burlesque tale is directed against the sentimental novels as well. It contains the customary mock-sentimental correspondence, the 'friendship of the soul' between Angelina and a person unknown to her, and the inevitable cottage in Wales. Araminta rhapsodizes over "The river silently meandering! The rocks! — The woods! — Nature in all her majesty. Sublime confidante! sympathising with my extremest felicity." Angelina takes solitary walks in the forest, sings ballads, and quotes appropriate lines from Goldsmith and Gray. While at an inn, she flies into ecstasies on discovering a harper; but her delight turns to disgust when he offers to play 'Bumper Squire Jones,' and proves to be "a mere modern harper . . . not even blind!"

Miss Edgeworth's caricature of the female social reformer is heavily ironical. 'Araminta' Hodges is pictured as having a "face and figure which seemed to have been intended for a man, with a voice and gesture capable of setting even man, 'imperial man,' at defiance." In her letters she expresses admiration for Angelina's mind, "formed to combat, in all its Proteus forms, the system of social slavery," and her energy which displays the "inborn independence" to

"exclaim against the family phalanx of her aristocratic persecutors." The apostrophe continues:

Surely — surely Arabella will not be intimidated from
the "settled purpose of her soul" by the phantom-fear of
worldly censure! The garnish-tinseled wand of fashion has
waved in vain in the illuminated halls of folly-painted
pleasure; my Angelina's eyes have withstood — yes, without a blink — the dazzling enchantment. And will she —
no I cannot — I will not think so for an instant — will she
now submit her understanding, spell-bound, to the soporific
charm of nonsensical words, uttered in an awful tone by
the potent enchantress *Prejudice*? The declamation, the
remonstrances of self-elected judges of right and wrong
should be treated with deserved contempt by superior
minds, who claim the privilege of thinking and acting for
themselves. The words *ward* and *guardian* appall my Angelina! but what are legal technical formalities, what are
human institutions, to the view of the shackle-scorning
Reason? Oppressed, degraded, enslaved, — must our unfortunate sex forever submit to sacrifice their rights, their
pleasures, their *will*, at the altar of public opinion; while
the shouts of the interested priests and idle spectators raise
the senseless enthusiasm of the self-devoted victim, or
drown her cries in the truth-extorting moment of agonizing
nature?

This is an example of Miss Hodges' rhetoric and of
the philosophy to which she converted the tractable,
novel-saturated Angelina.

The female Sancho Panza of the piece is the Welsh
maid, Betty Williams, the best of all the characters.
But aside from her, there is little to laugh at. Char-
acteristically Miss Edgeworth failed to recognize that
the best way to combat absurdity was not with com-

mon sense, nor even with preaching, but with laughter. Once more the contrast between the heroine's
extravagance and the everyday world is too great.
The characters are priggish and unnatural. Typical
of the spirit of the piece is the closing speech of Lady
Frances Somerset, cheery *raisonneuse*, who seals Angelina's cure with: "Tomorrow, as you like romances,
we'll read *Arabella; or, The Female Quixote*: and you
shall tell me which of all your acquaintance the heroine resembles most."

In the last days of its decline, the revolutionary
novel was burlesqued several times in novels written
partly against the sentimental novel. *The Illusions of
Youth; or, Romance in Wales and Common Sense in
London*, 1808, by Cordelia Cordova, is a four-volume
novel about a young girl, who, educated by novel-
reading in sentiment and the new philosophy, looked
on marriage as 'the grave of freedom' and refused all
offers, advantageous and otherwise. Threatened with
spinsterhood, she is rescued from 'the dangerous results of her folly' by a lordly lover, who marries her.
They settle in Wales. The only new note that the
author adds to the chorus is her complaint against
those "who condemn novels but continue to read
them." *The Corinna of England and a Heroine in the
Shade*, 1809, is by the author of the notorious novel of
gossip, *A Winter in Bath*. It, too, shows but little
variation. The central character is a female intellectual drawn in gross caricature of Mary Wollstonecraft. She preaches benevolence and freedom, is a
patroness of the arts, and tries to establish herself in

a salon, surrounded by geniuses, theatrical and otherwise. Her ward is a tender young girl, whose life she
almost, but not quite, ruins by her harmful sentiment
and philosophy.

By far the most vindicative of the anti-liberal
novelists was Mrs. Sarah Green. Within two years
she produced three satirical novels against the serious
novels of her day! The first and best of these, *Romance Readers and Romance Writers*, 1810, is her only
burlesque novel. Her over-zealousness is manifest
from the first. "Would that," she exclaims in her
preface, "would that, like the monster BRIAREUS, I
could strike a hundred blows in the same instant, and
that all the vampers of romance, who merit annihila-
tion, were in my presence! — they are the vermins of
literature — their spawn creep to our firesides, and
cover our chairs, our tables, our sophas, and our man-
telpieces; we find them in the bedchambers of our
daughters. . . ." Modern fiction, says Mrs. Green, is
coarse, inconsistent, unoriginal; then she proceeds
with a novel, which, in attacking the others is itself
coarse, inconsistent, unoriginal.

The heroine is a curate's daughter who is significantly named Margaret *Marsham*. Margaritta, as she
insists on being called, is a gawky country girl with
dry, mud-colored hair, a forehead marked with small-
pox, and two missing front teeth. Bitten with romance, she conceives of her sensible sister Mary as an
ignorant provincial; her too-gentlemanly uncle Ralph,
as a rustic squire; and her mild father, as the 'rigid'
parent of the sentimental novel. She is encouraged

in these notions, already derived from circulating library novels, by the immoral Lady Isabella Emerson, female pedant, atheist, and revolutionary. As a result of imprudent conduct based on radical opinions, Margaritta and Lady Isabella are both with child, at the end of the third and last volume, by men who are not their husbands. Deserted and miserable after a night spent in a London park, they determine to drown themselves. Lady Isabella has already jumped in the water when Margaritta's father arrives in time to prevent her from drowning and Margaritta from jumping.

In complaining of the sentimentalists' stilted vocabulary, Mrs. Green allows the Reverend Mr. Marsham to address his daughter in the following measured language: "Stuff, nonsense, quit this affectation of hard words, this pedantic jargon, so disgusting in the general conversation of a young female." Uncle Ralph responds to an oral invitation from the fashionable rector: "We are highly sensible of the honour you do us, sir; on such an occasion we cannot refuse your polite invitation, and will certainly honour ourselves by waiting on you." At his dinner party, the rector proposes a toast to Mary Marsham, with three cheers: "'Pardon me, sir,' said Frederic Harrington, gravely, 'the name of Miss Marsham, though it may excite homage, yet should never be toasted with such bacchanalian applause.'"

It is quite without satirical design that Mrs. Green disposes of her characters at the end. "Retirement the most secluded, was now become absolutely requi-

site for the most conspicuous actors in this piece."
Margaritta's entire family, their nerves completely
shattered by the disgrace she has brought upon them
retire to — Wales! The poor ex-heroine is obliged to
pass herself off as a young widow; for, as her curate
father remarked, "A little deception which does no
harm must sometimes be practiced in a deceptive
world." She is permitted to retire to Wales also, but
not in company with the rest; her cottage, we are
told, is at some distance from theirs. But the wicked
Lady Isabella Emerson is denied even this poor privilege. She is relegated not merely to Devonshire, but
to "the remotest part," where she takes refuge in "a
small, rural cottage, plain and humble."

The indefatigable Mrs. Green published a few
months later *The Reformist!!!* — a satirical novel
against reform in religion, manners, and politics; and
the next year, 1811, *Good Men of Modern Date*, which
contains a woman character who adopts Rousseau's
system of education for her children, with dire
results.

The satirists and burlesquers of the revolutionary
novels can all be convicted of the fault of over-
seriousness. Resentment so strong as theirs defeated
its own purpose. The violent end-of-the-century
radicalism ran but a brief course in the novel, and it is
doubtful if it swerved one iota from that course because of the burlesques against it, most of which, even
for the readers of the time, could have possessed no
more than an occasional flash of humor or interest.

VII. JANE AUSTEN'S SENSE AND OTHER PEOPLE'S SENSIBILITY

THE bad novels of the seventeen-eighties and nineties, which, according to sober-minded critics, were so detrimental to the public morals, cannot be altogether deplored when we consider that one of the most gifted of English writers found in her reaction against their extravagance and artificiality not only the impulse to write but also a direction for her peculiar genius in irony and satire. Jane Austen was from her early teens until her death an eager reader of novels, even the atrocious novels of her contemporaries; but unlike the Arabellas, the Susannas, and the rest of the 'female Quixotes,' she read them even in her girlhood, with sane detachment and critical reservation. Her sense of absurdity and fun preserved her from the unprofitable rôle of a mere literary critic, and, as a child of sixteen, she evinced her positive genius in a burlesque of current fiction, gayer, wittier, and potentially more effective as an 'antidote against silliness' than anything her elders had done. The opinion of J. E. Austen-Leigh that this early burlesque novel reflects a mind that worked "in a very different direction" from the mind that produced her later works is in contradiction of the easily recognized relationship that satire bears to realism. What could be more natural than that a youthful critic of the novels of her day, endowed with creative ability, should in maturity seek to correct their faults and supply their defects? Fifty years before, Fielding had progressed to realism along exactly the same path; and fifty years later, Thackeray was to follow in the footsteps of them both. Not only is Jane Austen's attitude as a novelist manifest in her youthful effort, but also her technique, crude and undeveloped, and even some of her favorite situations and characters. She never completely abandoned the rôle of burlesque critic; this is evidenced by the incomplete *Sanditon*, interrupted by her death. Moreover, it is possible to detect, lurking about the opening and closing chapters of all her novels, that same imp of sportive ridicule that supplied a motive to her earliest writing.

The small volume entitled *Love and Freindship and other Early Pieces* was not published until 1922. Of the half dozen juvenilia that it contains, the title piece is very much the best. The spontaneity of its style and its bubbling, irresistible humor mark it as the work of a young person who not only enjoyed reading the novels that she satirized, but still more enjoyed making fun of them. Didacticism, which starched and devitalized the fiction of the talented Maria Edgeworth and most other novelists of the time, burlesque and serious, is conspicuously absent from this as from all Jane Austen's works. Like Sheridan and Fielding, she realized that bad novels were too ineffectual to do any serious harm; and in the juvenile *Love and Freindship* she merely laughed at their excesses and invited her readers to do the same.

The form is in ironical imitation of the Richardsonian novel, the story being told in letters from the heroine, Laura, to the daughter of her friend. Laura, like Clarissa Harlowe and dozens of her descendants, expresses the hope that the fortitude with which she has endured her many past afflictions will prove a 'useful lesson' to her young correspondent. Laura is an 'ideal' sentimental heroine. Her father was a native of Ireland and an inhabitant of Wales; her mother was the natural daughter of a Scotch peer by an Italian opera singer; she herself was born in Spain and educated at a convent in France. She acknowledges that she was beautiful, was mistress of every accomplishment customary to her sex, and was possessed of a mind that was "the rendezvous of every good quality and of every noble sentiment." "A sensibility too tremblingly alive to every affliction of my Freinds, my Acquaintance and particularly to every affliction of my own, was my only fault, if a fault it could be called."

Her education completed, she retired to the home of her parents in the romantic Vale of Usk. The neighborhood was a small one — it contained only Isabel! But Isabel was twenty-one and had seen the world:

She had passed 2 years at one of the first Boarding-schools in London; had spent a fortnight in Bath and had supped one night in Southampton. Beware my Laura (she would often say) Beware of the insipid vanities and idle Dissipations of the Metropolis of England; Beware of the unmeaning Luxuries of Bath and of the stinking fish of Southampton.

Late one evening a noble and beauteous youth takes refuge in the home of Laura's parents. His name is Lindsay. Laura, 'for particular reasons,' conceals it under that of 'Talbot,' but she never refers to him afterwards except as 'Edward.' Although he was tolerably proficient in geography, he had, like the mock heroine Susanna, mistaken west for east and consequently found himself benighted in South Wales when he expected to arrive in Middlesex. He and Laura fall in love at their first meeting; he proposes, she accepts, and they are married that very night by Laura's father, who, "tho' he had never taken orders had been bred to the church." At Edward's aunt's home they are met by belated parental opposition, so they elope in the angry father's carriage to the home of Augustus and Sophia. In a tender scene Edward and Augustus renew an old friendship and their wives form a new one; but the concomitant emotion proves too much for the two heroines, and they faint alternately on a sofa near by. The four young sentimentalists resolve to remain united forever, but shortly Augustus, who, like a true man of feeling, scorns to turn his mind to money matters, is arrested for debt and sent to Newgate, whither Edward loyally follows him. The excessive sensibility of Laura and Sophia makes a visit to prison unthinkable for them, so they set out for Scotland, where Sophia has a cousin named Macdonald.

At an inn they encounter an elderly gentleman who, Laura's 'instinctive sympathy' informs her, is her grandfather. She follows him to his room, is acknowledged and embraced. Sophia follows immediately after and is also acknowledged as a granddaughter. Two beautiful young men named Philander and Gustavus enter successively and are acknowledged as grandsons by the grandpaternal stranger. Fearing that other grandchildren may follow, he presents them each with a fifty-pound note and departs. The two girls are so shocked at the crudity of this action that they faint away. When they return to consciousness, Gustavus and Philander and all the fifty-pound notes have disappeared.

Sophia's cousin opportunely arrives and takes them to Macdonald Hall, where they form an instant friendship with his daughter Janetta. They discover that her tyrannical parent expects her to marry one Graham, who is sensible, well informed, and agreeable, but has never read *The Sorrows of Werther*, has hair that is *not* auburn, and, in short, possesses no soul. They convince Janetta that she does not love Graham and persuade her to elope to Gretna Green with a Captain M'Kenrie. On the day of the elopement, as Sophia is majestically removing some bank notes from a private drawer, she is interrupted by the indignant Macdonald. Her tender spirit wounded by his reproaches, she taunts him with his daughter's approaching elopement and she and Laura are invited to leave:

. . . After having walked about a mile and a half we sate down by the side of a clear limpid stream to refresh our exhausted limbs. The place was suited to meditation. A grove of full-grown Elms sheltered us from the East . . . . A Bed of full-grown nettles from the West . . . . Before us ran the murmuring Brook and behind us ran the turn-pike road. We were in a mood for contemplation and in a disposition to enjoy so beautiful a spot. A mutual silence which had for some time reigned between us, was at length broke by my exclaiming — 'What a lovely scene! Alas why are not Edward and Augustus here to enjoy its Beauties with us?'

A few minutes later, a phaeton is overturned at their feet. Both their husbands are inside. Augustus is dead, Edward mortally wounded. In the midst of gasping out an account of his adventures, Edward also dies. Sophia faints an infinite number of times on the bank of a stream; Laura runs mad at intervals. Sophia develops galloping consumption, and, before she can be removed from the scene of the disaster, dies; her last words to her friend and the 'moral' to the story being:

"Beware of fainting fits. . . . Though at the time they may be refreshing and agreable yet believe me they will in the end, if too often repeated and at improper seasons, prove destructive to your Constitution. . . . My fatal swoon has cost me my life. . . . Beware of swoons Dear Laura. . . . A frenzy fit is not one quarter so pernicious; it is an exercise to the body and if not too violent, is I dare say conducive to Health in its consequences. . . . Run mad as often as you chuse: but do not faint. . . ."

After the funeral, Laura takes refuge in a romantic village in the highlands of Scotland, where she continues to live in melancholy solitude, mourning the deaths of her father, her mother, her husband, and her friend. All the rest of the characters are as appropriately accounted for.

Love and Freindship was written in the early seventeen-nineties, several years before burlesque of the sentimental novel became the fashion. Superior to almost all that followed, it might well have served as a model for them if it had been known. Laura and Sophia, except that they are sketched with more lightness and skill, might exchange places with Susanna, Rosella, Angelina, or any of the rest. They have all the favorite characteristics of the mock sentimental heroine. They scorn to talk about money, but are not above stealing it; they are eager to tell the history of their adventures and they demand that casual strangers do the same; they induce other young girls to their way of thinking and bring them to grief; they recognize friends and enemies at sight with no other clues than intuitive sympathy or instinctive antipathy; they elope without reason, take long journeys to the wrong places, are benighted, and find refuge in romantic cottages. Edward and Augustus are 'beauteous' puppets who move about for the accommodation of the heroines and serve as *provocateurs* of sensibility, love, and fainting fits. They play proportionately as much part in the story as the seriously intended heroes do in the novels of sentiment. The rest of the characters, too, are merely accessary to the sentimental activities of the heroines; the women either have romantic names and fantastic notions and become their 'soul friends,' or else they have prosaic names, practical views, and become their despised enemies. The picaresque Gustavus and Philander are an amusing exception. Having stolen nine hundred pounds from their respective mothers, who consequently starved to death, they lead a life of crime and adventure as strolling players. The best (and only) play which their company performs is *Macbeth*. The manager plays Banquo, his wife Lady Macbeth, Gustavus the three witches, and Philander all the rest.

With perfect good nature, the youthful Jane Austen turns into ridicule the stock devices of the contemporary novelists. The letters are all from and to the same person, as nearly all the letters of *Evelina* had been. Coincidence, the willing slave of most of her contemporaries, is overworked to a ludicrous degree. In the final scene, for example, the heroine discovers, one after the other, every character of the story that has been left alive: they all *happen* to have assembled on the night coach for Edinburgh. This gives the author the opportunity of tying the loose threads together with satirical meticulousness, as she later does in *Northanger Abbey*.

Much of the material was worked over in her later novels. Laura and Sophia, either or both, are easily recognized as light sketches of Marianne Dashwood in *Sense and Sensibility*; and Marianne serves in her turn as the model for Catherine Morland. Sir Edward, whose only claim to being the 'tyrannical' father is that he has a mild desire to see his son well settled in life, is found again in General Tilney of

Northanger Abbey, who opposed his son's marriage to Catherine because she was not rich enough. The incident of the overturned phaeton, which united the heroines with the dead Augustus and the dying Edward — and which, by the way, was seriously employed by Mrs. Roche to bring her lovers together in *The Children of the Abbey* — is repeated in the first scene of *Sanditon*. Sir Edward Denham, also in *Sanditon*, is a mock sentimental hero who uses the same highflown language as the Edward of *Love and Freindship*. The germ of one of Miss Austen's most delightful characters has been discerned in the 'knocking scene.' Laura is seated with her mother and father at the fireside of their cottage in Wales:

. . . we were on a sudden, greatly astonished, by hearing a violent knocking on the outward door of our rustic Cot.

My father started — "What noise is that," (said he.) "It sounds like a loud rapping at the door" — (replied my Mother.) "It does indeed." (cried I.) "I am of your opinion; (said my Father) it certainly does appear to proceed from some uncommon violence exerted against our unoffending door." "Yes (exclaimed I) I cannot help thinking it must be somebody who knocks for admittance."

"That is another point (replied he;) we must not pretend to determine on what motive the person may knock — tho' that someone *does* rap at the door, I am partly convinced."

Here, a 2d tremendous rap interrupted my Father in his speech, and somewhat alarmed my mother and me.

"Had we not better go and see who it is? (said she) the servants are out." "I think we had." (replied I.) "Certainly, (added my Father) by all means." "Shall we go now? (said my Mother,) "The sooner the better." (answered he.) "Oh! let no time be lost" (cried I.)

A third and more violent Rap than ever again assaulted our ears. "I am certain there is somebody knocking at the Door." (said my Mother.) "I think there must be," (replied my Father) "I fancy the servants are returned; (said I) I think I hear Mary going to the Door." "I'm glad of it (cried my Father) for I long to know who it is."

I was right in my conjecture; for Mary instantly entering the Room, informed us that a young Gentleman and his Servant were at the door, who had lossed their way, were very cold and begged leave to warm themselves by our fire.

"Won't you admit them?" (said I.) "You have no objection, my Dear?" (said my Father.) "None in the World." (replied my Mother.)

Mary, without waiting for any further commands immediately left the room and quickly returned introducing the most beauteous and amiable Youth, I had ever beheld. The servant, she kept to herself.

G. K. Chesterton[1] detects "in the aggravating leisure and lucidity" of the father's remarks "the unmistakable voice of Mr. Bennett." Miss Annette Hopkins,[2] however, points to a scene from *Tristram Shandy* of which this is an unmistakable parody, and remarks that the voice of the father, instead of being Mr. Bennett's, is Laurence Sterne's. It is indeed the voice of both, and the father here is simply the first sketch, drawn from Sterne, of Mr. Bennett in *Pride and Prejudice*.

Lesley Castle, the only other of the early works of even slight interest here, is a take-off of both romantic

[1] Preface to *Love and Freindship and other Early Works* (New York, Frederick A. Stokes Company, 1922), p. xii.
[2] "Jane Austen's *Love and Freindship*," in *South Atlantic Quarterly*, January, 1925.

and sentimental novels. The first letter contains a mock description of the venerable, mouldering Lesley Hall in Scotland. There is a sober, respectable son who has been deserted by his wife, whose father, "gay, dissipated, and Thoughtless at the age of 57," is spending the family fortune in the idle pleasures of town. The most interesting character is Miss Charlotte Lutterell, whose passions in life are reading receipt books and cooking pies. She is a parody of the famous bread-and-butter-slicing Charlotte in *The Sorrows of Werther*, and perhaps served as a preliminary sketch of Charlotte Lucas in *Pride and Prejudice*.[3] There are ten letters in all, but they are dull, and the author showed good judgment in leaving the piece a fragment.

Sense and Sensibility was first drafted about 1795 as "Elinor and Marianne," a letter novel; it was revised and given its present title in 1797, was further revised in 1810–11, and was published in 1811.[4] It bears a strong trace of the burlesque method. The two heroines, who personify the abstractions of the title, are, when introduced, very much like the burlesque characters of *Love and Freindship*.[5] Marianne "was sensible and clever; but eager in everything; her sorrows, her joys, could have no moderation. She was generous, amiable, interesting; she was everything but prudent." The sights and sounds of nature cause

[3] So thinks Miss Annette Hopkins. See her article on *Love and Freindship* in the *South Atlantic Quarterly*, January, 1925.

[4] See *Jane Austen*, by R. Brimley Johnson.

[5] Cf. Chapter v, page 95; account of Mrs. Jane West's *A Gossip's Story*.

her to fly into raptures; she judges the people she
meets entirely by her first impressions; she reads with
ecstasy the poems of Scott and Cowper, and concurs
with her lover in "admiring Pope no more than was
proper," allowing no merit in any work of literature
that was not of the romantic or sentimental schools.
Certain incidents near the beginning of the novel —
Marianne's transport of grief at leaving her childhood home, her protestation that friendship should
be based on 'instinctive sympathy' alone, and that
conduct should be entirely controlled by sensibility —
all point to her kinship with the mock sentimental
Laura and Sophia. The sensible Elinor has her prototypes in Augusta and Lady Dorothea, who are foils
for the supersensitive heroines in *Love and Freindship*,
as Elinor is for Marianne. It is possible that the early
draft of *Sense and Sensibility* showed an even stronger
tendency to burlesque than the final version, which
even in its present form depends for much of its point
on its satire against the novel of sensibility of the day.

Northanger Abbey made its belated appearance in
1818, with the following "Advertisement by the
Authoress":

This little work was finished in the year 1803, and intended for immediate publication. It was disposed of to a
bookseller, it was even advertised, and why the business
proceeded no farther, the author has never been able to
learn. That any bookseller should think it worth while to
purchase what he did not think it worth while to publish,
seems extraordinary. But with this, neither the author nor
the public have any other concern than as some observation is necessary upon those parts of the work which

thirteen years have made comparatively obsolete. The public are entreated to bear in mind that thirteen years have passed since it was finished, many more since it was begun, and that during that period, places, manners, books, and opinions have undergone considerable changes.

The delay was fortunate in this respect at least: the public of 1818 was far more ready to laugh at the Gothic novel than that of 1803 had been. In 1803 the subtle irony of *Northanger Abbey* would have passed ineffective and perhaps unnoticed in the great mass of terror novels that found such a large and sympathetic audience. Even the forthright satire of Barrett's *The Heroine* came none too late in 1813; and the accident may be accounted lucky that caused the two novels to issue forth in their most effective order, Barrett's heavy artillery being succeeded by Miss Austen's more accurate and no less deadly rifle fire.

In this gay comedy of realism versus romance, Jane Austen followed the conventional outline already traced by Mrs. Lennox in her imitation of *Don Quixote*. Catherine Morland, an attractive but by no means extraordinary young girl, is, like Arabella, sent into the world, her head crammed with romantic notions drawn from novels which represent life as it is not. She passes through a series of realistic experiences and emerges normal, sensible, happily married, and permanently cured of romantic nonsense. But here all resemblance ceases; for *Northanger Abbey* is, what no true burlesque novel can be, a depictment of real and living characters. Like Fielding's abortive parody of *Pamela*, it is, strictly speaking, not a burlesque novel at all. We have seen how in *Joseph Andrews* the parody-burlesque was prominent at first, was neglected for the greater part of the novel, and then was emphasized at the end. *Northanger Abbey* is like it in that respect, but is different in that parody is seldom employed and that the burlesque element is never strong enough to eradicate realism. Catherine Morland has a distinct entity of her own, even when she is most under the influence of the Radcliffian school of fiction; and what is true of the principal character is true of the whole novel. It is a work that stands on its own merits, not merely on the defects of others.

The burlesque part is directed chiefly against the terror-romanticists, and the author makes it clear that she is attacking them as a group. Catherine tells Isabella Thorpe how delighted she is with *The Mysteries of Udolpho*; she wishes she could spend her whole life in reading it; if it had not been to meet Isabella she would not have come away from it for all the world.

"Dear creature, how much I am obliged to you; and when you have finished Udolpho, we will read the Italian together; and I have made out a list of ten or twelve more of the same kind for you."

"Have you, indeed? How glad I am! What are they all?"

"I will read you their names directly; here they are in my pocketbook. Castle of Wolfenbach, Clermont, Mysterious Warnings, Necromancer of the Black Forest, Midnight Bell, Orphan of the Rhine, and Horrid Mysteries. Those will last us some time."

"Yes; pretty well; but are they all horrid? Are you sure they are all horrid?"

"Yes, quite sure; for a particular friend of mine, a Miss Andrews; a sweet girl, one of the sweetest creatures in the world, has read every one of them. I wish you knew Miss Andrews, you would be delighted with her. She is netting herself the sweetest cloak you can conceive. . ."

Later we learn that *Sir Charles Grandison* is an "amazing horrid book" and that Miss Andrews could not get through the first volume. Catherine herself finds it very entertaining but "not like Udolpho at all." The clownish John Thorpe thinks that most novels are stuff and nonsense and that "there has not been a tolerably decent one come out since Tom Jones, except the Monk."

Through her reading of 'horrid' novels Catherine has become interested in everything that is old and mysterious. She is bitterly disappointed at not being able to visit Blaise Castle, which she has been told is the oldest in England, has towers and long galleries by the dozens, and is exactly like 'what one reads of.' When the rain prevents her from fulfilling her engagement with the Tilneys she regrets that the weather at Bath is not such "as they had at Udolpho, or at least in Tuscany and the South of France! — the night that poor St. Aubert died! — such beautiful weather!" On the way to Northanger the surrounding landscape puts her in mind "of the country that Emily and her father traveled through in *The Mysteries of Udolpho.*"

It becomes obvious, as the novel proceeds, that, although the Gothic novel in general is the subject of burlesque, Mrs. Radcliffe has been selected as a typical author and *The Mysteries of Udolpho* as the typical novel. When Henry Tilney gives Catherine a mock description of Northanger it suggests to her already receptive mind another Castle of Udolpho where she can reënact the experiences of Emily St. Aubert. When she arrives, we have a scene that is almost a parody. She *does* retire to her chamber with misgivings, *does* discover a mysterious chest, *does* find a lost manuscript. All this is narrated with marvellous art, and the incident is brought to one of the most effective anti-climaxes in all literature when she learns that the precious manuscript is only an old laundry list — and not very old at that!

Catherine has meanwhile become convinced, on grounds insufficient for any one whose mind was not bewildered with novel-reading, that her host, General Tilney, has murdered his wife; she regards him with horror and avoids him whenever she can. Later she is mortified to learn from Henry Tilney that Mrs. Tilney has died a natural death and that the General's grief had almost sent him into a decline. Suddenly and uncivilly dismissed from Northanger, she believes it is because her host has discovered her former suspicions. But even this consolation is denied her; she must drink the cup of realism to its bitter dregs. Her only offence was in not being as rich as John Thorpe had led the greedy old General to believe.

Catherine's cure is so gradually and convincingly brought about that the reader scarcely needs to be told of it in the following guarded little essay on the romantic method:

Charming as were all Mrs. Radcliffe's works, and charming even as were the works of all her imitators, it was not in them perhaps that human nature, at least in the midland counties of England, was to be looked for. Of the Alps and Pyrenees, with their pine forests and their vices, they might give a faithful delineation; and Italy, Switzerland, and the south of France might be as fruitful in horrors as they were there represented. Catherine dared not doubt beyond her own country, and even of that, if hard pressed, would have yielded the northern and western extremities. But in the central part of England there was surely some security of existence even of a wife not beloved, in the laws of the land, and the manners of the age. Murder was not tolerated, servants were not slaves, and neither poison nor sleeping potions to be procured, like rhubarb, from every druggist. Among the Alps and Pyrenees, perhaps, there were no mixed characters. There, such as were not as spotless as an angel, might have the dispositions of a fiend. But in England it was not so: among the English, she believed, in their hearts and habits, there was a general though unequal mixture of good and bad. Upon this conviction, she would not be surprised if even in Henry and Eleanor Tilney some slight imperfection might hereafter appear; and upon this conviction she need not fear to acknowledge some actual specks in the character of their father, who, though cleared from the grossly injurious suspicions which she must ever blush to have entertained, she did believe, upon serious consideration, to be not perfectly amiable.

The sentimental novel is burlesqued too, and we find some echoes of *Love and Freindship*, with the satire refined and polished. Isabella and Catherine form a friendship at first sight, which, after a brief but violent course, ends as abruptly as it began. The parental disapproval of youthful marriage schemes, which the sentimentalists had made the excuse for much philosophizing about individual freedom, is gently satirized by having General Tilney delay, by disapproving it, the marriage of the hero and heroine:

... as this took place within a twelvemonth of the first day of their meeting, it will not appear, after all the dreadful delays occasioned by the General's cruelty, that they were essentially hurt by it. To begin perfect happiness at the respective ages of twenty-six and eighteen is to do pretty well; and professing myself, moreover, convinced that the General's unjust interference, so far from being injurious to their felicity, was perhaps conducive to it, by improving their knowledge of each other, and adding strength to their attachment, I leave it to be settled by whomsoever it may concern, whether the tendency of this work be altogether to recommend parental tyranny or reward filial disobedience.

The scornful indifference to money professed by the conventional novel character had been a source of the greatest amusement to Jane Austen in her youthful burlesques; it is still so in *Northanger Abbey*. Isabella Thorpe scoffs at the suggestion that money could influence her affection for James Morland or her approval of Catherine's marriage to her brother; nevertheless, when she discovers that the Morlands have only moderate means, she clearly perceives the inadvisability of both matches and remarks that "after all the romanticists may say, there is no doing without money." It is amusing to notice, however, that although Miss Austen stresses the importance of money and the folly of the sentimentalists in disregarding it, she allows her hero, otherwise a normal and sensible young man, to express no disappointment or even surprise when he learns that his future wife is a comparative pauper. There are limits, it seems, even to Miss Austen's realism.

Besides the burlesque of the romantic and sentimental novels, there is, in the holiday spirit of the book, a considerable amount of playful criticism of the novelist's art in general. In the mock heroic manner of Fielding, the author announces that her heroine is no paragon and that, contrary to most, she will not be the subject of exciting misfortune and romantic adventure. When Catherine leaves for Bath, we are given a short sketch of her sister Sarah and are led to expect that she will be the sympathetic recipient of Catherine's letters, but, "It is remarkable . . . that she neither insisted on Catherine's writing by every post, nor exacted her promise of transmitting the character of every new acquaintance, nor a detail of every interesting conversation that Bath might produce." Thenceforth the Richardsonian letter-writing confidante, created and made useless with one stroke, disappears from the novel. Mrs. Allen is carefully described, again in the Fielding manner, so that "the reader may be able to judge in what manner her actions will tend to promote the general distress of the work, and how she will probably contribute to reduce poor Catherine to all the desperate wretchedness of which a last volume is capable — whether by her im-

prudence, vulgarity, or jealousy — whether by inter-
cepting her letters, ruining her character, or turning
her out of doors." After describing the Thorpes:
"This brief account of the family is intended to super-
sede the necessity of a long and minute detail of Mrs.
Thorpe herself, of her past adventures and sufferings,
which might otherwise be expected to occupy the
three or four following chapters, in which the worth-
lessness of lords and attorneys might be set forth; and
conversations which had passed twenty years before
be minutely repeated." Beyond saying that "he is
the most charming young man in the world," it is impossible for the author to give any description of
Eleanor Tilney's suitor. She is forced, however, "to
add (aware that the rules of composition forbid the
introduction of a character not connected with [her]
fable) that this was the very gentleman whose negligent servant left behind him that collection of wash-
ing bills, resulting from a long visit to Northanger, by
which [her] heroine was involved in one of her most
interesting adventures."

Some time after the publication of *Emma* in 1815,
Jane Austen wrote her *Plan of a Novel*, "according to
hints from various quarters." It is a humorous sally
of two or three pages, never intended to be published,
but written for the amusement of herself and her
friends. Its tone of mock seriousness strongly recalls
the childhood burlesques. The heroine is to be a
faultless character with much sentiment, tenderness,
beauty, and accomplishment. Early in her adventurous and migratory career she must meet with the

hero, "all perfection of course — and only prevented from paying his addresses to her, by some excess of refinement." She is to be pursued by a relentless villain, obliged to earn bread for herself and her poverty-stricken father, and finally forced to take refuge with him in Kamchatka. Here her father, worn out with worry and travel, "finding his end approaching, throws himself on the ground, and after four or five hours of tender advice and parental admonition to his miserable child, expires in a fine burst of literary enthusiasm." At the end the hero is to arrive in the nick of time to rescue her from the villain, and "having just shaken off the scruples which fettered him before," he is to be united to the fair unfortunate.

The unfinished pages of *Sanditon*, written in the last years of Jane Austen's life, furnish even further proof that the spirit of literary satire was an important motivation for her works. When Charlotte Heywood, addict of circulating library novels, is introduced to Lady Denham's companion:

. . . she c^d not separate the idea of a complete Heroine from Clara Brereton. Her situation with Lady Denham so very much in favour of it! — She seemed placed with her on purpose to be ill-used. Such Poverty & Dependance joined to such Beauty & Merit, seemed to leave no choice in the business. — These feelings were not the result of any spirit of Romance in Charlotte herself. No, she was a very sober-minded young Lady, sufficiently well-read in Novels to supply her Imagination with amusement, but not at all unreasonably influenced by them; & while she pleased herself the first 5 minutes with fancying the Persecutions which *ought* to be the Lot of the interesting Clara, especially

in the form of the most barbarous conduct on Lady Denham's side, she found no reluctance to admit from subsequent observation, that they appeared to be on very comfortable Terms.

Sir Edward Denham seems to have been destined for
an important part in the incompleted story; in him
we have actually a young man whose head has been
turned from reading silly novels. He overwhelms
Charlotte with descriptions of his 'undescribable'
emotions excited by nature; he bewilders her with the
frequency and inaccuracy of his quotations from the
romantic poets; by unrestrained display of sensibility, he forces her to consider him a Man of Feeling.
But it soon becomes apparent that he conceives of
himself as a Lovelace also, and that he has designs of
seduction on the unprotected companion of his
wealthy aunt:

I am no indiscriminate Novel-Reader. The mere Trash
of the common Circulating Library, I hold in the highest
contempt. You will never hear me advocating those puerile
Emanations which detail nothing but discordant Principles
incapable of Amalgamation, or those vapid tissues of ordinary Occurrences from which no useful Deductions can be
drawn.... The Novels which I approve are such as display
Human Nature with Grandeur — such as shew her in the
Sublimities of intense Feeling — such as exhibit the progress of strong Passion from the first Germ of incipient
Susceptibility to the utmost Energies of Reason half-
dethroned, — where we see the strong spark of Woman's
Captivations elicit such Fire in the Soul of Man as leads
him — (though at the risk of some Aberration from the
strict line of Primitive Obligations) — to hazard all, dare
all, atcheive all, to obtain her.

The author then discloses that Sir Edward has read more sentimental novels than have agreed with him, and that his fancy "had been early caught by all the impassioned, & the most exceptionable parts of Richardsons; & such Authors as have since appeared to tread in Richardson's steps, so far as Man's determined pursuit of Woman in defiance of every opposition of feeling & convenience is concerned, had since occupied the greater part of his literary hours, & formed his Character."

The view of Jane Austen's artistic development which it is now possible, and even obligatory, to take, since the publication of the juvenilia and *Sanditon*, shows her to be anything but a solitary genius, out of touch with the literary activities of her period. It is not even necessary to consult the abundant evidence in her letters to see that she was an eager reader and critic of contemporary works: her novels themselves present overwhelming proof. Her incentive to write and much of her material were derived, as Fielding's had been, from her just sense of the inferiority of contemporary reading matter. But she was never so explicitly didactic as the older realist, and the weapon of her irony was lighter and more keenly pointed; otherwise, her career as a fiction writer follows the same lines as his. Beginning with the pure burlesque of *Love and Freindship* she passed through the transition stage of *Sense and Sensibility* and *Northanger Abbey*, and from a critic of literature to a critic of real life in *Pride and Prejudice*, *Mansfield Park*, and the rest; still continuing, however, to

laugh at the absurdities of other novels — and sometimes at her own — whenever a suitable occasion
arose. In her we see illustrated again that principle
of reaction that seems to be responsible for so much
of our best literature. If the novels of others had not
been so bad, her own would have been less good, or
anyhow, different: an ironical jest no doubt appreciated by this consummate mistress of the art of
irony.

VIII. GOTHIC NONSENSE

A NOTHER haunted castle!" was the greeting accorded *The Castle of Ollada* in *The Critical Review* in 1795. "Surely the misses themselves must be tired of so many stories of ghosts, and murders. . . ." Twenty-three years later weary critics were still informing their fair readers "what a vast quantity of useful spirits and patience" they were generally forced to exhaust before stumbling upon anything they could recommend; "through what an endless series of gloomy caverns, long and winding passages, secret trap doors" they were forced to pass. A dramatist of the day, George Colman the Younger, whose father had burlesqued the sentimental novel of the fifties in *Polly Honeycombe*, voiced his complaint in rhyme:

> A novel now is nothing more
> Than an old castle and a creaking door,
> A distant hovel,
> Clanking of chains — a galley — a light —
> Old Armour and a phantom all in white —
> And there's a novel!

In serious vein, Sir Walter Scott, reviewing Maturin's *The Fatal Revenge* in *The Quarterly Review* for May, 1810, regrets the passing of Richardson, Mackenzie, and Miss Burney, of Fielding and Smollett. The only modern novelists who find favor with him are Maria Edgeworth and Charlotte Smith. He considers the imitators of Mrs. Radcliffe and Lewis dull, flat, and repetitious, and especially condemns their matter-of-fact explanations of mysterious happenings. The wax doll behind the black veil in *The Mysteries of Udolpho* he condemns as a 'pitiful contrivance.' The incident cannot be reperused without 'contempt.' We wonder if Sir Walter had perused the recent *Santa Maria; or, the Mysterious Pregnancy*, and what his feelings were when he came across the following remarkable passage: "Rodolph eagerly opened the chest — when — ! ! ! to his infinite astonishment and horror, he beheld —— a frightful vacuity! ! !"

The 'sweet Miss Andrews' of *Northanger Abbey* had her living prototypes in hundreds of English girls. Even in remote America there was one young romance addict who has left behind evidence that she shared with her English sisters the joy of devouring the 'horrid' novels that poured with such generous abundance from the Minerva and other presses. From 1806 to 1822, Madame M. M. de Rieux, wife of the French *émigré* to Virginia, Justin Pierre Plumard, Comte de Rieux, kept a yearly list of the books she had read. There are 1106 titles, about five hundred of which are novels. Of these five hundred more than one hundred proclaim by their titles the Gothic nature of their contents. Fifty-six include the words 'castle,' 'abbey,' or 'priory'; twelve the words 'monk,' 'nun,' or 'vow.' In the then appropriately romantic setting of the mountains of western Virginia, the youthful Madame de Rieux turned with eagerly hurrying fingers the pages of *The Nocturnal Visit, Julia; or, the Illuminated Baron, The Mysterious Penitent, Love and Horrors*. Abundant and thrilling as were the contents of those boxes shipped from England, there were some unforgivable omissions. There is no record of her having received *The Nun's Picture*, by Regina Maria Roche; *Melmoth the Wanderer*, or *The Fatal Revenge* by Charles Robert Maturin; *Mystery, The Impenetrable Secret, The Fatal Vow, The Unknown, Very Strange but Very True*, or *Astonishment! ! ! ! !*, by Francis Lathom. Who could have been the correspondent, hard-hearted or negligent but altogether reprehensible, who denied her the supreme bliss of perusing *The Pillar of Mystery, a Terrific Romance*, and *The Abbess of St. Hilda, a dismal, dreadful, horrid Story!* [1]

Terror romanticism, which had been dormant in English fiction for a century, had incongruously made its appearance in the blustering pages of Smollett's *Ferdinand, Count Fathom*, 1753. For the next twenty-five years it ran an intermittent course, with Horace Walpole and Clara Reeve as its chief exponents. It was in 1789 that Ann Radcliffe, queen of the Gothic novelists, commenced her career with *The Castles of Athlin and Dunbayne*, which was followed by *A Sicilian Romance*, 1790, and *The Romance of the Forest*, 1791. In 1794 she published *The Mysteries of Udolpho*, most popular of all the Gothic romances;

---

[1] The latter two titles are cited by the Rev. Montague Summers in his introduction to *Horrid Mysteries*, by the Marquis of Grosse (London, 1927).

and in 1797 *The Italian*, regarded by modern critics
as her ablest work. The popularity of Mrs. Radcliffe's novels encouraged an almost incredible number of less able writers, whose tales of mystery, blood,
and terror were issued in unchecked numbers for the
next twenty years.

Fresh blood was infused from Germany. The late
seventeen-eighties and the seventeen-nineties saw the
'discovery' of German literature by the English
reading public. Goethe's sentimental, and Tieck's
romantic tales had been known for some time. Schiller introduced the new material of robber-romanti-
cism. Translations, imitations, and thefts from the
German not only increased the bulk but heightened
the extravagance of the English literature of horror.
The German writer of the time (for example, Kotzebue, whose dramas furnished an all but inexhaustible
supply of plots and situations for the English Gothi-
cists) laid absolutely no restraint upon his imagination. In the words of a critic of 1826,[2] he

. . . confounds the monstrous conceptions of whatever
is most strange, terrific, and impossible, with the legiti-
mate province of the imagination. He 'sups his full of
horrors,' and has only a nightmare for the result. He cares
not how violently and absurdly he violates all the laws of
the natural world; it is not enough if he has spurned the
bounds of real creation, and it matters not whither he may
speed in the insanity of his course. He has the complacent
conviction that he must be soaring in the elevation of

[2] Review of Thomas Roscoe's *German Novelists* in *The Monthly Review*, October, 1826.

genius, only because he has quitted the region of common sense. No German writer of novel or romance seems ever to have the most distant suspicion that it is possible to fall into absurdity, nor to be moved with the slightest dread of the ridiculous: nothing is too revolting and unnatural in horror, too puerile and inconsistent in design, too grovelling and absurd in detail, for his diseased invention. In relation of domestic fortunes he mistakes frothy rhapsody for 'the sentiment of the heart,' voluptuous impurity of thought for the workings of the finer passions, a loose morality for metaphysical causation, affectation for pathos, buffoonery for humour, and ribaldry for wit.

This diatribe was just in all respects, except that it should have been made to apply to the English romanticists as well; for they, especially after they had come under the influence of the Germans, laid no limit on extravagance. In 1795, Matthew Gregory Lewis, graduate with horrors from the German school of literature, capped the climax of sensationalism with *The Monk*, which ought to have been the end but proved to be the beginning of his career of literary excess. From then on the lid was off. Authors produced and readers devoured romantic novels in numbers as great as their quality was absurd and grotesque.

It can readily be imagined that the Gothic novel with all its flimsy trappings of haunted castles, secret chambers, swinging tapestries, and creaking doors; with its automaton heroines (differing from each other only in being dark or fair) who shrieked and fainted, and who sang romantic ditties and spoke sentimental soliloquies; its heroes who rhapsodized and ranted, and its villains who swore fiercely and pursued relentlessly; it can readily be imagined, that this incontinent type of fiction came in for a large share of abuse from the critics and ridicule from the burlesquers. The dual aim of the burlesque novels written at this time makes it difficult to classify them. The demon of Gothic romance seldom appeared in the novels unaccompanied by the weeping lady of sentiment; consequently, the same burlesque usually ridiculed both excessive sensibility and excessive Gothicism. Many of those discussed in a previous chapter as burlesques of the sentimental novel were to a greater or less extent burlesques of the Gothic novel as well: notably, Beckford's *Modern Novel Writing* and *Azemia*, the anonymous *Susanna*, Sarah Green's *Romance Readers and Romance Writers*, and Mary Charlton's *Rosella*.

Among the most repeatedly burlesqued novelists of the time was Matthew Gregory Lewis, who, as it ironically happens, was himself the first to write burlesque against the Gothic school. *The Effusions of Sensibility*, written in 1791, has already been mentioned for its ridicule of sentimentalism; it contains also a parody description of a castle with antique towers and several passages of landscape description which burlesque the style of the newly popular Mrs. Radcliffe. For example, on the day that Lady Honoria Harrowheart was obliged to quit her 'ancestral' home for London:

Fair and smiling blushed the young and rubicund morn when I stepped into my father's postchaise and four, on

Friday last. The azure atmosphere smiled with touching serenity; the feathered songsters poured forth their early orisons from the May-besprinkled bushes; and the heifers, hastening to their daily labours, lowed cheerfully to hail the gold-streaked dawn. But my sad heart was incapable of sharing the calm pleasures which on all sides offered themselves to my eyes. In vain did the atmosphere smile — I could not smile at the atmosphere. In vain did the birds trill their warbling songs — I could not trill my song in concert with theirs. In vain did the heifers low — I could not low in return. . . .

The burlesque was written when Lewis was sixteen; in 1795, when he was twenty, he published *The Monk*. It drew forth such torrents of abuse as no English novel before and few since. The fact that Lewis on the title page of his second edition acknowledged that he was a member of Parliament added to his notoriety. He was scored by both the professional critics and the general public on the grounds of indecency, want of taste, plagiarism, and irreverence. His sardonic suggestion that the obscene passages be deleted from the Bible was hailed as the height of impiety. The third edition of his romance, universally denounced but also universally read, was caused to be seized by the Society for the Suppression of Vice; and he was obliged to expurgate the fourth.

The most effective of Lewis's assailants was T. J. Matthias, author of *The Pursuits of Literature*, a satirical poem in four parts, published 1794–97. His well kept anonymity was maddening to his contemporaries, for in his Dunciad-like poem he abused almost every writer of the time who had the smallest claim to fame. His contempt for Gothic romances in general is voiced in several notable passages:

> Is it for me to creep, or soar, or doze,
> In modish song, or fashionable prose,
> To pen with garreteers obscure and shabby,
> Inscriptive nonsense in some fancied *Abbey*?

And again

> Shall nought but ghosts and trinkets be display'd,
> Since Walpole ply'd the virtuoso's trade,
> Bade sober truth revers'd for fiction pass,
> And mus'd o'er Gothic toys through Gothic glass?

But these lines were written and published before he had read *The Monk*. Having done so, he was prompted to devote the fourth and last part of his poem to 'Monk' Lewis, whom he compared to the notorious Edmund Curll and declared indictable at common law; whom he denounced as 'another Cleland,' invoking the ministers of law and justice to punish this 'indecent and blasphemous author.' Even Lewis, vain as he was of his notoriety, was stung to retaliate the following year with *Impartial Strictures on the poem called " The Pursuits of Literature": and particularly a vindication of the Romance of " The Monk."*

A three volume parody-burlesque called *The New Monk*, by "R. S. Esq.," was published by the Minerva Press in 1798. In its five hundred pages almost every character and incident of the original is turned into ridicule. Lewis's ascetic monk, Ambrosio, who moves great audiences with his austere eloquence, becomes Joshua Pentateuch, a Methodist parson who makes converts by preaching hell fire and damnation; Ambrosio's sinister lust is replaced by Pentateuch's gluttonous appetite for roast pork. The Spain and Madrid of Lewis's romance are transformed into England and London, and Germany into Ireland, where, instead of a Bleeding Nun, a Bleeding Physician is encountered. The fateful convent where Antonia suffered is reduced in the parody to Mrs. Rod's Boarding School for Young Misses; Ambrosio suffered arduous but at least dignified imprisonment by the Spanish Inquisition, but Pentateuch is thrown into Newgate.

The New Monk is at its best in an incident where 'R. S.' turns Lewis's own words (and his own book) against him. Ambrosio, of *The Monk*, had one day discovered the young and innocent Antonia reading the Bible. He expressed surprise and disapproval that she should be allowed to read in unexpurgated form a book that contained many indecent passages, calculated to corrupt untutored minds. At Ambrosio's instigation, the mother of Antonia copies out the Bible in her own hand, omitting the offensive parts, so that it may be fit for her daughter's perusal. The scene is exactly duplicated in the parody, except that *The Monk* is substituted for the Bible. Thus Lewis's own novel is denounced in the very words that he himself had used against the Bible.

In spite of the excellent opportunity which the extravagance of *The Monk* afforded, and in spite of the clever framework which 'R. S.' set up, his parody-burlesque does not come off. The contemporary crit-

ics would have welcomed eagerly any witty attack on
a book that they despised so much, but even one of
them was forced to admit that, although there is
"considerable humour in some parts . . . the undertaking, upon the whole, was too great for the author's
stock of wit." Few writers can be witty for five hundred pages at the expense of some one else's book, and
'R. S.' was certainly not one of them. Moreover he
himself is frequently guilty of such irreverence and
vulgarity as even Lewis would have blushed at. His
strictures on the much-abused Methodists, together
with many indecent passages (usually not on the subject of sex), as well as the too great length of his book,
were the causes of its being unenthusiastically received, in spite of its timeliness.

Lewis's romantic ballads, published in two installments as *Tales of Terror*, 1799, *Tales of Wonder*, 1800,
and finally the two groups combined in 1801 as *Tales
of Wonder*, were parodied by more than one author.
In the second edition of *Tales of Terror*, 1801, Lewis
himself reprinted several of the parodies, along with
the originals, and referred to them humorously in the
rhymed "Introductory Dialogue" at the beginning of
the volume. When *Rejected Addresses*, which contained
a poetical parody on Lewis, appeared in 1812, Lewis
remarked to a friend: "Many of them are very fair,
but mine is not at all like; they have made me write
burlesque, which I never do." "You don't know your
own talent," answered the friend. But Lewis did
know it; he was aware, although the world was not,
that he was author of *The Effusions of Sensibility*. It

is not at all unlikely that he was also responsible for some of the parodies of his own ballads that were published in *Tales of Terror*. Lewis had more humor than his contemporaries gave him credit for. One can imagine him in mischievous enjoyment of the public's laughter over these parodies of himself that he perhaps had written, and at their gullibility in taking seriously some of the other tales he had intended as burlesque.

In 1801, 'Mauretius Moonshine' addressed to Lewis an heroic epistle in rhyme entitled *More Wonders!* 'Moonshine' says he had allowed *The Monk* to pass unnoticed:

> When, first, you made the gaping million drunk,
> Did I expose the baldness of your *Monk*,
> Did I discover the mysterious hole,
> From whence your putrid carcasses you stole?

But the latest outrageous plagiarisms in *Tales of Wonder* have provoked him to attack. In a dream he has seen a host of ravished books descend from their shelves and each tear away the part that belonged to it; in the end very little of Lewis's work was left. In 1801 also appeared, anonymously, *The Old Hag in a Red Cloak*, a rhymed burlesque in which Lewis is represented as the son of Mother Goose and a German romancer. Mother Goose, indignant at her son for having tried to usurp her place, in a mock-Gothic scene causes all of his characters to fly off to hell and the devil. Like Lewis's romantic ballads, the piece ends in didactic vein:

If you wish me the moral, dear Mat, to rehearse,
'Tis, that nonsense is nonsense, in prose or in verse;
That all, who to talents claim any pretense,
Should write not at all, or should write COMMON SENSE.

Tales of the Devil, 1801, "from the original gibberish of Professor Lumpwitz, S. U. S. and C. A. C. of the University of Snoringberg," were four rhymed burlesque tales of terror in ridicule of Lewis and the German romanticists. But their author must have been a pupil of the 'professor,' for his satire is dull, obvious, elephantine. The same may be said for the author of an unnamed skit that appeared in *The Satirist* for April, 1810. At a Valentine party Lewis's Monk is made to read a pseudo-horrible valentine which alarmed all present, "except one or two philosophical ladies."

The works of 'Monk' Lewis and Mrs. Radcliffe were by far the most popular objects for the burlesquers of the Gothic romance; there were few indeed which did not at least mention them both.

The Satirist for April, 1808, printed a short "romance in the modern style," entitled "The Organ-Blower," which was a burlesque Gothic tale. The brave knight Isadore is promised the hand of the fair Seraphina if he will rescue her and her father from a demon who torments them nightly with a gruesome serenade on the organ in a church near by. Sir Isadore accomplishes his task under mock-macabre circumstances, by slaying with his sword not the demon, but the organ-blower. The skit might well have passed in its day for an allegory in which Seraphina stood for the young lady novel-reader; the demon, for the Gothic novel; and Sir Isadore for the critic, who, with the sword of satire, slew the organ-blower-author.

"Never did knight-errantry require the inimitable ridicule of *Cervantes* in *Spain*," wrote 'Mauretius Moonshine' in 1808, apropos of the Gothic romance, "more than this preposterous fashion does the burlesque gravity of some able writer, in *England*, at this moment." The able writer was soon to show himself. In 1813 appeared *The Heroine*, by Eaton Stannard Barrett, of which a contemporary said: "This work has been pronounced not inferior in wit and humour to Tristram Shandy, and in point of plot and interest infinitely beyond *Don Quixote*." [3] Although this praise is far too great and although Barrett's masterpiece must always suffer by the inescapable comparison, his imitation of *Don Quixote* is infinitely superior to any of those that came before. It is chiefly against the Gothic romance, at this time already toppling under the weight of its own imbecilities, that he directed his skilful, spirited burlesque. Realizing, as Mrs. Lennox, Maria Edgeworth, and the others had not, that so broad a form of humor does not mingle well with forthright didacticism, he offers pure ridicule as his antidote for folly, never once intruding upon his reader with a sermon.

[3] The popularity of the book, known also as *Cherubina, The Adventures of Cherubina*, and also as *The Adventures of a Fair Romance Reader*, is attested by the fact that it had a second English edition in 1814, and a third in 1815. The first American edition was in 1815, and it was reprinted in America five times subsequently before 1840. There have been two modern English editions, one in 1909 and one in 1927.

Cherry Wilkinson has saturated her mind with sentimental and Gothic fiction, especially *The Mysteries of Udolpho*. She determines to become a heroine herself. The obstacles are that her life is normal and happy, and that she is a plain farmer's daughter; but her ready imagination comes to her aid. The 'fat, funny' Wilkinson is only *pretending* to be her father; he is in a conspiracy with her distant relation Lady Gwyn to cheat her out of her rightful inheritance of money, lands and a title. Her real name is, let her see — Cherubina de Willoughby! She refuses to marry the handsome but unromantic Stuart, and, in order to avoid doing so, elopes in conventional heroine style, leaving a note on her toilet table addressed to "Gregory Wilkinson, Farmer," and signed "the much injured, Cherubina de Willoughby." The novel from then on concerns the burlesque adventures of Cherubina as Gothic-sentimental heroine, in London and on the estate of Lady Gwyn. In the end she is completely cured, marries Stuart, and settles down into a decent housewife.

The loose, picaresque structure of *The Heroine* allowed Barrett to bring in whatever incidents and characters he chose, and to use all sorts of devices for purposes of burlesque. There are several banquet scenes, a court trial, a mock siege, and a masquerade. The characters write poems, essays, and songs; they relate their life adventures whenever occasion offers. The satire depends almost entirely on incident and on these mock literary efforts of the characters, which Barrett takes pains to make both varied and lively.

He insured that the identity of his victims shall be unmistakable by appending a list of them to the second and subsequent editions. Fielding, Smollett, and Maria Edgeworth all escape; but they are the only novelists then well known at whom he does not cast at least a casual missile. Cherubina justifies a deviation from veracity by citing the example of Clarissa Harlowe; at the theatre she separates herself from the rest of her party in emulation of Evelina at the opera; Lord Altamont Mortimer Montmorenci reinstates himself in her favor, after a cowardly apology to Stuart, by showing her a passage from *la Nouvelle Héloïse*; she consoles herself in one of her wildest escapades by reflecting that Harriet Byron of *Sir Charles Grandison* too went mad about the country in masquerade costume. Some conception of the range of Barrett's satire may be gained by the following list of authors who are referred to by name: Ann Radcliffe, Sydney Owenson (Lady Morgan), Laurence Sterne, Edmund Burke, Regina Maria Roche, Samuel Johnson, Goethe, Jean Jacques Rousseau, Fanny Burney, Sir Walter Scott, Sophia Lee, Sir Francis Burdett, Mme. de Staël, Ossian, Milton, Napoleon Bonaparte, Mme. de Genlis, Mrs. Bennett, 'Monk' Lewis, Mme. de Montolieu, Samuel Richardson, Hannah More, Mrs. Griffiths, the Misses Culbertson, James Thomson, Peter Middleton Darling, and Lord Byron. But these names by no means represent the whole of the matter referred to by implication and inference in this amazing burlesque. The circulating libraries of the time would have to be reconstructed

and ransacked before an exhaustive list could be com-
piled; authors a century dead would have to be resur-
rected, and Grub Street give up its dust-covered
secrets. Barrett does not let escape him one fault or
absurdity in the novels of his time; and, as if gifted
with prophetic vision, he aims some surprisingly accurate criticisms at those that were to follow. For
example, when *The Heroine* appeared, none of the
Waverley novels had been written; and yet Sir
Whylom Eftsoones, Jerry Sullivan, and the adventures of Cherubina at Moncton Castle might well
have been invented in pleasant mockery of Scott's
novels, as they undoubtedly were of his poetry.

Among the diversions offered in *The Heroine* is
"The Memoirs of James Higginson, by Himself."
Higginson, in his endeavor "to avoid the vulgar
phraseology of the low, and to discuss the very
weather with a sententious association of polysylla-
bical ratiocination," distinguishes himself at once as
an accomplished imitator of the Leviathan of literature. Truth and modesty are the only virtues of
which he can permit himself to boast, but even these
have not in his case proven wholly satisfactory: "To
be unassuming in an age of impudence, and veracious
in an age of mendacity, is to combat with a sword of
glass against a sword of steel; the transparency of the
one may be more beautiful than the opacity of the
other; yet let it be recollected that the transparency
is accompanied with brittleness, and the opacity with
consolidation." The Brobdingnagian fancy of the
following poem by Higginson so delighted Oliver

Wendell Holmes that he could quote it from memory years after he had read it:

To Dorothy Pulvertaft

If Black-sea, White-sea, Red-sea ran
One tide of ink to Ispahan;
If all the geese in Lincoln fens
Produc'd spontaneous, well-made pens;
If Holland old, or Holland new,
One wond'rous sheet of paper grew;
Could I, by stenographic power,
Write twenty libraries in an hour;
And should I sing but half the grace
Of half a freckle on thy face;
Each syllable I wrote, should reach
From Inverness to Bognor's beach;
Each hairstroke be a river Rhine,
Each verse an equinoctial line.

The Heroine is pure fun from start to finish. Even in her most sober moments we are not required to take Cherubina quite seriously, nor does she seem to regard herself otherwise than as an adventurous young girl out on a lark. She takes the business of being a 'heroine' seriously enough to make it interesting for herself and others, but she is always playing a part, and even when the farce becomes pretty rough she continues to play it with all the determination of an imaginative child that refuses to be disillusioned. She not only seeks, but compels romantic adventure, forcing the circumstances of her normal, humdrum life into conformity with her conception of a heroine's. She even endows those around her with some-

thing of her own zealous spirit. One by one, her companions fall under her spell and good naturedly join
her in her rollicking chase after adventure. An old
lecher named Betterton, who at first tried to seduce
her, is melted by her naïve charm into a sort of benevolent uncle and provides an elaborate entertainment for her in the form of a Gothic chamber and a
ghost that sneezed and cursed. Kindly Jerry Sullivan, her faithful Sancho Panza from the first, openly
regards her as a frolicsome young miss who will soon
be tired of play-acting and become herself again.
Even her *bona fide* and none too imaginative suitor,
Stuart, views her escapades with a tolerant eye and
aids her in them, foreseeing her inevitable return to
the normal. There is even the slightest suggestion of
Mistress Millamant in Cherubina. Just as that capricious Restoration heroine must have her period of
flirtation before she can 'dwindle into a wife,' so
Cherubina must have her romantic adventures,
mock-heroic though they be.

Justly Barrett's most famous work, it is nothing
like so well known today as it deserves to be. It
was "read and applauded" by Sir Walter Scott. Jane
Austen declared herself "much amused" and "exceedingly diverted" by it, and speaks of it in a letter
as a "delightful burlesque on the Radcliffe style."
In 1835, Edgar Allan Poe published a long and enthusiastic review of it in *the Southern Literary Mes-
senger*. In summarizing his opinion he says, "Its wit,
especially, and its humor, are indisputable — not
frittered and refined away into that insipid com-

pound which we occasionally meet with, half giggle and half sentiment — but racy, dashing, and palpable." And again, "There are few books written with more tact, spirit, naïveté, or grace, few which take hold more irresistibly upon the imagination of the reader, and none more fairly entitled to rank among the classics of English literature."

Naturally Barrett cannot be given entire credit for the improvement that took place in the English novel in the second and third decades of the nineteenth century. This was due partly to the fact that the public was worn out with the silly novels of sentiment and supernatural terror, and demanded something better — or something different. It was due partly to the genius of Scott and of Jane Austen. But a share of the credit certainly belongs to Barrett, whose book was readable, witty, timely, and, what is more to the point, was widely read. *The Heroine* attacks, brilliantly and ably, contemporary faults in novelwriting; it points no elaborate moral lesson, but it was, nevertheless, moral, in its salutary influence on the taste of novel writers and novel readers. Barrett may not have given the actual *coup de grâce* to the demon of romance; but he certainly stood over the corpse in as truculent and triumphant a manner as did Falstaff over that of Hotspur.

As early as 1803 Barrett had first burlesqued contemporary fiction in a mock newspaper called *The Comet*. It was published in book form and contained satirical skits on political and social as well as literary subjects. Among the burlesque book advertisements

are "The Tortuous Twitches of Exquisite Sensibility," by the author of The Bloody Bodkin, "A Com-
pendium on the Art of Cutting Bread and Butter,"
and "The Glaring Eyeball: an Electrifying Romance,
humbly dedicated to the lethargic." It contains also
"A Tale of Horror," dedicated to Mr. Scott and Mr.
Lewis:

> A man once felt, on a certain night
> As he gazed aloft at the moon,
> That he was put in a lucky plight
> By a raven, that dropp'd on him in its flight,
> What was not a pleasant boon.
>
> He did not start when the boon did fall!
> And his face did not fear denote!
> And he did not utter a single squall!
> And his face did not turn any colour at all!
> And he did not cut his throat! ! !

Barrett's final work was *The Hero; or, the Adventures of a Night*, a companion piece to *The Heroine*,
published in 1817, the year of his death. It has never
before been recognized as Barrett's although its style
and burlesque method are very like his. However, in
the 1815 edition of *The Heroine* appears a hitherto
unnoticed advertisement of *The Hero*, as a forthcom-
ing publication "by the author of the Heroine." It is
asserted that the book was translated "from the Ara-
bic into Iroquese; from the Iroquese into Hottentot;
from the Hottentot into French; and from the French
into English."
The 'hero' is a wealthy profiteer of the early Napo-

leonic era. Although he is represented as a French citizen, his name is Dob. Afflicted with ennui, he retired to his country home outside of Paris, where he is visited by his son's friend, Dubert, who lends him the following English romances: *The Mysteries of Udolpho*, *The Tomb*, *Grasville Abbey*, *The Monk*, *Hubert de Sévrac*, *Celestina*, and *The Knights of the Swan*. Mr. Dob reads them all avidly, especially *The Monk*, and falls completely under their influence. Then one night, just before bedtime, as he is dozing in his chair, a monk appears suddenly and mysteriously before him and conducts him to a ruined abbey. Here he undergoes a long series of adventures exactly similar to those in the Gothic romances he has been reading. The last incident is a parody of the final scene of *The Monk*. Mr. Dob is seized by a fiend, lifted bodily in the air, and landed in a prison full of macabre horrors. There he is forced by threats of death and damnation to sign an agreement not to read in the future any novels except those by Fielding, Smollett, Miss Edgeworth, the author of *Pride and Prejudice*, and similar writers. At first he refuses, but the fiend threatens that if he hesitates longer he will be forced to read a chapter from the second part of Hannah More's *Coelebs in Search of a Wife*, whereupon Mr. Dob shudders, and signs. In the end the reader learns that the whole affair has been a plot of the young Dubert to get Mr. Dob's consent to his son's marriage to the penniless Ursula, which Mr. Dob had hitherto refused.

Each of the incidents of the burlesque is a parody

of a scene from one of the romances mentioned; care-
ful footnotes give the page and volume where the originals may be found in one of the six English romances mentioned, all of which had been translated
into French. Although it is similar to *The Heroine*,
its merit is far less. There are a few scenes in Barrett's best manner, but the incidents are monoto-
nously similar to each other and the humor is often
forced. The hero seems to be half aware that he is
being duped, and this proves fatal to the reader's interest, who sympathizes with the critic in *The Monthly
Review* whose smiles were 'distended into yawns' and
who wished that the two volumes had been com-
pressed into one.

At the end of the eighteenth century it had become
so commendable to abuse the novels of the day by
means of burlesque and other forms of satire that a
few inferior novelists foisted their own worthless productions upon the public in the fashionable guise of
burlesque novels. In 1798, the Minerva Press published *More Ghosts!* "by the Wife of an Officer."
The authoress asserts that the manuscript of her
work had been discovered in a farmhouse where she
was spending the summer and that it seems to her to
be a burlesque of ghosts and mysteries. It is obviously not a burlesque, however, and her claim that it
is seems merely a device to attract popular notice. It
is true that her ghost turns out at the end to be a real
person, but this fact is not disclosed to the reader
until all the mystery and sensation have been extracted from the situation. The novel is just as in-

sincere in other respects. It is filled with seductions and with hairbreadth escapes from seduction; there is even a suggestion of incest. Nevertheless, the 'Wife of an Officer' manages to give a 'moral' turn to her improper passages in time, or almost in time, to save herself from unfavorable criticism. For example, the hero, Thomas Grey, having just completed reading Ovid's *Art of Love*, wanders out into an orchard where he encounters a young lady who has been reading an equally inflammatory volume. The author carries her account of the subsequent seduction scene as far as she dares, then turns on the reader and warns him not to read novels that are calculated to arouse the passions. *More Ghosts!* is devoid of intentional humor, burlesque or otherwise; certainly the closing words to the reader are not *intended* to be funny: "Adieu, my patient companion."

Truth and Fiction, 1801, by Mrs. Elizabeth Sarah Villa-Real Gooch, is another novel in which the author attempts to win readers by abusing other novels. Her preface is a vociferous condemnation of almost every kind of novel that was then popular. Her purpose is, without wandering from 'the path of Nature,' to relieve 'the severities of TRUTH by the embellishments of FICTION.' Her leading object will have been accomplished if she is able to excite 'in the breast of her reader' those sensations 'which it is honorable for the breast to feel.' But her own novel is in the worst sentimental tradition. Moreover, in defiance of her strong prefatory attack on Gothic romances, she includes in her own novel an extensive episode entitled "The History of Antonio, Count Genzano; or, the Dominion of the Passions," which turns out to be a Gothic romance of the purplest dye.

No treatment of anti-romantic fiction would be complete without the mention of Thomas Love Peacock. His 'novels of talk' are, however, satires against the romantic movement in general, rather than burlesques of particular romantic novels. The title of *Nightmare Abbey*, 1818, is certainly a take-off of Gothic titles, and some of the incidents (like Scythrop's concealing the 'oppressed' Celinda in a lonely tower) are written in burlesque of situations in the conventional novels of the day. *The Sorrows of Werther* and *Horrid Mysteries* are mentioned as having partly inspired Scythrop's absurd romantic notions. Most of the satire is against romanticism in the abstract, however, and some of it is personal: the vacillating, lovesick Scythrop is Shelley; the transcendental Flosky is Coleridge; the pessimistic Cypress is Byron. *Headlong Hall*, 1815, contains a minor character named Miss Philomela Poppyseed, who recounts to the Reverend Doctor Gaster the plot of a "very moral and aristocratical novel" that she is preparing for the press:

[She] continued holding forth, with her eyes half shut, till a long-drawn nasal tone from the reverend divine compelled her suddenly to open them in all the indignation of surprise. The cessation to the hum of her voice awakened the reverend gentleman, who, lifting up first one eyelid, then the other, articulated, or rather murmured, "Admirably planned, indeed!"

"I have not quite finished, sir," said Miss Philomela,

bridling. "Will you have the goodness to inform me where I left off?"

The doctor hummed a while, and at length answered: "I think you had just laid it down as a position, that a thousand a year is an indispensable ingredient in the passion of love, and that no man, who is not so far gifted by *nature*, can reasonably presume to feel that passion himself, or be correctly the object of it with a well-educated female."

"That, sir," said Miss Philomela, highly incensed, "is the fundamental principle which I lay down in the first chapter, and which the whole four volumes, of which I detailed to you the outline, are intended to set in a strong practical light."

"Bless me!" said the doctor, "what a nap I must have had!"

Nearly all of Peacock's fiction contains satirical treatment of romantic themes, but the actual parody and burlesque that they contain is merely incidental. Charming as his novels are, they must, like *The Shaving of Shagpat* and *Farina* by his son-in-law, George Meredith, be omitted from this discussion of novels which ridicule other novels by burlesque imitation.

Finally, mention may be made of some of the dramatic burlesques of the terror romance. The earliest was *The Haunted Tower*, a comic opera by James Cobb, first published in 1790 and republished four times before 1830; its initial run was sixty nights. Gilbert à Beckett's *The Castle of Otranto*, "a romantic extravaganza in one act," was republished in Cumberland's collection of plays in 1837; the date of its first publication has not been determined. Its subject is that of Walpole's novel of the same name, of which it is an absurd travesty. An ephemeral publication of 1799–1800 called *The Meteors* printed a mock-drama entitled *The Benevolent Cut-throat*, "by Klotzboggen." It was written in ridicule of the overwhelmingly popular and prolific German dramatist Kotzebue, and is, according to F. W. Stokoe,[4] "obvious and clumsy."

Most famous of all the burlesque dramas of the time was the fragment of a play called *The Rovers; or, the Double Arrangement*, which was published in *The Anti-Jacobin* in June, 1798. The immediate occasion of it was the appearance in 1798 of a translation of Goethe's *Stella*. But *The Rovers*, the greater portion of which was by George Canning,[5] was directed also at *The Robbers* and several others of Schiller's plays, at a German play called *Cabal and Love*, at Kotzebue's *The Stranger*, and at a translation from the German, by a Mr. Render, called *Count Renyowsky; or, the Conspiracy of Kamtschatka*. It is a witty and effective attack on the whole group of German dramas of sentiment and horror. Here appeared first the famous "Rogero's Song," the sixth stanza of which was written by Mr. Pitt in his delight at the rest. Rogero, the hero of the piece, has been imprisoned for eleven years in a subterraneous vault, surrounded by coffins, death's heads, cross-bones, and all sorts of horrors. He sings to the tune of "Lanterna Magica":

[4] In his *German Influence in the English Romantic Period* (1926).
[5] Cf. p. 86.

Whene'er with haggard eyes I view
This dungeon that I'm rotting in,
I think of those companions true
Who studied with me at the U-
-niversity of Gottingen-
-niversity of Gottingen.

(Weeps, and pulls out a blue kerchief, with which he
wipes his eyes; gazing tenderly at it, he proceeds —)

Sweet kerchief, checked with heavenly blue,
Which once my love sat knotting in! —
Alas! Matilda *then* was true! —
At least I thought so at the U-
-niversity of Gottingen-
-niversity of Gottingen.

(At the repetition of this line, Rogero clanks his
chains in cadence.)

Barbs! barbs! alas! how swift you flew,
Her neat post-waggon trotting in!
Ye bore Matilda from my view;
Forlorn I languished at the U-
-niversity of Gottingen-
-niversity of Gottingen.

This faded form! this pallid hue!
This blood my veins is clotting in!
My years are many — they were few
When first I enter'd at the U-
-niversity of Gottingen-
-niversity of Gottingen.

There first for thee my passion grew,
Sweet! sweet Matilda Pottingen!
Thou wast the daughter of my Tutor, Law Professor at the U-
-niversity of Gottingen-
-niversity of Gottingen.

Sun, moon, and thou, vain world, adieu,
That kings and priests are plotting in:
Here doomed to starve on water gru-
el, never shall I see the U-
-niversity of Gottingen-
-niversity of Gottingen.

It is to this play that the decline in the popularity of
German horror drama in England has often been
attributed.

IX. 'WHEN KNIGHTHOOD WAS IN FULL BLOOM'

EIGHTEENTH–CENTURY historical fiction owed its beginning chiefly to the Gothic romance. The settings of the majority of the tales of terror were mediaeval, and the authors of them attempted, sometimes successfully, sometimes not, to provide a real historical background. It is true that in Walpole's *The Castle of Otranto* mediaeval Italy is hardly more than a nominal setting; but Clara Reeve assigned *The Old English Baron* quite definitely to fifteenth-century England during the minority of Henry VI and actually gave it some coloring of historical detail. Sophia Lee's *The Recess*, 1783–86, laid even more emphasis on historical background. From 1790 on, more and more Gothic romances appeared that might also be termed historical romances. Finally, in 1803, came Jane Porter's *Thaddeus of Warsaw*, the only historical novel that was not also Gothic — except for Thomas Leland's *Longsword*, 1762 — that had appeared since Defoe's *Memoirs of a Cavalier*. The devices used by the earlier writers to give an air of authenticity to their improbable tales were, to say the least, inadequate. Fifteenth-century characters spoke eighteenth-century English; French and Italian young ladies, though they might be living (supposedly) in the age of feudalism, invariably wrote

English poems in the manner of Gray, Cowper, or the Wartons. With monotonous regularity, each romance would begin with a declaration that it was not written by the author at all, but merely copied from an old black-letter manuscript, discovered in a trunk, or in the dungeon of an ancient castle; not infrequently the story was told by the ghost of some mediaeval celebrity, who had confided it to the author as he or she was wandering at midnight in the precincts of a ruined abbey.

More than twenty years before Scott, by the publication of *Waverley*, had set up a permanent model for the historical novel, it was made the object of burlesque in three charmingly written tales by James White, a writer who deserves more recognition than he has ever received either in his own day or since. The first of his works, *Earl Strongbow; or, The History of Richard de Clare and the Beautiful Geralda*, 1789, is, like the two others, partly burlesque, partly satire on contemporary manners and customs, and partly a seriously intended historical romance. *Earl Strongbow* begins with a travesty of the stock device of the 'discovered' manuscript. Just outside of Chepstow, when the author is on a walking tour, he discovers an old woman living in the ruins of a mediaeval castle. She guides him through the ruin and he becomes so charmed with the place that he decides to remain for several months. She produces a manuscript written by a man who had been a prisoner in that very castle during the reign of Charles II. The manuscript tells how the prisoner, walking on the battlements at midnight, encounters the armor-clad ghost of the twelfth-century Earl Strongbow, who begins to tell the story of his life in Norman French, which the prisoner fortunately understands. Thus we have the story of the twelfth century, told by a ghost to a person of the seventeenth, who writes it down in a manuscript which is discovered by the eighteenth-century author, who finally transmits it to the reader.

When the ghost of Earl Strongbow begins to converse, the prisoner expresses his surprise that he does not speak in the hollow tone "in which, it is said, the spirits of departed persons are accustomed to address the living":

> Be assured, replied the noble vision, that it is mere affectation, and intended to give an air of consequence to what they say. The souls of the deceased, when wandering in this upper world, have exactly the same tone of voice which was peculiar to them when enclosed in a mortal body.

He asks pardon for boasting, but reminds his listener that ghosts have no third person to speak for them. They are obliged to spend most of their time in insipid oblivion, sending scouts at Pentecost or Christmas to gather a little terrestrial scandal to relieve their boredom. They can remember everything that happened in the world while they were alive, but have to be told about subsequent events. Earl Strongbow says that he often makes tours of inspection about the scenes of his former life, and is diverted by the effeminacy of the age of Charles II as compared with the virility of his own age.

We handled the battle-ax, you wield the dice-box. We ran at the ring, you play ombre. Our breakfast was beef and ale, yours is toast and chocolate. Instead of wigs we wore helmets.

But as he proceeds with his narrative we see that life in the Middle Ages was not so ideal as the novelists pretend; for the Earl's romantic adventures are plentifully seasoned with realistic incidents. Fat political knights make long-winded meaningless speeches then as now, while the noble audience munch apples out of their helmets: thus is described a twelfth-century council of war. In the same semi-satirical, semi-realistic style a tournament, a siege, a battle, an abduction, and many other stock incidents of the conventional historical tale are recounted. James White's book is difficult to describe, being at times a seriously told romance, and at others a satire on contemporary and ancient manners, and frequently a burlesque of the very thing that he himself is doing, the writing of historical romances.

White's other two novels are of the same kind. *The Adventures of John of Gaunt, Duke of Gloucester*, 1790, is an account of John of Gaunt's journey into Wales, accompanied by the Black Prince and the Dukes of York and Gloucester; they are joined on their way by Geoffrey Chaucer and Owen Glendower. In his preface the author states that his story came from an old vellum-bound manuscript discovered in the house where Chaucer lived. The work, which contains a charming description of Chaucer's residence at Woodstock, is in the same satirical vein as the former one.

White's third and last novel was *The Adventures of Richard Coeur-de-Lion*, 1791. In the preface he complains that the young lady novel readers do not like his works; they prefer "those delicate histories in a series of letters, which heretofore they had been in the habit of reading." However, he will leave the follies of his own time to the incomparable authoress of *Cecilia*, "resolving to explore the remote doings of antiquity, to *show life*, as life was, in those heroic days, and evince that our forefathers were as foolish as we are ourselves." What follows is his masterpiece, an historical romance written with reality and with burlesque humor.

Richard Coeur-de-Lion, after his escape from the Duke of Austria's prison, is riding through the forest with his minstrel Fitzherbert.

At length they espied a black waggon, which was drawn by six sable horses, and driven by two persons in lugubrious apparel. In the waggon, upon a cushion of black serge that was stuffed with black horsehair, sate a sober-looking lady, neither young nor old. She was clad in a robe of black velvet; on her head she wore a coif of black satin, which was tied beneath her chin. In her hand was a piece of black gauze, which she was dotting with black silk, by way of pastime. She likewise blew her nose with a black handkerchief. At one side of her lay a black cat, and on the other a black dog. In fine, her accompaniments were all very black.[1]

The lady is in determined mourning for her husband. Being rich, she is importuned by many suitors, one of

[1] Cf. the description of the Green Knight in *Sir Gawaine and the Green Knight*.

whom woos her with "an irresistible violet robe, and a gorgeous pink gown." With great effort she has resisted the garments after having tried them on, and is now fleeing from further temptations of the suitor. Richard accompanies Lady Ursulina to her Castle of the Lake, where she immediately causes black to be put on all of her possessions, "the very horns of the oxen and of the kine [being] painted sable."

Richard, after many intervening adventures, undertakes the rescue of a young princess, who, when a child, had been captured by a caitiff knight. With difficulty he wins his way into her presence, having overcome the abductor with a magic potion and securely bound him in chains. But the unnatural maiden has meanwhile fallen in love with the monster and so Richard, instead of being welcomed, is reviled! Richard's conventional knight-errantry is stronger than his tact, however, and he is determined that the 'rescued' maiden shall be taken to her parents, even though he is obliged to tie her on his horse. On the way her cries for help attract a stranger knight who challenges Richard to combat. While they are jousting in approved style, there is what the author terms an 'under-battle' going on between Richard's minstrel and the princess:

"Wretch!" returned the Princess, "let me go incontinently, or, I vow to holy Mary, I will tear out both your eyes." She said, and having snatched his harp, which hung dangling at his girdle, dealt him many cruel blows with Amazonian intrepidity. With one hand she scratched his cheeks, and with the other pinched his ear. In fine, she plucked his beard (his beard, grey and venerable), causing

him to roar till the neighboring woods resounded. . . .
She spit upon his countenance, and kicked him on the shins.

Richard is victorious in his battle, but on the way
home, the princess, still tied behind, sticks pins in the
joinings of his coat of mail, and, with energetic appli-
cations of the same weapons to his courser's hinder
parts, causes the animal to rear and plunge.

The burlesque element is much stronger in *Richard
Coeur-de-Lion* than in White's other works, and yet
is never carried too far to prevent the reader's being
swept back into the romance whenever the author
desires it. The reviewers were less than lukewarm in
their praise of these novels. One of them regrets
White's "heterogeneous plan of combining *History*,
with *Romance*, *Chivalry*, and burlesque *Ridicule*: by
which last ingredient, the Dignity of Heroism is oddly
caricatured." Another speaks of his "misplaced talent" in mingling fiction with history, since it tends to
"poison the source of information for young readers." Still a third remarks, with point enough, that if
knight-errantry were still alive, White might be hailed
as another Cervantes.

If humor had been alive, as it so obviously was not,
in that decade of sentimental nonsense and counter-
feit romance, White's novels would have had the
appreciative audience that they deserved. Forty
years earlier, when Fielding, or forty years later,
when Thackeray was showing the novel-reading public what to laugh at, he would have been appreciated.
As it was, the proud, poverty-stricken author, soon
after the appearance of his third excellent novel,

starved himself to death in a lonely farmhouse near Bath to avoid accepting charity from his friends.[2]

The Jesuit; or, The History of Anthony Babington, Esq., 1799, was a seriously written historical novel, but its anonymous authoress showed in her preface that she was alive to the absurdities of the type that she was imitating. Posing as editor, she ridicules the conventional device of the manuscript by saying that hers came from the identical chest that Ireland's Shakespearean 'discoveries' came from, and offers her own volume as corroboratory testimony of Ireland's good faith. Babington, she asserts, had written his own story on his death bed, and "none but infidels and jacobins will venture to dispute the words of a dying man." Like James White, she is irritated by the contemporary novelist's criticisms of modern times in the light of ancient:

> I find great comfort in contemplating, by means of my researches into novels and history, that we have equal capabilities with our ancestors; that the world, though nearer its end, is not anathematized; and that those who do well are likely to fare well.

But her novel, which lacks the satirical humor of the preface, is no whit better than those she criticizes.

It remained for Benjamin Thompson, notable as the principal translator of Kotzebue's plays, to present the first unmitigated burlesque of historical fiction. *The Florentines; or, Secret Memoirs of the Noble Family de C***, 1808, is a mock romance of an Italian

---

[2] Cf. Miss J. M. S. Tompkins's article "James White, Esq., A Forgotten Humorist," in *Review of English Studies*, iii, p. 146.

family who lived during the Seven Years' War; its materials are love, battles, seductions, duels, sentiment, and bandits. The title page does not come until after the author's introduction, which is entitled "No Chapter, or the One Preceding Chapter the First." The author announces that he is not at all diffident, and intends to do or say whatever comes into his head, and to converse in any method he thinks proper — with the reader, himself, or the moon. The source of his story is in some family papers presented to him by his friend Timothy Sadboy Snooks, who, attracted by the fame of the 'Delta Crusean' school of writers, had made a journey to Italy. A Florentine courtesan had presented him with the papers; she had had them from a fat friar, who had borrowed them from the holy confessor in the family de C**, who had stolen them from . . . "In short," says the author, "I could make out a history as long as 'The house that Jack built.' Suffice it to say, I have them."

Thompson's humor is not always so Shandean nor so obvious; frequently the reader is cajoled into attending to the story for its own sake, only to discover by some subtly phrased aside or some absurd climax to an episode, that he has fallen into a trap and is himself the victim of the burlesquer's jest. In fact, Thompson may well have had the sophisticated purpose of writing a book to be taken seriously or humorously, according to the reader's temperament. It is conceivable that some novel addicts of the time may have read it without a smile; but the more wary, warned by the flippant passages, must have realized that it was a burlesque on contemporary conventionalities in novel writing, particularly on those of the historical novel. However that may be, and however pleasing the satire to the modern reader, it was, like James White's, very coldly received by Thompson's contemporaries.

Another book with the same double purpose was attempted, but far less well achieved, in *Baldwin; or, The Miser's Heir*, 1820, "a serio-comic tale by an Old Bachelor." The author was Richard Harris Barham, minor canon of St. Paul's, who also wrote under the pseudonym of 'George Henry Espaminondas.' His humor falls flat indeed. In *Castle Baynard*, 1824, by 'Hal Willis' (really A. H. Forrester, but better known under his other pseudonym of 'Alfred Crowquill'), the case was strangely reversed. The book was a youthful attempt at a historical novel in the manner of Scott. It was designed to be a serious novel with humorous passages, but was so extravagantly done that the whole was laughed at in a way that the author did not intend, the result being an unintentional travesty.

By 1825, the Waverley novels had stimulated many other imitators into activity. Scott's influence had helped to put an end to the Gothic novel, but, as one reviewer expressed it, there was now being produced a "whole deluge of novels and romances, which not only might not, but could not, have been written, had no Waverley pointed out one particular style and manner of novel-writing." He speaks of

James Fenimore Cooper as one example of a successful imitator, but complains that the best imitations
fall far short of the original, and that most of them
are very bad indeed.

It is interesting to recall here that Edward Waverley, the hero of Scott's first novel, began life as a
romantomaniac. He was allowed by his tutor to
roam at large in the library at Waverley-Honour, "a
large Gothic room, with double arches and a gallery,"
containing "such a miscellaneous and extensive collection of books as had been assembled together, during the course of two hundred years, by a family
which had always been wealthy, and inclined, of
course, as a mark of splendour, to furnish their
shelves with the current literature of the day, without much scrutiny, or nicety of discrimination."
With customary thoroughness, Scott discusses the
nature of the books his hero reads — they are chiefly
historical legends — and their effect upon his character. In chapter v, however, he assures his reader
that his tale is not "an imitation of the romance of
Cervantes," and that his intention "is not to follow
the steps of that inimitable author, in describing such
total perversion of intellect as misconstrues the objects actually presented to the senses, but that more
common aberration from sound judgment, which
apprehends occurrences indeed in their reality, but
communicates to them a tincture of its own romantic
tone and colouring."

The first satire in fiction form against the Scott and
Cooper type of novel was from the pen of the Ameri-

can writer, James Kirke Paulding, who had collab-
orated with Washington Irving on *The Salmagundi
Papers* in 1807, and had also published in 1813 a
parody of *The Lay of the Last Minstrel* entitled *The
Lay of the Scottish Fiddle*. His *Sketch of Old England,
by a New England Man*, 1822, and his *John Bull in
America; or, The New Munchausen*, 1824, are both
burlesque pieces directed against the contemporary
British travelers who wrote offensively about America. In 1823, he published a two-volume novel,
Koningsmarke, the Long Finne, a humorous work
which is divided into books, with introductory chapters in Fielding's mock-heroic style, stating what the
book is and is not to be. Scott is the main object of
attack, and is identified by name, although he is usually referred to as 'the Great Unknown' and as 'the
author of *Kenilworth*.' In book i, chapter i, the author
declares that, like the Great Unknown, he has made
no plan for his novel and does not even know how it
will end. He will not submit to chronology, since to
do so "must materially interfere with the interest and
variety" of his work. He will alter his direction whenever he chooses, will display a detailed knowledge of
ballads and nursery tales, and will, in imitation of the
Great Unknown, seize "any romantic or improbable
adventure" that comes to his mind; moreover, he
promises his reader to hold no intercourse with common sense, that foe to historical novelists. In the introductory chapter of book vi, he makes a spirited
defence of Cooper's recently published novel, *The
Pioneers*, against the charge of vulgarity. For a time

he steps out of his rôle of satirist and stands forth a staunch democrat and a loyal American. Books are not necessarily vulgar because they deal with plain people; moreover, they may be so even when they deal with nobles. The Great Unknown, "in a late popular work," introduces his readers to the court of a king where they are "presented with morals the most debauched and corrupt, with titled pimps, and prostitute duchesses, with a parent seeking to compass the purposes of revenge, by placing his only daughter in the power of a systematic seducer and voluptuary — not the rank of the actors, the splendours of the court, nor the false glitter thrown around the whole by the genius of the writer, can rescue the picture from the imputation of vulgar indecency."

The burlesque element in the story itself is not abundant nor is it so severe as the above censorious passage would lead one to believe. *Koningsmarke* has interest and humor of its own, apart from its ridicule of the historical novel. In style it resembles 'Diedrich Knickerbocker's' *History of New York*, which indeed Paulding mentions in terms of high admiration. Occasionally there are character sketches and descriptive passages that are parodies of Scott. The Mother Bombie of the novel seems to be a take-off of the Meg Merrilies type. The opening sentence is in mild parody of Scott: "The curious traveler along the western bank of the Delaware river, will hardly fail to notice. . . ." The chapter headings, in mockery of Scott, are Mother Goose rhymes. In spite of Paulding's defence of Cooper's novel, he indulges in some good-natured burlesque of Cooper in an episode about the 'Mud Turtle' tribe of Indians, and in several landscape and 'seasonal' descriptions. The book is not a masterpiece, but it is one of which a critic might conscientiously have said that it showed remarkable promise.

The first English corrective of the new type of historical novel was a three-volume burlesque in 1824 called *Scotch Novel Reading; or, Modern Quackery,* "by a Cockney," who claimed that his story was founded on facts. It is here that we find the latest example of the romance-mad young lady used as a vehicle of criticism. Alice Fennel is an attractive young London lady whose mind has become unduly affected by novels about Scotch life. At first she refuses to read any except those written by the 'Great Unknown'; later, however, her enthusiasm for everything Scotch induces her to read his imitators as well. She makes a laughing-stock of herself by affecting a Scotch brogue and by dressing in plaid and bonnet; she names the cook Jenny Deans, her maid Betty Boodle, and designates everything to eat by the name of haggis. Her father wants to marry her to Robert Butler, the son of a lifelong friend; but Robert hates fiction, especially Scotch fiction, and for a long time refuses to allow himself to be presented. At length having discovered by accident that Alice is the original of a portrait he has long adored, he determines to transform her into a suitable wife. He appears before her disguised as a Scotch Highlander, with red hair and moustaches, one eye, one arm, and no nose, posing as Duncan Macgregor, the last living descendant of Rob Roy. By means of Butler's stratagem, and by her experience with some real Scotch people who happen to visit in her home and who prove to be disagreeably different from what she had imagined, Alice is cured of her obsession with everything Scotch. Robert Butler confesses his deception, she forgives him, and the two are happily married.

The satire against Scott and his imitators is sometimes too violent and direct to be effective; but it is amusing to notice the discontent of the Cockney author that so much should be made over Scotland and a mere Scotsman, while England and her authors are neglected. The Scotch, he sarcastically supposes, have formed a mutual admiration society for the purpose of floating one another's books. But all this craze for Scott and his compatriots is a mere literary fad that will soon pass away. There was a time, he says, when only Miss Burney's books could be procured from a circulating library, and afterwards only Mrs. Radcliffe's, and still more recently only those of Rosa Matilda, Miss Owenson, and 'Monk' Lewis. To illustrate his point, he introduces a character — an elder sister of the heroine — who had formerly been mad about Byron's poetry, had named her servants after characters in *The Corsair*, and even on her wedding day dressed herself to resemble 'the bride of Abydos,' but who finally settled down into a sane appreciation of Byron. This, he implies, is what will happen with regard to the present Scott enthusiasts. Why should Scott (he vindictively pursues the sub-

ject), who is an excellent poet, waste his own time and
other people's money with his dull, voluminous novels, which are 'stale,' 'unintelligible,' 'puffed up with
historical registry matter,' each containing the same
wooden characters with no change except that of
name? Finally, he refuses to believe that one person
could write so many novels, preferring to think that
there is a cabal of writers as well as readers:

The pageantry of the old, vain maiden queen at Kenilworth, the worn-out story of Robin Hood, the king-craft of
James I, and many more historical records have furnished
matter for very many pages; and, if a man has any brains,
any genius at all, the deuce is in it, if he cannot patch up a
long story, aided by an imagination by no means of the
common order, quite the reverse. It is his imitators I find
most fault with: nothing now goes down but Scotch stories;
and Scotch dialect, by the way a very unpleasant one, is
thrust upon us, as if there was not another country under
the sun worth hearing of than poor, miserable little
Scotland.

Late in 1826 appeared *Brambletye House*, a serious
effort at a historical novel. It covered the same
period as Scott's *Peveril of the Peak*; that is, the mid-
seventeenth century. The reviewers accused it of
dulness, servile imitation of Scott, dragging in historical celebrities without sufficient reason, pomposity of style, and unpardonable inaccuracy. It was
by Horace Smith, co-author of the fourteen-year-old,
but still popular, *Rejected Addresses*, those clever
rhymed burlesques of every well known author of the
time. Even if his novel had not so richly deserved
attack, Horace Smith, himself a famous burlesquer,

could hardly have hoped to escape. Poetic justice was fulfilled less than a year later with the appearance of *Whitehall; or, The Days of George IV*, by Dr. William Maginn.

The 'editor's' preface stated that *Whitehall* was printed at Teynimhakawaranenopolis, capital of the great empire Yankeedoodoolia, in the year 2227, exactly four hundred years in the future, and that it was going to give quite as graphic and correct a picture of that day and place as the generality of novels now being published gave of the times four hundred years in the past. (Actually the scene is the London of the author's own day.) The satire is directed against the imitators of Scott — especially the author of *Brambletye House*.

Horace Smith had put into his novel a character which was a little too obviously a copy of Meg Merrilies, a character which Maginn burlesques as "the grand-daughter of Meg Merrilies." *Brambletye House* had introduced, with an absurd lack of motive, almost every famous character and incident of the time about which it was written: Cromwell, Samuel Pepys, Charles II, the Duke of Monmouth, Izaak Walton, Bishop Wilkins, the Duchess of Newcastle. Milton is shown dictating *Paradise Lost* to Waller and again to his daughters; the Plague and the Fire are both described. Maginn, in travesty, puts into his burlesque a number of famous scenes and characters which have nothing to do with the story; the best being an episode in which the Duke of Wellington, in soliloquy, regrets his victory at Waterloo, and weeps apologetically before a statue of Napoleon. Smith's awkward style, his anachronisms, and his pompous descriptions are also taken off.

The hero of the burlesque is a handsome young mulatto named John Jeremy Smithers, from 'Jamaiky.' He is very rich, very sentimental, philanthropical, and namby-pamby. When he is about to be sentenced at a court trial, he refuses to take refuge "under the cold and barren forms" of the law and tries to win his freedom by quoting Dante; but the judge remarks, "I dinna understand Gaelic," and sentences him to a term's imprisonment. The lieutenant of the Tower conjectures "from the twist of his tongue" that he is a "yankee-doodle":

"I am a MAN, Sir," was the answer. "I was born beneath the canopy of the Western sky, in the land discovered by the ill-treated Columbus! But the starspangled banner claims me not as a subject, though I hail as a patriot the glorious domain over which it floats in streaky triumph."

Smithers is a take-off of the very rich, very noble, young hero, usually from the colonies, who was popular in the sentimental novels of the time.[3]

[3] For example, *The Mysterious Marriage; or, the Will of My Father*, by Mrs. Catherine G. Ward. The hero is Tanjore Trelawney, an Anglo-Indian who visits England in search of a wife. A characteristic speech is that in which he addresses the father of his country sweetheart, disavowing any intention of marrying the rich Lady Alexina, who has been "brought out in the gay and splendid circles of the *bon ton*": "Now, Sir, I am a romantic fellow, and this mode of education is not at all to my taste; I would have the maid I love and wish to make my bride, blushing in the native sweets of innocence, like the lily of the valley — remarkable only for her retiring modesty, — lively as the bounding doe, but gentle and mild as the weaning lamb; this, Sir, is the creature whom I could adore: but I cannot make love in a drawing-room at St. James's, — I

Although Dr. Maginn carefully avoids mentioning Scott in this burlesque of a historical novel, it was impossible for him to burlesque Scott's imitators without burlesquing Scott as well, as the following description will show:

He was a tall man, standing six feet four inches, with a countenance indicative of determination, if not of ferocity. A circular mark, in which the blue color had begun to yield to the yellow, round his left eye, testified that he had not long before been engaged in a personal rencontre; while the pustulary excrescences that disfigured his aquiline nose, showed that he was not less accustomed to the combats of Bacchus than those of Mars. He wore a fur tiara, of enormous dimensions and a conical figure. A pewter plate, indented with the royal arms of England—gules sable, on a lion passant, guarded by a unicorn wavy, on a fess double of or argent, with a crest sinople of the third quarter proper, and inscribed with the names of several victories, won or claimed by the household troops of England, proved him to be a member of the Horse Guards. A red doublet, with a blue cuff, and lapelles, was buttoned with mother-of-pearl buttons reaching from his waist to his chin, where they were met by a black leather stock, garnished and fastened by a brass clasp, on which was inscribed *Dieu et mon droit*, the well known war-cry of the English nation. White kerseymere trowsers, buttoned at the knee, and a pair of D. D. boots — as they were called from the circumstance of their having been invented by a Duke of Darlington — completed the dress . . . of one of the Hanoverian Horse Guards of that period; . . . the absence of the hauberk, (or morion) and of the ponderous tar-

---

cannot, indeed, — so Lady Alexina will wait a long time, if she expects a dying swain in Trelawney."

Mrs. Ward also wrote: *The Daughter of St. Omer, My Native Land, The Bachelor's Heiress, The Primrose Girl*, and many other novels.

get of bull's-hide and ormolu, showed that the gigantic Hussar was not at present upon actual duty.

Horace Smith was later the object of a parody-burlesque by a far more gifted writer than William Maginn. Between 1831 and 1835 Edgar Allan Poe, an obscure, poverty-stricken youth in his early twenties, composed as his first venture into prose fiction a group of sixteen sketches which he vainly offered for publication as *Tales of the Folio Club.* It was originally planned that they were to be told by the various members of the Club — Mr. Blackwood Blackwood, Mr. Rouge-et-Noir, Mr. Horribile Dictu, etc. — as parodies of well known authors or as burlesques of literary groups and literary fads. When the tales were rejected in their original form, Poe revised them, toning down the burlesque element and offering them as serious stories. As such they were accepted, not as a group but separately, and published in several different contemporary magazines. Poe's sardonic, yet practical, hoax remained undetected for almost a hundred years. [4]

Horace Smith's three-volume historical novel, *Zillah, a Tale of Jerusalem,* 1829, was parodied by Poe in a brief story entitled *A Tale of Jerusalem,* which,

[4] See "The Devil Was in It," by James Southall Wilson, Edgar Allan Poe Professor of English [at the University of Virginia, in *The American Mercury* for October, 1931. In this entertaining account of a piece of literary detective work such as Poe himself would have delighted in, we find conclusive proof that Poe wrote *Tales of the Folio Club* in their original form "with his tongue in his cheek," and that when they were refused as burlesques, he made some revisions, "shifted his tongue to his other cheek," and offered them to the world to be taken at the world's evaluation.

according to the original plan of the Folio Club, was
to have been contributed by Mr. Chronologos Chronology, who "admired Horace Smith" and possessed
"a very big nose that had been in Asia Minor." Poe's
burlesque method in this as in the other skits was to
epitomize the characteristic features of the novel and
hold them up to ridicule. Horace Smith is scored for
his superficial efforts to give historical and local coloring to his novel, Poe quoting verbatim such phrases
as "true as the Pentateuch," "bigger than the letter
Jod," and Hebrew ejaculations like *El Emanu!*, *El
Elohim!*, etc., which Smith had culled from too obvious sources. *King Pest*, "A Tale Containing an
Allegory, by ——," is a burlesque of an episode from
Benjamin Disraeli's *Vivian Grey*. It was to have been
told by a gentleman who admired Sir Walter Scott,
and is in part a take-off of Disraeli's imitation of
Scott's habit of opening his tales with two unknown
travelers. *MS. Found in a Bottle* was to have been
told by Solomon Seadrift, who "looked like a fish,"
and was probably intended as a parody of a fake history of Sir Edward Seaward, which had recently been
perpetrated by Jane Porter and her brother. The
objects of the burlesque in the remaining tales can
only be guessed at.

Poe's *Tales of the Folio Club* in their original form
show several interesting developments in the writing
of parody-burlesques. They are the first group with a
framework to hold them together: the tales were to
have been told by the members of the Club, the member telling the best tale to be elected president for the

next meeting and the one telling the poorest to have the expense of the entertainment. Poe was also the first writer to use the epitomizing method of burlesque which was to be made popular later on by Thackeray and Bret Harte. The older writers had been accustomed to write parody-burlesques and burlesque novels almost as long as the originals. Poe demonstrated (although for himself alone) that a novel could be wittily and effectively burlesqued in a sketch of four or five pages. It is also interesting and significant to find in Poe another great writer who, like Fielding, Jane Austen, and, later, Thackeray, developed his style by early exercises in burlesque fiction.

Eccentric Tales, 1827, by 'W. F. von Kosewitz' (Witless) contained five comic stories in the manner of the Germans, the first being the only one to have the element of parody-burlesque. It is aimed at the English imitations of the German historical, chivalric, sentimental tale. It is about two brothers, Dickbauch (Tun-belly) and Stricknadel (Knitting-Needle), sons of the Baron von Bettelheuser, who, although they were born on the same day, are not twins, because they have different mothers. The Baron, aged sixty, was worn out in the service of Cupid and Mars:

He was a comely old gentleman; the remnant of his white hair was confined with a rusty black riband, and hung like a greyhound's tail down his back. His large and bushy moustachios completely concealed his lips from view, of which he was so vastly proud, that it would have been sacrilege to have dared to touch, or trim them; they were (he would say, while a smile of complacence illumined his wrinkled face, like the sun upon a ploughed field) his chief beauty and attraction in the eyes of the fair sex in his younger days; and he valued them as he did his rusty arms — for the conquests they had enabled him to make. He had a long memory and a short neck — a large body with little legs — and, finally, a great purse and a small income!

After their father's death the two sons, who have gained all their ideas of life from reading romances, set off as troubadours. Their chief burlesque adventure is that in which Dickbauch successfully woos a neighboring princess by moonlight, only to discover the next day that she is very old and very ugly. There are faintly amusing Shandean passages by the author: chapter five, printed at the end as an appendix because it might shock the reader, contains only two words: "Thou liest!"

'W. F. von Kosewitz' was none other than A. H. Forrester, whose *Castle Baynard*, published three years before under the name 'Hal Willis,' had been adjudged so much a failure as to be an unintentional travesty.

It cannot be maintained that parody or burlesque has ever seriously affected the course of the historical novel. The vogue created by Scott has lasted well over a century, and even today shows no signs of abating. But both Scott and those who have followed him have presented opportunities for good-natured fun, and the burlesquers have usually contented themselves with writing skits that are more humorous than critical. There seem actually to have

been no burlesques of the historical novel in the decade after Scott's death, except those which, as we
shall see, dealt primarily with the 'Newgate' novel.
Later on, however, Thackeray and many other Victorian burlesquers found Scott, James Fenimore
Cooper, G. P. R. James, and Alexandre Dumas easy
marks for comic skits and parody novels.

X. BURLESQUES BY AN
EMINENT HAND

IN THE summer of 1832 *Fraser's Magazine* published in two parts an anonymous novelette entitled
Elizabeth Brownrigge. The ironical dedication states
that the author has requested his laundress to ask at
the nearest circulating library for the latest most popular novel, which he intends to imitate and thus write
a salable book — a thing which he has often attempted
to do before but always failed at. She returns with
Eugene Aram. The resulting 'imitation' is actually
an able parody-burlesque of this most famous of the
novels about Newgate criminals.

This type of novel, which is today designated as the
'Newgate' novel, was intensely popular during the
eighteen-thirties. It was a fusion of three older types:
the picaresque tale, the Gothic novel, and the revolutionary novel. Its difference from them consisted in
shifting the emphasis from adventures, terror, and
political philosophy to a sophistical justification of a
criminal-hero. In general it presented the exploits
of some figure of Newgate fame, in a favorable light,
against a background of terror-romanticism. Its pretended purpose was to conduct a rational inquiry
into the nature and causes of crime; actually this purpose was subordinated to supplying the public demand for sentiment, sensationalism, and romance.

Obviously, a notorious villain, even as the centre of interest in a romantic novel, could never hope to win the readers' sympathy if his murders, rapes, and thefts were represented as plain murders, rapes, and thefts. The Newgate novelists found it necessary to envelop him in an atmosphere of the glamorous or picturesque and then to 'justify' his crimes with sophistry and fine writing.

William Godwin in *Caleb Williams* and *St. Leon* and M. G. Lewis in *The Monk* had laid the foundation for the Newgate novel in the closing years of the eighteenth century. Each of these novels contains a prominent character whose sins are laid not on himself but on his fellow men. But in the decades after the French Revolution, English opinion had turned too conservative to tolerate any literature that was flavored even mildly with liberalism. The victim-of-society hero virtually disappeared from fiction until 1832, when the spirit of reform again was in the air. It was then that Bulwer-Lytton, always sensitive to changes in public taste, revived him in *Eugene Aram*.

Fraser's Magazine carried on an active campaign of criticism and burlesque against Bulwer-Lytton and other authors of 'Newgate' novels from 1831 to 1840. Beginning certainly as early as 1832, Thackeray was a constant contributor to *Fraser's* and continued to be throughout the period mentioned and beyond. The majority of the articles against the Newgate novels and almost all of those against Bulwer are known to have been written by him. There is good reason for believing that Thackeray was also the author of

Elizabeth Brownrigge, although it was never acknowledged by him and has never appeared in the authorized editions of his works.[1] In style, in the method
and the object of its satire, and in its author's thinly
disguised detestation of Bulwer's fiction, it strongly
resembles Thackeray's *Catherine*, which also appeared
serially in *Fraser's*.

Every important character in *Elizabeth Brownrigge*
has its prototype in *Eugene Aram*. Elizabeth herself
is the feminine counterpart of Eugene, but those
qualities which gave to the student-ruffian an air of
nobility make the woman criminal sometimes ridiculous and frequently repellent. She is possessed of
youth, stately beauty, and an aloof and dominating
personality. She poses as being highly intellectual;
but her philosophical pronouncements, delivered
with an air of pompous dignity, are rhetorical and
meaningless. Like Aram she has a 'past' which is
continually referred to in a dark, mysterious manner
— Aram has murdered a man for his money, Elizabeth has beaten two female apprentices to death —
but like him she considers herself superior to human
law. Eugene Aram had been in love with a beautiful,
tractable maiden named Madeline Lester; Elizabeth
Brownrigge loves Alphonso Belvidere:

The pair . . . were formed in the very prodigality of nature. Each seemed to have been created, rich in every per-

---

[1] It was first reprinted in *Sultan Stork and other Stories and Sketches
by William Makepeace Thackeray (1829–1844) now first collected*. Richard
Herne Shepherd, editor. London, 1887. The preface contains an elaborate examination of the evidence of Thackeray's authorship.

sonal endowment, as the worthy counterpart of the other.
Young they were; but in them youth was blooming with all
its freshness, and devoid of all its frivolities. Beautiful they
were; but the beauty which rendered them the delight and
admiration of the eyes of others, was held of no estimation
in their own. Alphonso, who stood six feet two without his
shoes, united, in the compact and slender structure of his
person, the vigour of the Hercules with the elegance of the
Apollo. His features, which were cast in the perfect mould
of the Antinous, were colored with a deep, rich sunniness of
tone, which no pencil inferior to that of Titian could ever
have aspired to imitate; while the breadth of his forehead
bespoke the intellectual powers of a Newton or a Locke;
and the bright, lambent, and innocuous fires of his un-
fathomable eye beamed with the gentle virtues of a mar-
tyred saint. As his figure was characterised by strength
and grace, so was his countenance by intelligence and humility. He was distinguished among literary men as the
editor of a new monthly magazine; and his attire was of
that simple style of elegance which accorded well with the
cast of his person. . . . His coat, waistcoat, and nether garments, were formed *en suite* of snuff-coloured broad cloth;
his stockings were of white silk, variegated with horizontal
stripes of blue; and his only ornaments were the silver
buckles that glistened, with a modest and a moon-like
lustre, at his knees, on his shoes, and in front of his hat. [2]

All the men in *Eugene Aram* are transformed into
women in *Elizabeth Brownrigge* and all the women
into men. Even Jacobina, the cat with canine qualities, is changed by the parodist into Muggletonian, a
dog with feline qualities. We have seen how effective
this device was when employed by Fielding in *Joseph*

---

[2] This burlesque description is aimed not only at *Eugene Aram* but at
Bulwer-Lytton personally. He was a notorious dandy and had recently
been made editor of *The New Monthly Magazine*.

Andrews; it is scarcely less so in *Elizabeth Brownrigge*. To make a woman act and think as a man, and a man as a woman, is one of the easiest and most effective methods of travesty.

The trial scene, particularly Aram's famous speech in his own defence, is admirably parodied. Bulwer-Lytton, possessing the actual speech of the real Aram, was obliged to follow it accurately in his novel. It is such a patent example of sophistry that, having quoted it, he is constrained to make Rowland Lester, a friend of Aram, say that "he had expected a more warm, a more earnest, though, perhaps, a less ingenious and artful defence." Like Aram, without once denying her guilt outright, Elizabeth endeavors by artful insinuation to create a doubt in the minds of the jury. Her reasoning, only in a slight degree more obviously faulty than that of Aram, effectively convicts Aram, by indirection, of flagrantly falsifying moral values.

Few of the idiosyncrasies of Bulwer-Lytton's pretentious, affected style escape the burlesquer. Obvious quotations from well known authors, ineffective references to classic mythology, and unnecessary historical scenes and persons appear in the parody-burlesque. The following description of an ancient inn burlesques Bulwer-Lytton's habit of parading his wide but superficial learning:

I never approach the place, and see the sign of the red cabbage hanging aloft from the projecting branch of the aged elm by which that venerable and mouldering porch is overshadowed, but a world of historic and poetic associations are awakened in my mind; my memory reverts to the personages and the incidents of other times — to Queen Elizabeth and Queen Mary, to Lord Bacon and Lord Burleigh — to the success of the Protestant Reformation, and the defeat of the Spanish Armada.

It is clear that the all-but-Victorian author of *Elizabeth Brownrigge* was actuated by the most serious motives. To him *Eugene Aram* seemed a formidable menace to the public morals, and he ruthlessly tore it asunder to expose the unsound reasoning that lay beneath the smooth urbanity of its style. With a methodical precision unsuited to burlesque, he pointed out its faults both as a novel and a social study, and too strenuously exhorted his readers to think badly of it.

Newgate novels continued to be written and read, and *Fraser's* continued its warfare against them. In the abusive reviews and in the satirical and burlesque skits which it was publishing as late as 1840, Thackeray's increasingly powerful aid was enlisted, especially in those concerning Bulwer and his works. In May, 1839, it published the first installment of *Catherine*, Thackeray's sternly satirical burlesque novel against the Newgate writers as a group.

His attitude toward them is perhaps most forcefully summed up in a paragraph from his review of Fielding's works, which appeared a few years later in *The Times* for September 2, 1840:

Vice is never to be mistaken for virtue in Fielding's honest downright books; it goes by its name, and invariably gets its punishment. See the consequences of honesty!

Many a squeamish lady of our time would throw down one of these romances with horror, but would go through every page of Mr. Ainsworth's "Jack Sheppard" with perfect comfort to herself. Ainsworth dared not paint his hero as the scoundrel he knew him to be; he must keep his brutalities in the background, else the public morals will be outraged, and so he produces a book quite absurd and unreal, and infinitely more immoral than anything Fielding ever wrote. "Jack Sheppard" is immoral actually because it is decorous. The Spartans, who used to show drunken slaves to their children, took care, no doubt, that the slave should be really and truly drunk. Sham drunkenness which never passed the limits of propriety, but only went so far as to be amusing, would be rather an object to incite youth to intoxication than to deter him from it, and some late novels have always struck us in the same light.[3]

Thackeray, like the authors he was burlesquing, went to the Newgate calendar for a subject. He selected a certain Mrs. Catherine Hayes, who, after a life of crime, had been burned at Tyburn in 1726 for murdering her husband under singularly revolting circumstances. The effectiveness of the book as satire lies chiefly in the fact that instead of obscuring the disagreeable facts of his heroine's life under a romantic glamour, Thackeray purposefully reveals them in detail, intensifying horror and guilt by mock justification.

In several of his too frequent satirical asides to the reader he reveals the names of the novels of which he disapproves: *The Autobiography of Jack Ketch*, *Ernest Maltravers*, *Eugene Aram*, *Rookwood*, *Oliver Twist*,

---

[3] Quoted in *William Makepeace Thackeray, a Biography*, by Lewis Melville [pseud. for Lewis Saul Benjamin] (London, 1910), i, p. 168.

Devereux, and *Paul Clifford*. Even *Claude Du-Val*, a novel of the same sort that had been projected by Ainsworth but never written, is sneeringly referred to as the 'embryo Duval.'

As is to be expected, the sharpest criticisms are of Bulwer. Thackeray always, and especially when he was a young man, detested Bulwer's affected, flashy style. In the first chapter of *Catherine*, as in *Elizabeth Brownrigge*, the drinking scene at the 'Spotted Dog' from *Eugene Aram* is parodied; and in the same chapter Thackeray ironically apologizes for the low social rank of his characters and for their not being introduced with a flourish of trumpets. Having allowed the action of his story to skip a number of years, he bridges the gap with a passage of mock moralizing that the readers of the day could have had no difficulty in interpreting as a parody of Bulwer:

It is an awful thing to get a glimpse, as one sometimes does, when the time is past, of some little, little wheel which works the whole mighty machinery of FATE, and see how our destinies turn on a minute's delay or advance, or on the turning of a street, or on somebody else's turning of a street, or on somebody else's doing of something else in Downing Street or in Timbuctoo, now or a thousand years ago. Thus, for instance, if Miss Poots, in the year 1695, had never been the lovely inmate of a Spielhaus at Amsterdam, Mr. Van Silverkoop would never have seen her; if the day had not been extraordinarily hot, the worthy merchant would never have gone thither; if he had not been fond of Rhenish wine and sugar, he never would have called for any such delicacies; if he had not called for them, Miss Ottilia Poots would never have brought them, and partaken of them; if he had not been rich, she would certainly have rejected all the advances made to her by Silverkoop; if he had not been so fond of Rhenish and sugar, he never would have died; and Mrs. Silverkoop would have been neither rich nor a widow, nor a wife to Count von Galgenstein. Nay, nor would this history have ever been written; for if Count von Galgenstein had not married the rich widow, Mrs. Catherine would never have —

Oh, my dear Madam! you thought we were going to tell you. Pooh! nonsense, — no such thing! not for two or three and seventy pages or so — when, perhaps, you *may* know what Mrs. Catherine never would have done.

Dickens's sentimentality is ridiculed in a burlesque description of Mr. Hayes's courtship:

Miss Catherine, then, was a *franche coquette*, and Mr. John Hayes was miserable. His life was passed in a storm of mean passions and bitter jealousies, and desperate attacks upon the indifference-rock of Mrs. Catherine's heart, which not all his tempest of love could beat down. O cruel, cruel pangs of love unrequited! Mean rogues feel them as well as great heroes. Lives there the man in Europe that has not felt them many times? — who had not knelt, and fawned, and supplicated, and wept, and cursed, and raved, all in vain; and passed long wakeful nights with ghosts of dead hopes for company; shadows of buried remembrances that glide out of their graves of nights, and whisper, "We are dead now, but we *were* once; and we made you happy, and we come now to mock you: — despair, O lover, despair, and die"? O cruel pangs! — dismal nights! — Now a sly demon creeps under your nightcap, and drops into your ear those soft, hope-breathing, sweet words, uttered on the well-remembered evening. . . ."

Such passages of burlesque humor occur but rarely in *Catherine*, which is a book as disagreeable to read as Thackeray frequently declared it was to write. It was dictated by the stern voices of indignation and duty, and Thackeray, in the rôle of Spartan father, took care that his criminal characters should be 'really and truly' criminals. He makes no concession to sensibility or good taste; on the contrary, he re-cords the revolting crimes of Catherine Hayes and her accomplices with a detailed realism calculated to turn the reader's stomach against all such fare, however temptingly it might be seasoned by others. Effective in its day as an antidote to the Newgate novel, *Catherine* has little interest now except as it reflects the fiction of its decade and helps to indicate the develop-ment of Thackeray's method as a writer.

There can be little doubt that *Fraser's Magazine*, with the aid of *The Athenaeum* and *The Quarterly Review*, did much to quell the popularity of the New-gate novels; nor can it be denied that Thackeray's censorious reviews and satirical skits, especially those in the "Epistles to the Literati," made him the most conspicuous individual writer against them. Add to these the parody-burlesque *Elizabeth Brownrigge*, which he probably wrote, and the burlesque novel *Catherine*, both of which appeared in *Fraser's*, and we have no hesitation in giving to Thackeray and to *Fraser's* the lion's share of credit for the sudden ces-sation of novels with a criminal protagonist. Ains-worth, although he had planned a whole series of them, published not a single one after 1837, the date of the appearance of *Catherine*. Egan, Moncrieff, and Whitehead also ceased to write such novels after that. *Oliver Twist*, 1837, was the last novel by Dickens of which anyone could say that criminals were made romantically appealing. In the 1848 edition of *Paul Clifford*, Bulwer, who had long since stopped writing novels of the Newgate type, apologized for his youthful works in declaring that he had "emerged into an atmosphere which he believed more congenial to art."

Certainly more congenial to Thackeray's art was *The Tremendous Adventures of Major Gahagan*, which was appearing serially in *The New Monthly Magazine* at the same time that *Catherine* was appearing in *Fraser's*. Although the two works must have been composed about the same time they are utterly different. *Major Gahagan* is a humorous take-off of the extravagances of the novel of military life; the target is Thackeray's friend, Charles Lever, whose *Harry Lorrequer* had been published in 1837. Major Goliah O'Grady Gahagan, penniless Irish commander of a 'Battalion of Irregular Horse,' narrates his own unparalleled adventures in love, battle, and high society, during the Napoleonic Wars and during campaigns in India, Spain, and elsewhere.

. . . my life has been one of no ordinary interest; and, in fact, I may say that I have led a more remarkable life than any man in the service — I have been at more pitched battles, led more forlorn hopes, had more success among the fair sex, drunk harder, read more, and been a handsomer man than any officer now serving her Majesty.

When I at first went to India in 1802, I was a raw cornet of seventeen, with blazing red hair, six feet four in height, athletic at all kinds of exercises, owing money to my tailor and everybody else who would trust me, possessing an Irish

brogue, and my full pay of 120 *l.* a year. I need not say
that with all these advantages I did that which a number
of clever fellows have done before me — I fell in love, and
proposed to marry immediately.

The modest Major detests "more than all other vices
the absurd sin of egotism," but he cannot conceal that
he is probably the most wonderful fellow who ever
lived. His mock-modest accounts of his experiences
are strung out a little too long, but for a time the burlesque of Lever's dashing young subaltern heroes is
amusing. There are NO IRONICAL ASIDES; and whatever criticisms the burlesque contains are inherent in
the exaggerated style and in the caricatures. The
work has merit as a humorous narrative, independent of its burlesquing of Lever.

Thackeray was always an inveterate novel reader.
In his burlesques, in the critical asides of his serious
novels, and especially in the charming *Roundabout
Papers*, he constantly chats about his adventures
among novels. Like Jane Austen, he derived a double
pleasure from reading them: the sheer, unsophisti-
cated enjoyment of the story-reader and the ironical
amusement of the critic. Tenderly and sentimen-
tally he recalled in later years 'dear Scott' and his
'glorious cycle of romances.' The flowing pen of
G. P. R. James delighted the younger days of the
'lazy, idle boy' with *Darnley*, and *Richelieu*, and
Delorme. Alexandre Dumas he considered the greatest of the three: "I think of the prodigal banquets to
which this Lucullus of a man has invited me, with
thanks and wonder. To what a series of splendid

entertainments he has treated me!" Thackeray, the realist, never tired of paying tribute to these favorite romancers; and although he never tired of burlesquing them too, his satire was always tempered by his genuine admiration.

In *A Legend of the Rhine*, which appeared serially in *George Cruikshank's Table Book* during the latter months of 1845, he produced a mock historical romance which is a burlesque of James, Dumas, and Scott. The time of the story is "Many, many hundred thousand years ago, and at the exact period when chivalry was in full bloom":

'Tis a story of knights and ladies — of love and battle, and virtue rewarded; a story of princes and noble lords, moreover: the best of company. Gentles, an ye will, ye shall hear it. Fair dames and damsels, may your loves be as happy as those of the heroine of this romaunt.

On the cold and rainy evening of Thursday, the 26th of October, in the year previously indicated, such travellers as might have chanced to be abroad in that bitter night might have remarked a fellow-wayfarer journeying on the road from Oberwinter to Godesberg . . .

An elderly warrior, clad in full armor, riding an active and powerful war-horse, is described in the meticulous, pedantic manner of G. P. R. James, with much emphasis on such words as 'soldan,' *destrier*, 'saltire,' 'surcoat,' and 'mangonel'; but he carries a silk umbrella to shield him from the rain, and a portmanteau bearing the inscription 'Count Ludwig de Hombourg, Jerusalem,' with the last word scratched out and 'Godesberg' substituted in its place. There are many humorous anachronisms and mock romantic details. At a festival, the guests are served "with such tea as only Bohemia could produce"; a holy hermit, while witnessing a mortal combat, calmly puffs at his pipe; and Otto the Archer demands that a phantom princess serve him with "a pork-chop and some mashed potatoes." The marriage of the hero and the heroine is celebrated "by a tasteful display of fireworks," and thus gun-powder, the most destructive possible anachronism to a romance of chivalry, is introduced. One of the cleverest thrusts is made by the illustrating artist; he draws all the characters *who have been described* in mediaeval costume, the remainder in modern dress.

Although Scott and James are both specifically mentioned as objects of the burlesque, it was Dumas who furnished the immediate occasion for it. His *Othon l'Archeur*, 1840, was such a shameless imitation of *Ivanhoe* that Thackeray had accused Dumas of plagiarism in a public letter. *A Legend of the Rhine* is really a parody-burlesque of this early romance by Dumas, with the complicated purpose of burlesquing the style of the two older historical novelists as well as Dumas, and at the same time of reproving the latter for his theft. Dumas had lifted from *Ivanhoe*, with little alteration, the archery scene, the tournament scene, the description of the storming of Torquilstone, several characters, and a number of other incidents. Frequently Thackeray omits certain descriptions or incidents from his narrative as unnecessary since they have already been done "in the novel of

Ivanhoe." When the "simple tale is done," the supposed authoress — for Thackeray wrote under a feminine pseudonym — meaningly reveals her source:

I read it in an old, old book, in a mouldy old circulating library. 'Twas written in the French tongue, by the noble Alexandre Dumas; but 'tis probable that he stole it from some other, and that the other had filched it from a former tale-teller. For nothing is new under the sun. Things die and are reproduced only. And so it is that the forgotten tale of the great Dumas reappears under the signature of

THERESA MacWHIRTER.

But Thackeray had not yet finished with the subject of *Ivanhoe* and Dumas. The August and September numbers of *Fraser's* for the next year — 1846 — contained his "Proposals for a Continuation of Ivanhoe, in a letter to Monsieur Alexandre Dumas, by Monsieur Michael Angelo Titmarsh." He pretends that there is a woeful dearth of novels. Fashionable novels have grown wearisome; historical novelists — even Mr. James, that 'teeming parent of romance' — have fallen asleep; a certain celebrated author, since *The Last of the Barons*, has written nothing but a pamphlet on the Watercure. Novel readers in England are entirely dependent upon translations of French writers — Dumas, Eugene Sue, Soulié, and Paul Féval. But Thackeray likes the French habit of twenty-volume novels, in which favorite characters are continued. Why doesn't the great Dumas continue *Ivanhoe*? He draws up a list of proposals for such a continuation. These 'proposals' are really a first draft for Thackeray's celebrated *Rebecca and Rowena*, which was not published in its final and lengthened form until 1850.

Still writing under the pseudonym of 'Titmarsh,' Thackeray, in *Rebecca and Rowena*, pretends to be dissatisfied with the ending of *Ivanhoe* and declares that those people are sadly mistaken who think that as soon as a hero and heroine are married, all is happy. His 'middle-aged' novel will tell what really happened. Wilfred and Rowena have been leading a humdrum existence at Rotherwood. Rowena, always inclined to be self-complacent and a trifle priggish, has developed into a stout, quarrelsome matron. Conscious of her superiority in rank over Wilfrid and jealous of his former attachment for the Jewess, she has got him completely under her thumb and regulates him and the rest of the household according to twelfth-century notions of what is proper. Old Cedric has sulkily retired; Wamba has been cowed into silence; and Athelstane, more of a glutton than ever, pays patronizing visits to Ivanhoe and commiserates with him for being henpecked. The debonair Robin Hood, now Earl of Huntingdon, has gone respectable and developed into a stout, conscientious magistrate; and Friar Tuck has become as sleek and effeminate as the Abbot of Jorvaulx. Bold Richard of the Lion Heart has dwindled into an undignified mountebank, wearying his subjects with stale jests and half-remembered songs and ballads which he believes to be original compositions.

At length the desperate Wilfrid breaks the news to

Rowena that he is going to join his king on the battle-fields of France. Contrary to his expectation, she takes the announcement calmly, and later, when the news of Ivanhoe's death comes (the reader knows he is only severely wounded), she marries Athelstane, but virtuously takes the precaution of having her first marriage annulled by the Pope in case Ivanhoe should be still alive. Disguised as a hermit, Ivanhoe returns to Rotherwood, utters dark *doubles entendres* to Rowena, Athelstane, and their infant son Cedric, is recognized by the keen-eyed Wamba, and sighs out the aphorism that "only fools are faithful." Having disclosed his identity to the family solicitor and secured sufficient funds, he disguises himself more permanently in a wig and spectacles, sets up in the neighborhood as a country gentleman, attends a ball at York, dances a Sir Roger de Coverley with Rowena, takes up arms against the tyrant John and forces him to sign the Magna Carta. Athelstane is slain by a cannonball — this time really slain — and Ivanhoe is summoned to the bedside of the dying Rowena; she extracts from him the promise to look after her infant son, hers and Athelstane's, and, with her dying gasp, *never to marry a Jewess*. He places little Cedric in the Hall of Dotheboys in Yorkshire, travels to Palestine, distinguishes himself in many battles, and encounters old Isaac of York, who informs him that Rebecca is dead. He swoons and remains unconscious for several days. It is later revealed that Rebecca is alive and has become a Christian. The Jews all denounce her and throw her into prison. She remains there for four

years, three months, and twenty-four days before she
is rescued by Ivanhoe.

That she and Ivanhoe were married, follows of course;
for Rowena's promise extorted from him was, that he would
never wed a Jewess, and a better Christian than Rebecca
now was never said her catechism. Married I am sure they
were, and adopted little Cedric; but I don't think they had
any other children, or were subsequently very boisterously
happy. Of some sort of happiness melancholy is a characteristic, and I think these were a solemn pair, and died
rather early.

Rebecca and Rowena is something more than a farci-
cal imitation of *Ivanhoe*, excellent though it is in that
respect. What gives it a more stable quality than the
grotesque *A Legend of the Rhine* possesses, is that the
characters are not merely caricatures of their prototypes; they have an entity of their own. Thackeray,
not denying that Scott's was an accurate portrayal
of the youth of the characters, sets out to show what
these same persons were in middle age. His portrait
of the matronly Rowena is almost, if not quite, as
notable as that of a certain card-playing baroness at
Tunbridge Wells who had once been the brilliant
Beatrix Castlewood. We knew, before he told us,
that Rowena was destined for the rôle of the contented country squiress and Ivanhoe for that of the
docile husband; Scott, perhaps without intending to,
made all that clear. Thackeray elected to give details
that Scott, the romanticist, chose to ignore, and he
gives them with logic and consistency, remaining perfectly faithful to the youth of the characters. It is this

fundamental truth to nature that makes Thackeray's piece of fun-making a thing of lasting interest.

As a burlesquer, Thackeray has always been known best for his *Novels by Eminent Hands*, originally called *Punch's Prize Novelists* and published in *Punch* in 1847. These seven parody-burlesques, like Poe's *Tales of the Folio Club*, are brief epitomes of the novels they are attacking; they sum up their faults and idiosyncrasies and present a few of the characters and scenes in a style which is a ridiculous exaggeration of the original author's.

The first of them was "George de Barnwell, by Sir E. L. B. L., Bart.," which is not so much a parody of any one of Bulwer's novels as it is a burlesque of all his 'fashionable' and Newgate novels. Its introduction and three 'scenes' comprise less than fifteen pages. The introduction begins:

In the Morning of Life, the Truthful wooed the Beautiful and their offspring was Love. Like his Divine parents, He is eternal. He has his Mother's ravishing smile; his Father's steadfast eyes. He rises every day, fresh and glorious as the untired Sun-God. He is Eros, the ever young. Dark, dark, were this world of ours had either Divinity left it — dark without the day-beams of the Latonian Charioteer, darker yet without the daedal Smile of the God of the Other Bow! Dost know him, Reader?

It ends:

. . . Listen! I tell thee a tale — not of Kings — but of Men — not of Thrones, but of Love, and Grief, and Crime. Listen, and but once more. 'Tis for the last time (probably) these fingers shall sweep the strings. E. L. B. L.

De Barnwell's disagreeable crimes, like those of Bulwer's Eugene Aram and Ernest Maltravers, are smudged over, and he is represented as hobnobbing with all the notables of his period. He drinks Joe Addison under the table, writes a better paper for *The Spectator* than Dick Steele could (so did Henry Esmond by the way), defeats Dean Swift at capping verses, suggests an emendation to Mr. Pope's *Homer*, and knows more about the French king than Lord Bolingbroke does. During all this his identity has been elaborately withheld by the author:

Meanwhile who was he? where was he, this youth who had struck all the wits of London with admiration? His galloping charger had returned to the City; his splendid court-suit was doffed for the citizen's gabardine and grocer's humble apron.

George de Barnwell was in Chepe — in Chepe, at the feet of Martha Millwood.

At the close of the burlesque, a benevolent clergyman draws the 'moral' in his speech to de Barnwell on the day before de Barnwell is hanged:

"Yes, indeed, my brave youth! and the Tragedy of Tomorrow will teach the World that Homicide is not to be permitted even to the most amiable Genius, and that the lover of the Ideal and the Beautiful, as thou art, my son, must respect the Real likewise."

In "Codlingsby, by D. Shrewsberry, Esq.," Thackeray makes rather ill-natured fun of Benjamin Disraeli's *Coningsby*. Rafael Mendoza poses as the proprietor of a mean clothing-shop, but is in reality rich and powerful, and has at his beck and call all the great people of the kingdom. Adjoining the shop is an apartment of the utmost magnificence; the carpet is of white velvet, with edges of seed pearls; the divans are of carved amber, covered with ermine. Seated on a mother-of-pearl stool before an ivory piano, is a gorgeously dressed young woman wearing an aigrette composed entirely of diamonds. She casually lights Mendoza's pipe with a ten thousand pound note. Mendoza informs young Codlingsby that his family has Saxon blood:

An ancestress of ours made a *mésalliance* in the reign of your King John. Her name was Rebecca, daughter of Isaac of York, and she married in Spain, whither she had fled to the Court of King Boabdil, Sir Wilfred of Ivanhoe, then a widower by the demise of his first lady, Rowena. The match was deemed a cruel insult among our people; but Wilfred conformed, and was a Rabbi of some note at the synagogue of Cordova. We are descended from him lineally. It is the only blot upon the escutcheon of the Mendozas.

Disraeli never forgave Thackeray for this parody, and caricatured him with much bitterness and some truth as the snobbish St. Barbe in *Endymion*.

"Phil Fogarty, by Harry Rollicker," was the third in the series of *Novels by Eminent Hands*. Phil Fogarty belongs to the Fighting Onety-Oneth, which is conducting a siege of a French town. Having distinguished himself by his reckless bravery, he is knocked down by a cannon ball aimed by the Emperor Napoleon himself. Six weeks later he recovers — a prisoner on parole in Paris. He hob-nobs with Napoleon, Murat, Ney, Tallyrand, and other notables, and receives the thanks of the Emperor for being attentive to Josephine. In a duel with his rival, the Maréchal Cambacères, he shoots away the bridge of that worthy's nose, much to the amusement of everybody except Napoleon, who in a fit of rage orders Fogarty himself to be instantly shot:

> This was too much. "Here goes!" said I, and rode slap at him.
> There was a shriek of terror from the whole of the French army, and I should think at least forty thousand guns were leveled at me in an instant. But as the muskets were not loaded, and the cannon had only wadding in them, these facts, I presume, saved the life of Phil Fogarty from this discharge.

He rides straight at the Emperor, leaps over him, scarcely grazing his cockade, and dashes away "with an army of a hundred and seventy-three thousand eight hundred men" at his heels.

On reading this entertaining burlesque, Charles Lever "declared that he might as well shut up shop and did actually alter the character of his novels."[4]

"Barbazure, by G. P. R. Jeames, Esq., etc.," is a humorous version of the story of Bluebeard, which is a parody of G. P. R. James's *Richelieu*. Besides the parody of this particular novel, there is burlesque of other scenes and characters from the works of this popular but pedestrian imitator of Scott. James

---

[4] *William Makepeace Thackeray, a Biography*, by Lewis Melville [pseud. for Lewis Saul Benjamin], i, p. 289.

wrote fifty-seven romances, and in seventeen of these, none of them published after the appearance of "Barbazure," horsemen, singly, in pairs, or in parties, make an early appearance. Near the end of James's career, Thackeray was to reflect in one of the *Roundabout Papers* on the "strange fate which befell the veteran novelist," who had been appointed her Majesty's consul-general in Venice, — "the only city in Europe where the famous 'Two Cavaliers' cannot by any possibility be seen riding together." "Barbazure" opens with a burlesque of the scene. For the rest, it is too much a repetition of what Thackeray had already done in *A Legend of the Rhine* to add very much to his credit as a burlesquer.

"Lords and Liveries, by the Authoress of 'Dukes and Déjeuners,' 'Hearts and Diamonds,' 'Marchionesses and Milliners,' etc., etc.," is a burlesque of the novels of fashionable life by Mrs. Catherine Grace Gore, who was celebrated in her own day for the brilliancy of her epigrams, the exactness of her portraiture, the vivacity of her style, and her high moral tone, maintained despite the laxity of the gay circle in which she moved and about which she wrote. The headings of her chapters were quotations from several different foreign tongues, and the persons in her novels used French, German, Spanish, and Italian phrases almost as much as they used English. Thackeray's essays and humorous pieces contain many references to the works of Mrs. Gore, Miss Braddon, Mrs. Henry Wood, and Lady Morgan; sometimes he was impatient at their triviality, but usually he regarded them with tolerant amusement. The young hero of "Lords and Liveries" has just returned from abroad, a man of the world at twenty-three:

"Corpo di Bacco," he said . . . "what a lovely creature that was! What eyes! what hair! Who knows her? Do you, mon cher prince?"

"E bellissima, certamente," said the Duca de Monte-pulciano, and stroked down his jetty moustache.

"Ein gar schönes Mädchen," said the Hereditary Grand Duke of Eulenschreckenstein, and turned up his carroty one.

"Elle n'est pas mal, ma foi!" said the Prince de Boro-dino, with a scowl on his darkling brows. "Mon Dieu, que ces cigarres sont mauvais!" he added as he too cast away his Cuba.

"Try one of my Pickwicks," said Franklin Fox, with a sneer, offering his gold *étui* to the young Frenchman; "they are some of Pontet's best, Prince. What, do you bear malice? Come, let us be friends," said the gay and careless young patrician; but a scowl on the part of the Frenchman was the only reply.

"Crinoline," the next in the series of *Novels by Eminent Hands*, is an unfinished satire of the French authors who write about English life with too little knowledge of the subject. Thackeray good-humor-edly rallies Dumas, Eugene Sue, Soulié, and others, as he had already done in *Paris Sketches*. The central character of the burlesque is "Munseer Jools de Chacabac," a newspaper writer who considers himself well qualified for the task of writing about the English by having read *The Vicar of Wakefield* in the original. He obtains all the information he gets from

Lord Yardarm, who answers all questions with the only French he knows, which is "Wee, wee."

"The Stars and Stripes" is as much a satire of the American people as it is of the novels of James Fenimore Cooper. Part I recounts a conference between the French king and the American ambassador at the time of the American Revolution. Benjamin Franklin is purposely late for the appointment with Louis XVI, and, when he enters the royal presence, bows slightly to the queen, refuses to greet the king at all, and scornfully neglects to remove his hat. He is accompanied by the Indian Tatua in native costume, whose "manly chest was . . . tattooed and painted," and who wore around his neck "innumerable bracelets and necklaces of human teeth, extracted (one only from each skull) from the jaws of those who had fallen by the terrible tomahawk at his girdle." Tatua contemptuously accepts the star of the Order of the Bath from Louis, and promises to give it to one of his squaws, that his papooses may play with it. Franklin whittles his cane the while and makes insulting remarks about the British and the French. In Part II we are introduced to Leatherlegs, who boasts of his knowledge of Pawnee, Sioux, and Canadian French. The narrative continues with an account of the daring exploits of the American seaman, Tom Coxswain, and of the victory of the *Repudiator* over two British frigates.

It was Thackeray's desire to include in the *Novels by Eminent Hands* two other burlesques which he had written, one of Dickens and one of himself; but the

editor of *Punch* objected to printing a burlesque of
Dickens and consequently Thackeray refused to include the one of himself. There was, nevertheless, a
burlesque of Thackeray published about this time,
which unfortunately seems not to have survived.
Thackeray mentions it in his preface to Appleton and
Company's New York edition of his minor works,
published in 1852, just as he was leaving America
after his first lecture tour:

The prize novels contain imitations of the writings of
some contemporaries who still live and flourish in the novelists' calling. I myself had scarcely entered on it when these
burlesque tales were begun, and I stopped further parody
from a sense that this merry task of making fun of the
novelists should be left to younger hands than my own;
and in a little book published some four years since, in
England, by my friends Messrs. [James] Hannay and
Shirley Brooks, I saw a caricature of myself and writings
to the full as ludicrous and faithful as the prize novels of
Mr. Punch. . . .
    . . . I own to a feeling of anything but pleasure in re-
viewing some of these misshapen juvenile creatures, which
the publisher has disinterred and resuscitated. There are
two performances especially (among the critical and biographical works of the erudite Mr. Yellowplush) which I
am very sorry to see reproduced; and I ask pardon of the
author of the "Caxtons" for a lampoon, which I know he
himself has forgiven, and which I wish I could recall.

This handsome apology was worthy of Thackeray
and it was no more than Bulwer-Lytton's due on account of the malignant, and often personal, satire and
criticism which Thackeray and the rest of the Fraser-
ians had heaped upon the author of *Eugene Aram*.

Thackeray expressed his regret more than once that he should have been concerned in what was little short of a conspiracy against a fellow-author.

But Thackeray's avowal that he had put aside the 'merry task' of writing parody and burlesque of other novelists is not entirely consistent with some of his later work. Nearly all his novels, both early and late, contain fragmentary examples of literary satire, as does almost all he wrote. Even that rollicking extravaganza, *The Rose and the Ring*, is not free from it. Embedded in the *Roundabout Papers* is found Thackeray's last out-and-out burlesque novel, a travesty of the 'sensation' novels of Wilkie Collins, called *The Axe with a Notch — a Story à la Mode*. *The Moonstone* and *No Name* had just appeared in 1860 and 1862, and Thackeray could not resist a good-natured burlesque of these popular novels in a mock supernatural-historical-ratiocinative story about a blackmailing ghost that wrote worthless checks.

It is important to note that one of Thackeray's most admirable novels was a direct outgrowth of his early burlesques of the Newgate school of fiction. *Barry Lyndon* is an implicit, rather than outspoken, protest against the novels of criminal life. In *Catherine*, which had been written a few years earlier, Thackeray had so intruded his own distaste between the characters and the reader that the illusion of real life was never produced; but in *Barry Lyndon* he brilliantly allowed the villain-hero to be his own biographer, and to record his life of crime in its true repellent colors. Barry does not attempt to conceal unpleasant realities because from his perverted point of view they are praiseworthy. The reader follows him with fascinated interest, but with a detestation for him that all of Thackeray's obtrusive moralizing in *Catherine* had not been able to create. Its very indirectness helps to make it a far more powerful moral document than Thackeray had produced before, and it is a worthy offset to the unsound productions of his showily brilliant contemporaries, Bulwer and Ainsworth.

The obvious development of *Barry Lyndon* from Thackeray's earlier work gives us the third name in the trilogy of great realistic novelists who served their apprenticeship in the writing of burlesque. Thackeray's progression to realism is in no essential different from that of Fielding and Jane Austen. All three of them began with writing pure burlesque; then each of them wrote at least one novel which, while not burlesque, was motivated by reaction against the popular novels of their time; finally, each arrived at the maturity of writing novels based on real life rather than on other novels. The fact that three of the greatest English novels *Tom Jones*, *Pride and Prejudice*, and *Vanity Fair*, can be traced in their evolution back through *Joseph Andrews*, *Northanger Abbey*, and *Barry Lyndon* to *Shamela*, *Love and Freindship*, and *Catherine*, gives greater significance and interest to the study of burlesque literature; nor is it surprising to find these three great realistic novelists sharpening their wit with the same instrument that served the authors of *les Précieuses ridicules* and *Love's Labour's Lost*.

XI. THE DECLINE OF THE
BURLESQUE NOVEL

THE early Victorian period saw the rise of the comic magazine. Political, social, theatrical, and literary satire crowded the pages of *Punch* and its rivals: *Funny Folks*, *The Comic News*, *Fun*, *Judy*, and *Punch and Judy*. The new form of burlesque novel which Thackeray had inaugurated in his *Novels by Eminent Hands* was ideal for periodical publication: it was short, it had obvious appeal for literary readers, and it lent itself well to illustration by Cruikshank, Daniel Maclise, 'Alfred Crowquill,' and dozens of other talented cartoonists in which the age abounded. The almanacs and other year-books, such as *Cruikshank's Comic Almanack* and *The Puppet Showman's Album*, and ephemeral periodicals which survived, some of them, for no more than half a dozen issues, like *The Shotover Papers*, *The Bat*, *The Mask*, *Tennis Cuts and Quips*, *The Tomahawk*, also contained many burlesques and parodies of well-known novels.

In 1867 Bret Harte published his *Condensed Novels*, a volume of prose parodies written by the same method as Thackeray's. It was followed in 1870 by *Condensed Novels and other Papers*, which contained the old parodies and a number of new ones; in 1871 appeared *Sensation Novels Condensed*, which again consisted of repetitions and additions. Concise, witty, salient, these deserved and received wide public approval. Even today they can be read with enjoyment, just as Thackeray's can, by a reader who has some acquaintance with the novels that are satirized.

In *Miss Mix*, Bret Hart's parody of *Jane Eyre*, Jane is transformed into Mary Jane and the virile Mr. Rochester into the gorilla-like Mr. Rawjester, who absent-mindedly ties a poker into hard knots with his nervous fingers, heaves a brass candle-stick at the head of the submissive, infatuated governess, and, disguised as a highwayman, ties, gags, robs his guests, locks them in the cellar, and then sets fire to the mansion:

"Burn!" he said, as he shook his fist at the flames. Then sinking on his knees before me he said hurriedly, —

"Mary Jane, I love you; the obstacles to our union are or soon will be removed. In yonder mansion were confined my three crazy wives. One of them, as you know, attempted to kill me! Ha! this is vengeance! But will you be mine?"

I fell, without a word, upon his neck.

Athos, Porthos, Aramis, and D'Artagnan, in Harte's *The Ninety-nine Guardsmen*, interrupt a love passage between Louis XIV and Louise de la Vallière. They respectfully refuse to obey the angry monarch's command, first to arrest each other, and then to arrest themselves:

"What does this mean?"

"It means, your majesty," said Aramis, stepping forward, "that your conduct as a married man is highly improper. I am an abbé, and I object to these improprieties. My friends here, D'Artagnan, Athos, and Porthos, pure-minded young men, are also terribly shocked. Observe, sire, how they blush!"

Athos, Porthos, and D'Artagnan blushed.

"Ah," said the King thoughtfully. "You teach me a lesson. You are devoted and noble young gentlemen, but your only weakness is your excessive modesty. From this moment I make you all marshals and dukes, with the exception of Aramis."

"And me, sire?" said Aramis.

"You shall be an archbishop!"

The four friends looked up and then rushed into each other's arms. The King embraced Louise de la Vallière, by way of keeping them company. A pause ensued. At last Athos spoke, —

"Swear, my children, that, next to yourselves, you will respect the King of France; and remember that 'Forty years after' we will meet again."

The most popular of all Harte's comic pieces was *Lothaw*, a parody of Disraeli's *Lothair*, which reached four editions as a separate volume. Like all of his similar works, it is piquant without being malevolent and critical without being dull.

Another burlesquer of exceptional ability was Sir Francis Cowley Burnand, for many years editor of *Punch*, and the first man to be knighted for his services on that periodical. *Strapmore!*, *The Incompleat Angler*, *The New Sandford and Merton*, and almost all the rest of his parody-burlesque novels will delight the modern reader almost as much as they did the reader of the eighteen-eighties. Walter Parke also deserves mention for *The Skull Hunters*, an uproarious burlesque of the Wild West 'thrillers' of Captain Mayne Reid, whose novel, *The Scalp Hunters*, and almost fifty others like it have 'thrilled to the core' more than one generation of English and American youths. The hero of Parke's inimitable burlesque is Captain Washington Busterville; the heroine is Isabella Maria Elvira Serafina Inez de Fandango, who "possessed 20 per cent. more than the usual amount of beauty which falls to the lot of all Spanish ladies born in Mexico or elsewhere." The modest Captain Busterville narrates his own adventures:

> The prairie was on fire!
> And not only this but tremendous herds of wild beasts, driven by the flames, were rushing towards us!
> "Onward, onward, quick!" I exclaimed to the lady, "or we shall both be everlastingly obliterated!"
> Motionless with terror, she rode on quicker than possible, while I followed at a still greater speed.
> But we had scarcely galloped a few inches, when, on looking towards the east, a frightful yell, like that of a million infuriated baboons, greeted our ears. I knew it only too well. It was the war-cry of the Prawnee Indians.
> They appeared on the horizon; they were rushing towards us; their name was Legion!
> "Jee-roosalem!" I exclaimed, "this is indeed unlucky! . . ."

Other burlesquers of special merit were E. H. Yates, R. B. Brough, The Reverend Edward Bradley ('Cuthbert Bede'), and H. F. Lester. Charles H. Webb, an American humorist, achieved distinction in *St. Twel'mo*, a parody of Mrs. Augusta Ann Evans

Wilson's *St. Elmo*. Andrew Lang, for his *Letters to Dead Authors* and not for his dull parodies of Rider Haggard, deserves to be listed among the better literary satirists.

Victorian burlesques were not always aimed at a particular book or author. By 1840, the post-Scott English novel had been molded into several conventional types: the historical, the fashionable, the maritime, the 'sensational,' and others. *The Comic Almanack*, illustrated by Cruikshank, and supported by the pens of Thackeray, Albert Smith, and Gilbert à Beckett, published in 1846 "Hints to Novelists," suggesting how to begin some of the various types of novels that had been successful. The Read-Up, or Jamesian, should open with: "If we examine closely the records of the past. . . ." The Pseudo-Graphic, or Weak Boz-and-Water: "Any one whom business or pleasure has taken across Hungerford Bridge may have observed. . . ." The Topographical, or Transatlantic: "The long chain of rocky mountains, which, reaching from Oregon to New York. . . ." The Eclogic, or Gorean: " 'Then you will be sure and come?' said Lillie Effingham, as the party of handsome young girls and men with whom she was riding turned through the opening. . . ."

Mrs. Gore and the rest of the 'fashionable' novelists were easy victims for the literary satirist. Thackeray, particularly, was never weary of laughing at them. His *Paris Sketches* contain an essay "On Some French Fashionable Novels"; among the *Character Sketches* is one on "The Fashionable Authoress." In the "Letter to Alexandre Dumas" already mentioned, he deplores the dearth of novels in the middle forties, but adds:

Fashionable novels we get, it is true; the admirable Mrs. Gore produces half-a-dozen or so in a season; but one can't live upon fashionable novels alone, and the mind wearies rather with perpetual descriptions of balls at D ————— House, of fashionable doings at White's or Crocky's, of ladies' toilettes, of Gunter's suppers, of dejeuners, Almack's, French cookery, French phrases and the like, which have been, time out of mind, the main ingredient of the genteel novel with us.

Besides Mrs. Gore, the principal fashionable novelists were Robert Plumer Ward, Benjamin Disraeli, Bulwer-Lytton, Mrs. Mary Elizabeth Braddon Maxwell, Mrs. Henry Wood, 'Ouida,' and Rhoda Broughton, not to mention dozens of lesser ones. They were easily the most popular target among the burlesque writers, and richly deserved to be. Besides the parodies of particular novels and authors listed below, there were, in magazines like *Punch* and *The Comic News*, mock descriptions of the type, which satirized its shallowness, its snobbishness, and its over-colored pictures of high society.

On March 7, 1868, *Punch* announced the formation of the "Sensational Novel Company, Ltd.," with the object of obtaining "the most startling, most thrilling, most exciting, plot by the most original romancers," whether in England or abroad. The members of the company are not mentioned by name, but a list of mock titles of their novels is given

by which we identify, among others: Charles Reade,
Dickens, E. W. Southworth, W. E. Suter, Julia
Kavanagh, Wilkie Collins, and Eugene Sue. The
first novel published by the company was *Chikkin
Hazard*, F. C. Burnand's clever parody-burlesque of
Charles Reade's novel *Foul Play*. The 'sensation'
type of novel, so popular among the readers and so
notorious among the critics of the middle nineteenth
century, had grown directly out of the earlier Newgate novel, and was characterized by its sensational
incidents, its dealing with social problems, and its
over-elaborate attempts at verisimilitude. Next to
the fashionable novel, the Victorian burlesquers
found more material in this than in any other type of
novel. A receipt for a sensational romance is found in
The Comic News for November 12, 1864:

Take a converted Jewess, an athletic parson, and a
Jesuitical colonel of volunteers. Put them in a yacht, and
shipwreck them on a coast of Italy. Bring Garibaldi down
to their rescue. Introduce a quarrel, followed by a duel on
Mount Vesuvius. Wind up with a struggle on the summit.
Lead your victim to the highest pitch of excitement; describe the rolling of the combatants; the noble language of
the herculean curate; the oaths of the Jesuit rifleman. Boil
up the lava to the edge of the crater, and continue in the
next number.

The historical novel continued to be the object of
burlesque, even after the first popularity of Scott had
waned. Besides the parodies of James, Ainsworth,
Dumas, and others mentioned below there were a
number of ironical descriptions of the type in the

humorous magazines. Among the "Eligible Plots for Sale or Hire" in *Funny Folks*, for December 12, 1874, was that of an historical romance:

Plot comprises Baronial castle with moat, portcullis, practicable draw-bridge, and convenient "lowest dungeon beneath the castle moat," in excellent repair. Ardent lover with taste for masquerade, enacting Red Cross Knight in Holy Land. Wicked old baron takes advantage of performance to persecute lovely object of adoration with addresses. Rejected addresses. Sudden appearance of minstrel at castle gate. Masquerading lover in nick of time. Attempted rescue. Lover defeated and convenient occupation of practicable lowest dungeon beneath castle moat. Baron triumphant! No matter; a time will come. So will squadron of Red Cross Knights. Attack on castle, defeat of Baron, rescue of Beauty, ditto of Valour, and indissoluble union. Throw in magicians, jesters, black-dwarfs, &c, at discretion. This plot has paid Scott and lot — handsomely.

Of the half a dozen other burlesques of the historical romance as a type, only one is interesting, and that one merely because its author was Mark Twain. In 1870, *Express* published *An Awful, Terrible Medieval Romance*; it was published again in 1871, bound in the same volume with his *Burlesque Autobiography*. Afterwards, Mark Twain himself rightly judged it to be worthless, and within a year or two bought and destroyed the plates.

Other type-burlesques were written on the nautical novel, the military novel, the 'boat-race' novel, the 'muscular Christian' novel, the novel of social reform, the Wild West novel, and the French novel

about English life. Appearing in the comic magazines, usually in groups of three or four, they are
mostly slight, inconsequential skits, that have no
other importance than to show what kinds of novels
were popular enough to justify ridicule.

It is not surprising that Dickens, the most widely
read author of the time, should have been the one
most often parodied. Disraeli is next, and after him
and very close together, come Ouida and Victor
Hugo; then Miss M. E. Braddon, Wilkie Collins,
G. A. Lawrence, William Black, Charles Reade, Rider
Haggard, and Thomas Hardy. Rhoda Broughton,
the first of whose 'daring' novels was published in the
sixties, was the object of four burlesques before 1883,
one of them by the popular F. C. Burnand. After
that she was not burlesqued at all, although she continued to produce a novel every other year for several
decades. An eloquent explanation is found in the remark she made to a friend, just before her death in
1920: "I began my career as Zola. I finish it as Miss
Yonge. It's not I that have changed, it's my fellow-
countrymen."

The traces of literary satire that are to be found in
the serious Victorian novels can receive no notice
here. Blanche Amory and 'Mes Larmes' of *Pendennis*, Julia Mills and the Desert of Sahara of *David
Copperfield*, and Mr. Knag, the circulating library
proprietor in *Nicholas Nickleby*, must serve as re-
minders of the many characters whose conduct was
affected by the novels they had read. "The Tale of
Baron Grogswig" and "The Bagman's Tale" in *Pick-*

wick Papers illustrate Dickens's early fondness for burlesque narrative. In Trollope's *The Three Clerks*, Charley Tudor, an amateur author, writes a tale called "Crinoline and Macassar; or, My Aunt's Will," which is a burlesque of the Braddon type of fashionable novel. The passages from Arthur Pendennis's first attempt at novel-writing, "Leaves from the Lifebook of Walter Lorraine," are burlesque in effect.

The years from 1867 to 1888 marked the height of the popularity of parody and parody-burlesque novels. During that time more than a hundred were published in England alone: in comic magazines, in newspapers, and as separate volumes. In 1879 *The World*, a London daily newspaper, conducted a parody contest in which prizes were offered for the best prose burlesques "in the manner of Mr. Bret Harte." *The Weekly Dispatch* in 1881, 1882, 1883, and 1885, conducted similar contests, until, as the editor was forced to assert, the talent of his contributors had been exhausted. Meanwhile the art of parody was being seriously discussed in newspaper editorials, in essays, and in reviews; more than thirty articles on the subject appeared within the period mentioned. In 1883, Walter Hamilton published the first volume of his *Parodies of the Works of English and American Authors*. The public demanded more and yet more until in 1888 the sixth and final octavo volume appeared; the supply of parodies had given out, although the demand for them had not. Hamilton's collection contains more than four thousand parodies in verse (most of them of nineteenth century authors) and the most extensive list of prose parodies that has yet appeared.

The parody-burlesque novels of the time were almost all modelled upon those of Thackeray and Bret Harte; but most of the scribblers who produced them, lacking the wit and critical insight of their masters, produced mere facetious imitations, unworthy of the space that the magazines too readily accorded them. It is difficult to conceive how these abortive attempts at humor could have been received with even temporary favor. They had no merit except timeliness. Their feeble puns and far-fetched analogies, their self-conscious, inaccurate sallies at wit, found, however, a favorable audience among Victorian readers.

By 1890, the craze for parodies had attained to such a pitch that literary critics became alarmed about the public morals. "Is parody in accordance with the golden rule?" inquired one reviewer of Hamilton's anthology. Percy Russell, in *A Guide to British and American Novels*, 1894, expressed very strongly indeed the disapproval that had by then become widespread: "It is well . . . to warn the reader that in general literature no taste is so perilous to the mind and character as that for parody. It is a taste that grows intense by over-indulgence, and in excess it ends by becoming a curse rather than a recreation." At first, he goes on to say, it produces harmless laughter, but "may all too readily guide into a confirmed taste which eventually can make only a mockery and a jest of things and thoughts which should remain forever sacred." Such was the apprehensive state of mind to which the late Victorian parodists had brought their critics. Almost a hundred years before, Isaac D'Israeli had written, at the dictate of common sense, the final answer to all such arguments on the subject: "We maintain that, far from converting virtue into paradox, and degrading truth by ridicule, parody will strike at what is chimerical and false; it is not so much a piece of buffoonery as a critical exposition." Most of the literary satire of fifty years ago was, however, 'buffoonery' and little else; it deserves contempt, but hardly serious blame. The worst that can be said of it is that it has unfortunately provided the standard by which many modern readers judge all such writing.

It is hoped that this history has demonstrated that in an earlier day the burlesque novel frequently performed the useful task of criticism and the pleasant one of entertainment. More than any other literary form, perhaps, it has been degraded into triviality by the inept and uninspired; but in the hands of capable writers it has often attained to positive merit. The effectiveness of criticism by the burlesque method has been demonstrated in poetry and the drama by Homer, Aristophanes, Chaucer, Shakespeare, and Molière, to mention only the greatest names. In the field of the novel, Cervantes, by means of *Don Quixote*, pointed out to Fielding, Jane Austen, and Thackeray that one road to criticism of life lay through criticism of literature. As a consequence, each of these three English writers arrived at his realistic method after an apprenticeship in burlesque. Perhaps the greatest claim to distinction that the burlesque novel has is in serving the youth of these writers, and thus assisting at the birth on English soil of that Sancho Panza of literature, the realistic novel.

APPENDIX

APPENDIX

A list of burlesque and parody-burlesque novels that appeared between 1830 and 1900, with brief descriptions of the more important ones. The greater number of them appeared in the humorous periodicals. Some few appeared in annuals and almanacs. Many were published in anthologies, after they had appeared elsewhere. Some others, notably Burnand's, were published separately in volume or pamphlet form. Still others appeared in newspapers, especially between 1860 and 1890, when parody contests were popular. The most extensive list of prose parodies, excepting my own, is that in Walter Hamilton's *Parodies of the Works of English and American Authors* (see *ante*, Chapter XI, p. 243).

WILLIAM HARRISON AINSWORTH

Parody-burlesques of *Rookwood* (1834):
Blueacre. By E. H. Yates and R. B. Brough. Published in *Our Miscellany*, 1857, as "a romance by W. Harrassing Painsworth." It contains burlesque of Ainsworth's other novels and of his style in general.

Parody-burlesque without title. Anonymous. 1884. Published in *Tennis Cuts and Quips.*

GRANT ALLEN (pseud. Cecil Power)

Parody-burlesque of *The British Barbarians, a Hill-top Novel* (1895):
The Barbarous Britishers, a tip-top novel. By Henry Duff Traill. 1896.

THOMAS SHAY ARTHUR

General burlesque of Arthur's novels:
John Jenkins; or, The Smoker Reformed. By Bret Harte. Published in *Condensed Novels and other Papers,*

1870. Burlesques Arthur's "reform" novels, the most famous of which, *Ten Nights in a Bar-room*, was made into an even more famous play. John Jenkins murders two of his children in a fit of drunken anger. He wins his wife's pardon and the parson's commendation by promising to give up the "unclean habit" of — smoking!

Sir James Matthew Barrie

General burlesque of Barrie's novels about Thrums:

Thrums on the Old String. By R. C. Lehman. Published in *"Mr. Punch's" Prize Novels*, 1892, as "by J. Muir Kirrie, author of 'A Door in Convulsions' (*A Window in Thrums*), 'Bald Tight Fiddlers' (*Auld Licht Idylls*), 'When a Man Sees Double' (*When a Man's Single*), 'My Gentleman Meerschaum' (*My Lady Nicotine*)."

Walter Besant

General burlesque of Besant's novels:

The de Cognac. By R. C. Lehman. Published in *"Mr. Punch's" Prize Novels*, 1892, as "by Walter Decant, author of 'Chaplin off His Feet' (*The Chaplain of the Fleet*), 'All Sorts of Editions for Men' (*All Sorts and Conditions of Men*), 'The Nuns in Dilemma' (*The Monks of Thelema*), 'The Cream He Tried' (*The Seamy Side*), 'Blue-the-money Naughty-Boy' (*Ready-Money Mortimer*), 'The Silver Gutter Snipe' (*The Golden Butterfly*), 'All for a Farden Fare' (*All in a Garden Fair*), 'The Roley Hose' (*The Holy Rose*), 'Caramel of Stickinesse' (*Armorel of Lyonesse*)."

William Black

Parody-burlesque of *A Princess of Thule* (1874):

A Princess of Lundy. By H. F. Lester. Published in *Ben D'Ymion and Other Parodies*, 1887, as "by the author of 'Jib-booms and Jury-masts, a Yachting Romance' (*White Wings, a Yachting Romance*), 'The

Strange Adventures of a Fat 'un' (*The Strange Adventures of a Phaeton*), 'Sweet Meadows and Pall Mall' (*Green Pastures and Piccadilly*), 'The Adorable Sinner' (*The Beautiful Wretch*)."
Parody-burlesque of *The Strange Adventures of a Phaeton* (1872):
Strange Adventures of a Pen-Holder. By R. C. Lehman, published in "*Mr. Punch's*" *Prize Novels*, 1892, as "by Wullie White, author of 'They Taught Her to Death' (*A Daughter of Heth*), 'A Pauper in Tulle' (*A Princess of Thule*), 'My Cloudy Glare' (*Macleod of Dare*), 'Green Pasterns in Piccadilli,' (*Green Pastures and Piccadilly*), 'Ran Fast to Royston' (*Stand Fast, Craig Royston!*)." Contains general burlesque of Black's style.
Parody-burlesque of *In Silk Attire* (1869):
In Silk Attire. Anonymous. Published in *The Tomahawk*, July 17, 1869, as "by W —— m B ——k."

RICHARD DODDRIDGE BLACKMORE
Parody-burlesque of *Lorna Doone* (1869):
Marian Muffet: A Romance of Blackmore. By R. C. Lehman, published in "*Mr. Punch's*" *Prize Novels*, 1892, as "by R. D. Exmoor, author of 'Born a Spoon' (*Lorna Doone*), 'Paddock Rowel' (*Cradock Nowell*), 'Wit and Witty' (*Kit and Kitty*), 'Tips for Marriers' (*Cripps, the Carrier*), 'Scare a Fawn' (*Clara Vaughan*), ''Brellas for Rain' (*Alice Lorraine*)," with Lorna as "Little Miss Muffet" and Carver Doone as the spider.

CHARLOTTE BRONTË
Parody-burlesque of *Jane Eyre* (1847):
Miss Mix. By Bret Harte. Published in *Sensation Novels Condensed*, 1871.

RHODA BROUGHTON
Parody-burlesques of *Red as a Rose is She*, (1870):
Jimmy, or, Green as the Grass is He. By "Maid Marion." *The Shotover Papers*. Oxford. 1874–5.

Green as a Leek Was He. By Howell Davies. *The Weekly Dispatch*, February 25, 1883. Published as "by the author of 'Goeth Down Like a Skittle' (*Cometh Up as a Flower*)."

Parody-burlesque of *Not Wisely but Too Well* (1867):

Not Proper but Too True. By T. Alderson Wilson. *The Weekly Dispatch*, February 25, 1883.

General burlesque of Miss Broughton's novels:

Gone Wrong. By Sir F. C. Burnand, 1881. Published as "by Miss Rhody Dendron, authoress of 'Cometh Down like a Shower' (*Cometh Up as a Flower*), 1867, 'Red in the Nose is He' (*Red as a Rose is She*), 'Good! Buy Sweet Tart!' (*Goodbye, Sweetheart*), 'Not Slily, But Don't Tell' (*Not Wisely But Too Well*)."

EDWARD BULWER, LORD LYTTON

Parody-burlesque of *What Will He Do With It* (1858):

The Wrongful Heir; or, What Will They Do With Him. By Walter Parke. Serially in *Judy*, beginning May 12, 1869. Contains some excellent parody of Bulwer-Lytton's dramatic verse. The Epilogue reads: "And now, *lector dulcissimus*, I must say *vale*. The time has come for me to make my Bulwerian bow, previous to my Lyttonian departure, and send for three cabs to carry home the showers of wreaths wherewith I perceive you have already overwhelmed me. I am sure I have convincingly, by the enticing aid of Fiction, proved to you that the Sublime and the Infinite are One, — even a great many more; — that the mysteries of the Rosyposycrucians are not entirely insoluble to men of genius, and that, whatever vicissitudes beset our mortal lot, in the end, Virtue either will or will *not* prevail. In doing this, I have fulfilled all that can reasonably be expected of a human being. Finis."

General burlesques of Bulwer's novels:

The Dweller of the Threshhold. By Bret Harte. Published in *Sensation Novels Condensed*, 1871.

The Diamond Death. Anonymous. Date unknown.
The Puppet Showman's Album. Published as by "Sir
Pelham Little Bulwer, Bart."

Burlesque without title. Anonymous. Published in
The Individual, a Cambridge undergraduate magazine,
November 15, 1836, as "from an unpublished romance,
by the author of 'Eugene Aram.'" It is a general burlesque of Bulwer-Lytton's style. The burlesquer evokes
from the words "NO NOTHING!" an elaborately phrased
meditation on the Beautiful and the True. "The Athenian shapes . . . of ancient and sculptural Greece" floated
before the sight of "the humble and patient scholar,"
as "pageants of INCARNATE INTELLIGENCE, denied to
the rest of mankind, poor gnomes! — toiling in the dark-
some furnace of the earth." There is some parody of
Eugene Aram.

HALL CAINE

Parody-burlesque of *The Bondman* (1890):
   The Fondman. By R. C. Lehman. Published in "*Mr.
Punch's*" *Prize Novels,* 1892, as "by Called Abel, author
of 'The Teamster' (*The Deemster*)."
General burlesque of Caine's novels:
   *Golly and the Christian, or, The Minx and The Manx-
man.* By Bret Harte. Published in *Condensed Novels:
The Two Series Complete,* 1903. General burlesque with
parody of *The Christian,* 1897 and *The Manxman,*
1894.

LEWIS CARROLL

(See Charles Lutwidge Dodgson.)

WILKIE COLLINS

Parody-burlesque of *No Name* (1862):
   No Title. By Bret Harte. Published in *Sensation
Novels Condensed,* 1871.
Parody-burlesque of *The Dead Secret* (1857):

The Dread Secret. By F. P. Delafond. *The Weekly Dispatch*, October 2, 1881.

Parody-burlesque of *The Woman in White* (1860):

The Woman in Tights. By William Evison Rose. *The Weekly Dispatch*, February 25, 1883.

Parody-burlesque of *The Moonstone* (1868):

The Moonstone and Moonshine. Anonymous. *The Mask*, August, 1868.

For parody-burlesques of *No Thoroughfare*, see Dickens.

HUGH CONWAY
(See Frederick John Fargus.)

JAMES FENIMORE COOPER

General burlesques of Cooper's novels:

The Stars and Stripes. By W. M. Thackeray. Published in *Novels by Eminent Hands*, 1847. Contains some good satire on America and Americans.

The First of the Pongimonkees. By Albert Smith. Published in *A Bowl of Punch*, 1848. Contains some parody of *The Last of the Mohicans*, 1826. The hero is named Corduroy Leggings, and the story is about a party of dishonest Red Men who escaped from Catlin's Museum of North American Indians.

Muck-a Muck. By Bret Harte. Published in *Sensation Novels Condensed*, 1871.

MARIE CORELLI

Parody-burlesque of *Wormwood, a Drama of Paris* (1890):

Germfood. By R. C. Lehman. Published in "*Mr. Punch's*" *Prize Novels*, 1892, as "by Mary Morally, author of 'Ginbitters' (*Wormwood*), 'Ardart' (*Ardath*)."

Parody-burlesque of *Ziska: the Problem of a Wicked Soul* (1897):

Zut-ski: the Problem of a Wicked Feme Sole. By Bret

Harte. Published in *Condensed Novels: The Two Series Complete*, 1903.

FRANCIS MARION CRAWFORD

Parody-burlesque of *Mr. Isaacs* (1882):
Mr. Jacobs, A tale of the drummer, the reporter, and the prestidigitateur. By Arlo Bates. Boston, 1883.

MARY ANN EVANS CROSS (pseud. George Eliot)

Parody-burlesque of *Middlemarch* (1873):
Muddlemarsh. By H. F. Lester. Published in *Ben D'Ymion and Other Parodies*, 1887, as "by the author of 'Madam Tree'd' (*Adam Bede*), 'Lamech Jones' (Refers to Lamech, father of Jubal in George Eliot's poem *The Legend of Jubal*, 1870), 'The Spill on the Horse' (*The Mill on the Floss*), 'Ananias Anaconda' (*Daniel Deronda*)." This parody-burlesque is very polite and restrained.

THOMAS DAY

Parody-burlesque of *The History of Sandford and Merton* (1786):
The New History of Sandford and Merton. By Sir F. C. Burnand. 1872. Over two hundred pages in length, very amusing and very popular; virtue is punished and vice rewarded; boys are taught what *not* to do.

DANIEL DEFOE

Parody-burlesques of *Robinson Crusoe* (1719):
Stories for Little Girls: The Story of Miss Crusoe. By Bret Harte. San Francisco. 1865.
The Real Adventures of Robinson Crusoe. By Sir F. C. Burnand. 1893. Burlesquer claims to have the actual facts from the diary of John Robbingson Crewsoe.

LOUISE DE LA RAMÉE (pseud. "Ouida")

Parody-burlesques of *Under Two Flags* (1867):
Blue Blooded Bertie; or, Under Two Fires. Anony-

mous. Serially in *Funny Folks*, August 21, 1875. Burlesques improbability of incident and exaggerated nobility of characters. At the end Cigarette shoots her rival and then Bertie, but simultaneously with the action comes remorse. Cigarette is swifter than her bullet and intercepts it with her own fair head. As she lies dying in Bertie's arms, the general blows his whistle and the twenty-two thousand soldiers who have loved her draw near and shake the desert air with their sobs. Cigarette requests to be buried in England, since she has never been there and this is a good opportunity. "In Kensal Green Cemetery there is a marble slab, carved in the shape of a cigar box. On its lid is this inscription: 'Here lies all that is left of CIGARETTE. Peace to her ashes!' "

Into New Bags. By Walter Parke. *Funny Folks*, July 29, 1876.

Parody-burlesque without title. Anonymous. *The World*, July 2, 1879.

Parody-burlesque without title. By H. Atton. *The Weekly Dispatch*, October 2, 1881.

Cigarette; or, a Bad Weed-ah. By Darjew. *The Weekly Dispatch*, October 2, 1881.

Under Two Fig Trees. By H. F. Lester. 1886. A humorous novel suggested by Ouida, rather than a parody.

Parody-burlesque of *Strathmore* (1865):

Strapmore. By Sir F. C. Burnand. Published before 1878 (5th edition, 1878) in "Our Novel Shilling Series." Republished in a collection of the author's parody novels called *Some Old Friends*, 1892.

Parody-burlesque of *Ariadne* (1877):

Without title. By Gossamer.. *The Weekly Dispatch*, September 13, 1885.

General burlesque of Ouida's novels:

Bluebottles. *A Novel of Queer Society*. Anonymous. Serially in *Judy*, beginning July 7, 1880. Described as a novel "idylised *à la* Ouida."

CHARLES DICKENS

Parody-burlesque of *Christmas Stories* (1843–1847):
Old Joliffe: Not a Goblin Story. By Miss M. A. Planché (afterwards Mrs. Mackarness). 1845. Published as "by the Spirit of a little Bell, awakened by 'The Chimes.'" Contains very subtle but very effective burlesque of Dickens's sloppy-sentimental style. The author's purpose was to show up "that catering to the morbid appetite of the Public for horror, which is the chief characteristic of a certain class of publications."

Parody-burlesque of *The Haunted Man*.
The Haunted Man. By Bret Harte. 1871.

Parody-burlesques of *Dombey and Son* (1847–8):
Dombey and Daughter: a Moral Fiction. By Renton Nicholson. Published in monthly parts during 1847, simultaneously with *Dombey and Son*. Less a burlesque than an avowed attempt to combat unreality with reality: "I think I may, without arrogance, predict that these pages will be read with pleasure by those whose tastes are not vitiated, and who prefer a simple story, representing scenes of real life, to the monstrous productions of a feverish imagination, which have late been received with unmerited though almost universal applause."

Dolby and Father. By "Buz." New York, 1868. There is some burlesque of Dickens's style, but the main purpose is to score the intolerance of the English (especially of Dickens in his *American Notes* and *Martin Chuzzlewit*), toward Americans, and the too great tolerance of Americans toward those who have injured them. The scene is New England.

Parody-burlesques of *No Thoroughfare* (1867), [with Wilkie Collins]:
No Thoroughfare, the Book in Eight Acts. Anonymous. *The Mask*, February, 1868.

No Thorough Fair; or, a Pretty Pass in the Mountains. Anonymous. Serially in *The Serio-Comic Magazine*, beginning in March, 1868. The parody-burlesque, which consists of "five acts and an overture (composed by Offenbach)," contains examples of punning such as: "The clock of St. Paul's has just struck one, and all the other clocks have struck too," and "The streets are empty but the moon is full."

No Throughfare. By "C——s, D——s, Bellamy Brownjohn, and Domby." Boston, 1868. The scene is transferred to Boston and Dickens is scathingly attacked for his *American Notes.*

Parody-burlesque of *Hard Times* (1854):

Hard Times (Refinished). 1857. By E. H. Yates and R. B. Brough. Published in *Our Miscellany* as "by Charles Diggins."

Parody-burlesques of *American Notes for General Circulation* (1842):

English Notes, intended for Very Extensive Circulation! By "Quarles Quickens." Boston, 1842. The best of the burlesques of *American Notes,* but not very good at that. Republished in 1920 by Joseph Jackson and George H. Sargent in a not very convincing attempt to prove that it is by Edgar Allan Poe.

Current American Notes. By Charles Stretch. 1842. Published as "by Buz."

Change for the American Notes; or, Letters from London to New York. By Henry Wood. 1843. Published as "by an American Lady" and thought at the time to be so; but see *The Dickensian,* August, 1908, for proof that the author was Henry Wood, a Yorkshireman.

Some Notes on America to be rewritten: suggested, with respect, to Charles Dickens, Esq. Anonymous. Philadelphia. 1868. A belated attempt to correct, rather than to satirize.

General burlesques of Dickens's novels:

A Christmas Carol: Being a few scattered staves, from a familiar composition, rearranged for performance, by a Distinguished Musical Amateur, during the Holiday Sea-

son at H-w-rd-n (Hawarden). Anonymous. *Punch*, December 26, 1885. Less a parody-burlesque of Dickens than political satire: Bendizzy's ghost appears to Scrooge-stone.

The Cloven Foot: being an adaptation of the English novel, 'The Mystery of Edwin Drood,' to American scenes, customs, and nomenclature. By Orpheus C. Kerr. New York, 1870. Published, with slight modifications, in London as *The Mystery of Mr. E. Drood.* Specimen of an Adaptation, in *The Piccadilly Annual* for December, 1870. An adaptation of Dickens's novel, with some burlesque; but the principal aim is to prove the author's theory "that the notorious lack of the higher order of imaginative writing in this country is due rather to the physical, social, and artistic crudity of the Country than to . . . deficiency . . . of genius."

Parody-burlesque without title. Anonymous. *The World*, July 2, 1879. Parody of Chapter XV of *Martin Chuzzlewit* (1843).

Parody-burlesque without title. Anonymous. 1884. Published in *Tennis Cuts and Quips.* Concerns Mr. Hitquick and The Hitquick Club.

BENJAMIN DISRAELI, EARL OF BEACONSFIELD

Parody-burlesques of *Coningsby* (1844):

Anti-Coningsby; or, The New Generation Grown Old. By "an embryo M. P." (William North). 1844. Two volumes of satire against Disraeli as a writer and as a politician.

Codlingsby. By W. M. Thackeray. Appeared in *Novels by Eminent Hands*, 1847. Previously published in *Punch.* Contemporary newspaper criticism says: "We marvel if Disraelli (sic) could ever again write one of his Oriental absurdities, after his trick has been so marvelously exposed, his fustian so ludicrously reproduced, his style surpassed with such ease even in those parts upon which he most piques himself. It seems to us that if he had been labouring under the author's delusion up to that time, he could not continue in it. He may have believed his melodious assemblage of words was eloquence, and that his descriptions had a gloing truth about them, until Thackeray shoed him how easy such eloquence is, how Holywell-street can be painted with an Oriental brush which shall make the Rose of Sharon gro in its gutters, and the splendour of Damascus glitter in its back parlours."

Parody-burlesques of *Endymion* (1880):

Splendimion; or, The Asian Mystery. By Walter Parke. Serially in *Funny Folks,* beginning December 18, 1880. Published as "a Grand 'Diz'— torical Romance, by the author of 'Vivian Blue' (*Vivian Grey*), 'Hythair' (*Lothair*), 'Cunningsby' (*Coningsby*), 'Black and Tancred' (*Tancred*), 'Henrietta de Temple Bar' (*Henrietta Temple*), 'The Wondrous Tail de Hal Roy!' *Alroy*" Burlesques as usual Disraeli's politics and his penchant for high society, French phrases, gaudy descriptions.

Ben D'Ymion. By H. F. Lester. 1887. *Ben D'Ymion and Other Parodies.* Published as "by the author of 'Loafair' (*Lothair*)."

Parody-burlesques of *Lothair* (1870):

Lothaw; or, The Adventures of a Young Gentleman in Search of a Religion. By Bret Harte. 4th edition May, 1871. Republished in *Condensed Novels: The Two Series Complete,* 1903. It is a very amusing parody-burlesque: "The heroine was . . . slim, but shapely as an Ionic column; her face was Grecian, with Corinthian temples; Hellenic eyes that look from jutting eyebrows like dormer-windows in an Attic forehead, completed her perfect Athenian outline." The Cardinal arrives at the dinner party, saying, "And how do you do, my dears?" in the several different languages that he spoke fluently.

Hythair; or, A Peer's Perplexities. By Walter Parke. *Funny Folks,* September 2, 1876.

Parody-burlesques of *Sibyl* (1845):

Parody-burlesque without title. Anonymous. *The World*, July 2, 1879.

Nihilism in Russia. Anonymous. Published in *The World*, September 17, 1879. Parodies style of *Sibyl*.

Parody-burlesque without title. Anonymous. 1884. Published in *Tennis Cuts and Quips*.

Parody-burlesques of *Tancred* (1847):

Tancredi; or, The New Party. By the Rev. Edward Bradley (Cuthbert Bede). 1856. Published in *The Shilling Book of Beauty* as "by the Right Hon. B. Bendizzy."

De Tankard. Anonymous. Published in *The Puppet Showman's Album* as "by Benjamin Dizzyreally, Esq., M. P." (n. d.) Contains good parody of the style of *Tancred*.

General burlesque of Disraeli's novels:

Endymion; or, a Family Party in Heaven. By William Edmondstowne Aytoun. 1842. Parody-burlesque of *Ixion in Heaven*, which had appeared in *The New Monthly Magazine* in 1832–3. The parody-burlesque was reprinted in Sir Theodore Martin's *Memoir of William Edmonstowne Aytoun*, 1867; and again in the Scholartis Press edition of *Ixion in Heaven*, 1927. It is an amusing take-off of a book which was itself a burlesque. It has no connection with Disraeli's *Endymion*, which was not published until 1880.

CHARLES LUTWIDGE DODGSON (pseud. Lewis Carroll)

Parody-burlesque of *Alice in Wonderland* (1865–6):

Alice in Numberland. Anonymous. Serially in *Fun*, beginning October 9, 1878, as "by the author of 'Through an Opera Glass' (*Through the Looking Glass*), 'The Bunting of the Ark' (*The Hunting of the Snark*)." A very poor parody.

SIR ARTHUR CONAN DOYLE

Parody-burlesque of Sherlock Holmes stories:

The Stolen Cigar Case. By Bret Harte. Published in *Condensed Novels: The Two Series Complete*, 1903.

ALEXANDRE DUMAS

Parody-burlesques of the D'Artagnan romances:

Prrranprrran, the King's Chrysalis! Anonymous. Published in the Christmas number of *The Comic News* for 1864, as "a historical romance by Alexandre Dumoth." Athos becomes a temperance lecturer; Aramis starts a new religion and marries a fortune; Porthos goes on the stage, changing his name to Paul; D'Artagnan becomes a ticket-of-leave man.

The Ninety-nine Guardsmen. By Bret Harte. Published in *Sensation Novels Condensed*, 1871. Excellent parody of some scenes from *le Vicomte de Bragelonne*, as well as burlesque of Dumas' humor and his narrative style.

GEORGE ELIOT

(See Mary Ann Evans Cross.)

FREDERICK JOHN FARGUS (pseud. Hugh Conway)

Parody-burlesque of *Dark Days* (1883):

Much Darker Days. By Andrew Lang (under the pseudonym, A. Huge Longway). 1884. Published as "by the author of 'Scrawled Back' (*Called Back*), 'Unbound' (*Bound Together*), 'The Mystery of Paul Targus.'" This parody-burlesque appeared as a Christmas annual, which attacked the original as being "morally dismal and artistically inefficient." The preface to the second and revised edition of 1885 stated: "Parody is a parasitical, but should not be a poisonous, plant. The Author of this unassuming jape has learned, with surprise and regret, that some sentences which it contains are thought even more vexatious than frivolous. To frivol, not to vex, was his aim, and he has corrected this edition accordingly."

Parody-burlesque of *Called Back* (1885):

Hauled Back. Anonymous. Published as "by U-Go Gone-Away Hug-away." 1885.

CHARLES GIBBON

Parody-burlesque of *For Lack of Gold* (1871):
Wi' Flush O' Siller. By Walter Parke. *Funny Folks*,
August 5, 1876.

JOHANN WOLFGANG VON GOETHE

Parody-burlesque of *The Sorrows of Werther* (1774):
The New Werther. Anonymous. Published in *Fraser's
Magazine* for November, 1846. Burlesque of the senti-
ment and tearfulness of Goethe's novel.

MRS. CATHERINE GRACE FRANCES GORE

General burlesques of Mrs. Gore's novels:
Mammon's Marriage. By the Rev. Edward Bradley
(Cuthbert Bede). Published in *The Shilling Book of
Beauty*, 1856, as "by Mrs. Bore, authoress of 'Mammon
and Salmon' (*Mammon; or, the Hardships of an Heiress*),
'Mothers and Grandmothers' (*Mothers and Daughters*),
'Peers and Peris' (*Peers and Parvenus*)." General burlesque of her "fashionable" novels.
Lords and Liveries. By W. M. Thackeray. Published
in *Novels by Eminent Hands*, 1847, as "by the authoress
of 'Dukes and Déjeuners' (*Peers and Parvenus*), 'Hearts
and Diamonds' (*The Diamond and the Pearl*), 'Marchionesses and Milliners.'" It is a general burlesque
of her novels.

MRS. ALICE SEYMOUR GREY

General burlesque of Mrs. Grey's novels:
The Baby Wife. By the Rev. Edward Bradley (Cuth-
bert Bede). Published in *The Shilling Book of Beauty*,
1856, as "by Mrs. Grayling, authoress of 'The Gambler's
Grandmother' (*The Gambler's Wife*), 'The Cantatrice'
(*Opera-Singer's Wife or Prima Donna*)." Mrs. Alice
Seymour Grey also wrote *Passages in the Life of a Fast
Young Lady*.

Sir Henry Rider Haggard

Parody-burlesques of *She* (1887):

He. By Andrew Lang and W. H. Pollock. 1887. Published as "by the author of 'It' (*She*), 'King Solomon's Wives' (*King Solomon's Mines*), 'Bess' (*Jess*)."

Hee! Hee! Anonymous. Published in *Punch*, February 26, 1887, as "by Walter Wierd author of 'Solomon's Ewers' (*King Solomon's Mines*)."

Parody-burlesque of *King Solomon's Mines* (1886):

King Solomon's Wives; or, The Phantom Mines. By Andrew Lang and W. H. Pollock. 1887. Published as "by Hyder Ragged"; with the hero's name changed from Allan Quartermain to Ananias Quarterman.

General burlesque of Haggard's novels:

The Book of Kookarie. By R. C. Lehman. 1892. This general burlesque of Haggard's novels had appeared previously in *Punch*, as "by Reader Faghard, author of 'Queen Bathsheba's Ewers' (*King Solomon's Mines*) 'Yawn' (*Dawn*), 'Guess' (*Jess*), 'Me' (*She*), 'My Ma's at Penge' (*Maiwa's Revenge*), 'Smallun Halfboy' (*Allan Quartermain*), 'General Porridge, D. T.' (*Colonel Quaritch, V. C.*), 'Me a Kiss' (*Beatrice*), 'The Hemisphere's Ire' (*When the World Shook*)."

James Hannay

General burlesques of Hannay's naval tales:

Jigger of the "Dodo." By E. H. Yates and R. B. Brough. Published in *Our Miscellany*, 1857, as "by the author of 'Sketches in Sky Blue' (*Sketches in Ultra Marine; Nautical Tales*), 'Sangster's History of the Umbrella,' 'Dietrichsen's Almanack,' 'Singleton Glo'ster' (*Singleton Fontenoy: a Naval Novel*)."

Mrs. Belle Boyd Hardinge

Parody-burlesque of *Belle Boyd in Camp and Prison*. London. 1865:

Mary McGillup. By Bret Harte. Published in *Sensa-*

tion Novels Condensed, 1871, as "a Southern novel, after Belle Boyd." It is a very satirical burlesque of Mrs. Hardinge's biographical novel. Belle Boyd was a well-known Confederate spy during the War between the States. After the war she went to London, where she married. It was there also that she made her stage *début* as Pauline in *The Lady of Lyons*. While still resident in England she published her book, with an introduction by a self-avowed sympathizer of the Southern cause. Harte's burlesque attacks the book and the author for unveracity, conceit, and prejudice.

Thomas Hardy

Parody-burlesque of *Far from the Madding Crowd* (1874): *Not Far from the Lowing Herd*. By Edwin Clarke. Published in *The Weekly Dispatch*, October 2, 1881, as "by the author of 'A Pair of Pink Ears' (*A Pair of Blue Eyes*), 'Up in the Greenwood Tree' (*Under the Greenwood Tree*)."

General burlesques of Hardy's novels: *A Rustic Zenobia*. By H. F. Lester. Published in *Ben D'Ymion and Other Parodies*, 1887, as "by the author of 'A Mad World, My Masters!', 'Three on a Walking Tour' (*Two on a Tower*), 'Under the Graveyard Turf' (*Under the Greenwood Tree*), 'All Among the Tombs.'"

Bo and the Blacksheep, A Tale of the Sex, by R. C. Lehman. Published in "*Mr. Punch's*" *Prize Novels*, 1892, as "by Thomas of Wessex, author of 'Guess how a Murder Feels' (*Tess of the D'Urbervilles*), 'The Cornet Minor' (*The Trumpet Major*), 'The Horse that Cast a Shoe' (*The Mayor of Casterbridge*), 'One in a Turret' (*Two on a Tower*), 'The Foot of Ethel Hurt Her' (*The Hand of Ethelberta*), 'The Flight of the Bivalve' (*The Return of the Native*), 'Hard on the Gadding Crowd' (*Far from the Madding Crowd*), 'A Lay o' Deceivers' (*A Laodicean*)." The story of Little Bo-peep told *à la* Thomas Hardy.

BRET HARTE

Parody-burlesque of *The Luck of Roaring Camp* (1868):
  The Luck of Tory Camp. By J. C. Rose. Published in
  The Weekly Dispatch, September 13, 1885, as "by Bread
  Tart." Contains political satire.
General burlesque of Harte's novels:
  His Finger. Anonymous. Published in *The Shotover
  Papers* (Oxford), 1874–5. Parody of Harte's style.

ANTHONY HOPE HAWKINS

General burlesque of Hawkins' novels:
  Rupert the Resembler. By Bret Harte. Published in
  Condensed Novels: The Two Series Complete, 1903. Burlesque of *The Prisoner of Zenda* (1894), and *Rupert
  of Hentzau* (1898).

VICTOR HUGO

Parody-burlesques of *l'Homme qui rit* (between 1865–
69):
  Anticipations of the Derby and *Realities of the Derby.*
  Anonymous. 1869. These two short skits "by a French
  Visitor" tell of the experiences of a Frenchman at the
  Derby in a style which burlesques *l'Homme qui rit.*
  Touchatout, l'Homme qui Rit. Anonymous. 2nd ed.
  Paris. 1869. This "nouveau roman de Victor Hugo"
  was published in New Orleans the same year under the
  title *Parodie de l'Homme qui rit.*
  Grinplaine; or, the man who doesn't laugh. By Walter
  Parke. Serially in *Funny Folks*, beginning November 20,
  1875, as "a romance of un-English history." The burlesquer makes fun of Hugo's ignorance of English
  history.
Parody-burlesques of *Quatre-vingt-treize* (1865–70):
  "31." Anonymous. Published in *Fun*, August 14,
  1878, as "by the author of '93,' 'The History of a
  Grime' (*l'Histoire d'un crime*)." It contains general
  burlesque of Hugo's style:

Chapter I. Searching.

"She was lost! In this world nothing is lost! It is only mislaid. *She* was Miss Lade: yet she was lost! Where was she? She was in London. London is in England. It is a great city — as large as Paris! It is as hard to discover a person in London as 'to find a needle in a bottle of hay.' That is an English phrase. They bottle hay, and rack it, like wine! It is made into chaff. The Scotchman lives on oats, the Irishman on potatoes, the Englishman on chaff!"

One and Three. By Sir F. C. Burnand. Published in *Some Old Friends*, 1892; originally published in "Our Novel Shilling Series" (n.d.) as "by (that distinguished French novelist) Fictor Nogo."

Parody-burlesques of *les Misérables* (1862):
les Misérables pour rire, parodie. By A. Vémar, Paris, 1862.

Fantine. By Bret Harte. Published in *Sensation Novels Condensed*, 1871, as "after the French of Victor Hugo." Excellent parody of Hugo's style.

Parody-burlesque of *What Cheer 'Ria?*:
Quel Bonheur Marie! Anonymous. *The Bat*, June 2, 1885.

Parody-burlesque of *les Travailleurs de la mer* (1866):
The Spoiler of the Sea. By F. P. Delafond. *The Weekly Dispatch*, September 13, 1885.

General burlesque of Hugo's novels:
The Cat. Republished without date or name of author in Walter Hamilton's *Parodies of the Works of English and American Authors*, Vol. VI. 1888.

Ferguson Wright Hume

Parody-burlesque of *The Mystery of a Hansom Cab*:
The Mystery of a Wheelbarrow; or, Gaboriau Gaborooed. Anonymous. 1888.

GEORGE PAYNE RAINSFORD JAMES

Parody-burlesque of *Mary of Burgundy* (1833):
Magnum of Burgundy, a Romance of the Fronde. By Albert Smith. Published in *A Bowl of Punch*, 1848.
General burlesques of James's novels:
Barbazure. By W. M. Thackeray. Published in *Novels by Eminent Hands*, 1847, as "by G. P. R. Jeames, Esq., etc." It has some parody of the Bluebeard theme in *Richelieu*, 1828.
The Page, a Romaunt from English History. By Edmund Hodgson Yates and R. B. Brough. Published in *Our Miscellany*, 1856, as "by Gustavus Penny Royal James."
The Robber of Idleburg. By Walter Parke. Published in *The Comic News*, 1864. James was the author of a novel called *The Robber* and of another called *Heidelburg*.
The Passage of Prawns. Anonymous. Published in *The Puppet Showman's Album* (n.d.), as "by George Prince Regent James."

HENRY JAMES

General burlesque of James's novels:
The Portrait of a Hybrid. By H. F. Lester. Published in *Ben D'Ymion and Other Parodies*, 1887, as "by the author of 'The Cosmopolitans' (*The Bostonians*), 'Crazy Miller' (*Daisy Miller*), 'Whitewashington Square' (*Washington Square*), 'An Interminable Episode' (*An International Episode*)." *The Portrait of a Lady* (1881), and other novels by Henry James, handled with gloves on.

JEROME KLAPKA JEROME

Parody-burlesque of *Three Men in a Boat* (1889):
One Man in a Coat. By R. C. Lehman. Published in *"Mr. Punch's" Prize Novels*, 1892, as "by Jericho Jerrygo, author of 'Stage Faces' (*Stageland*), 'Cheap Words of Chippie Chappie' (*Some Thoughts of an Idle Fellow*)."

RUDYARD KIPLING

General burlesques of Kipling's Indian and Army tales:
Burra Murra Boko. By R. C. Lehman. Published in
"*Mr. Punch's*"*Prize Novels*, 1892, as "by Kippered
Herring, author of 'Soldiers' Tea' (*Soldiers Three*), 'Over
the Darodees' (*Under the Deodars*), 'Handsome Heads
on the Valets' (*Plain Tales from the Hills*), 'More Black
than White' (*In Black and White*), 'Experimental Dit-
tos' (*Departmental Ditties*)."
Stories Three. By Bret Harte. Published in *Condensed
Novels: The Two Series Complete*, 1903. The three stories
are: *For Simla Reasons, A Private's Honor*, and *Jungle
Folk*.

GEORGE ALFRED LAWRENCE

Parody-burlesques of *Guy Livingstone; or, Thorough*
(1857):
*One Against Three: A Romance of the School of 'Guy
Livingstone.'* Anonymous. Published in *The Shotover
Papers; or, Echoes from Oxford*, 1874-5.
Guy Heavystone; or, "Entire." By Bret Harte. Pub-
lished in *Sensation Novels Condensed*, 1871 as "a muscu-
lar novel, by the author of 'Sword and Gun' (*Sword and
Gown*)."
Guy Deadstone; or, The Muscular Christian. By Walter
Parke. Published in *Judy*, 1869. Guy Deadstone quotes
Sophocles, while riding furiously to the hounds.
Guy Dyingstone. By Walter Parke. Published in
Funny Folks, 1875.

CHARLES LEVER

General burlesques of Lever's military novels:
Phil Fogarty, a Tale of the Fighting Onety-Oneth. By
W. M. Thackeray. Published in *Novels by Eminent
Hands*, 1847, as "by Harry Rollicker." Parodies inci-
dents from *Charles O'Malley* (1841).
Terence Deuville. By Bret Harte. Published in *Sensa-*

sation Novels Condensed, 1871. Parodies incidents from *Charles O'Malley* also, and is in other respects strikingly like Thackeray's burlesque.

The Tremendous Adventures of Major Gahagan. By W. M. Thackeray. 1838–9.

Tom Kinnahan; or, The Frays and Fights of a Horse Marine. Anonymous. Published in *The Puppet Show-man's Album*, (n.d.), as "by Charles Heaver, author of the 'Confessions of Larry Jollycur' (*Harry Lorrequer*)."

EDNA LYALL

Parody-burlesque of *Donovan* (1882):

Sonogun. By R. C. Lehman. Published in "*Mr. Punch's*" *Prize Novels*, 1892, as "by Miss Redna Trial, author of 'Wee Jew' (*We Two*), 'A Lardy Horseman' (*Hardy Norseman*), 'Spun by Prating' (*Won by Waiting*)."

CAPTAIN FREDERICK MARRYAT

Parody-burlesque of *Mr. Midshipman Easy* (1836):

Mr. Midshipman Breezy, a Naval Officer. By Bret Harte. Published in *Sensation Novels Condensed*, 1871.

General burlesque of Marryat's novels:

The Flying Dutchman. A Tale of the Sea. By W. E. Aytoun. 1842.

MRS. MARY ELIZABETH BRADDON MAXWELL

Parody-burlesque of *John Marchmont's Legacy* (1863); and of *Lady Audley's Secret* (1862):

Dr. Marchmont's Misery, A Tale of Society, Singularity and Sensation. By Walter Parke. Published in *Judy*, 1868, as "by the author of 'Lady Eleanor's Legacy' (*Eleanor's Victory*), 'Aurora F. Lloyd's Newspaper' (*Aurora Floyd*), 'Sir Jasper's Ten Aunts' (*Sir Jasper's Tenants*), 'The Lady's Mile-and-a-Half' (*The Lady's Mile*), 'The Tail of the Serpent' (*The Trail of the Serpent*), 'Only a Cod' (*Only a Clod*), 'The Captain of the

Vultures' (*Darrell Markham; or, The Captain of the Vulture*), 'Live Sea Weed' (*Dead Sea Fruit*), Etc. Et-cetera, and Settrer."

Parody-burlesque of *Lady Audley's Secret* (1862):

A New Lady Audley. By William Edward Clery (Austin Fryers). 1891.

General burlesque of Mrs. Maxwell's novels:

Selina Sedalia. By Bret Harte. Published in *Sensation Novels Condensed*, 1871, as "by Miss M. E. B — dd-n and Mrs. H-n-y W — d."

GEORGE MEREDITH

Parody-burlesque of *Diana of the Crossways* (1885).

Joanna of the Crossways. By R. C. Lehman. Published in "*Mr. Punch's*" *Prize Novels*, 1892, as "by George Verimyth, author of 'Richard's Several Editions' (*The Ordeal of Richard Feverel*), 'The Aphorist' (*The Egoist*), 'Shampoo's Shaving-Pot' (*The Shaving of Shagpat*)."

JULES MICHELET

Parody-burlesque of "*La Femme.*"

"*La Femme.*" By Bret Harte. Published in *Sensation Novels Condensed*, 1871. In 1843 Michelet published as a sort of social history of France, a series of lectures which he had already delivered; one of them was entitled "La Femme."

OUIDA

(See Louise de la Ramée.)

CECIL POWER

(See Grant Allen.)

VALENTINE CAMERON PRINSEP

Parody-burlesque of *Imperial India, an Artist's Journals* (1872):

Injyable Injia. By Sir F. C. Burnand. Published in

Some Old Friends, 1892, having previously appeared in *Punch*. The parody-burlesque is illustrated with caricatures of the drawings by Prinsep.

CHARLES READE

Parody-burlesque of *Griffith Gaunt; or, Jealousy*, 1865 (1866):

Liffith Lank; or, Lunacy. By Charles H. Webb. New York. 1866. Originally published in *The New York Times*.

General burlesques of Reade's novels:

Handsome is as Handsome Does. By Bret Harte. 1903.

Chikkin Hazard. By Sir F. C. Burnand. 1881. Appeared earlier in *Punch*. Published as "A novel by Charles Readit and Dion Bounceycore," really a parody burlesque in novel form, of the play, *Foul Play*, by Charles Reade and Dion Boucicault, dramatized from Reade's "greatly daring" romance *Foul Play*, 1869.

CAPTAIN MAYNE REID

General burlesque of Reid's novels:

The Pale-faced Warriors. By F. P. Delafond. *The Weekly Dispatch*, February 25, 1883.

The Skull Hunters; or, The Warriors of the Wild West — A Prairie Parody. By Walter Parke. 1887. Reprinted from an early number of *Judy*. Parody-burlesque of *The Scalp Hunters; or, Adventures among the Trappers*, with burlesque of his novels in general, such as: *Osceola, The Seminole; or, the Red Fawn of the Flower Land; The Wild Huntress; or, Love in the Wilderness; Rifle Rangers; or, Adventures in Southern Mexico; Wild Life; or, Adventures on the Frontier*.

WILLIAM CLARK RUSSELL

General burlesque of Russell's novels:

The Mate of the Marlinspike. By R. C. Lehman. Published in "*Mr. Punch's*" *Prize Novels*, 1892, as "by Shark Mussell, author of 'Erect with a Stove in Her' (*The Wreck of the Grosvenor*), 'My Gyp made to Wheeze' (*My Shipmate Louise*), 'The Romance of a Penny Parlor' (*The Romance of Jenny Harlowe*), 'A Hook for the Bannock' (*A Book for the Hammock*), 'Found the Gal on Fire' (*Round the Galley Fire*), 'The Mystery of the Lotion Jar' (*The Mystery of the 'Ocean Star'*), 'The Jokes o' Lead' (*On the Fo'k'sle Head*)."

GEORGE AUGUSTUS SALA

General burlesque of Sala's novels:
Full Fathom Five. By Walter Parke. *Funny Folks*, July 15, 1876. Published as "by the author of 'The Seven Sevres of Salmon' (*Seven Sons of Mammon*), 'The Badmington Steerage' (*Baddington Peerage*), 'The Secrets of the Limelight' (*Gaslight and Daylight*)."

OLIVE SCHREINER

Parody-burlesque of *Dreams* (1890):
Gasps. By R. C. Lehman. Published in "*Mr. Punch's*" *Prize Novels*, 1892, as "by Olph Schreion, author of 'Screams' (*Dreams*), 'The Allegory of an Asian Ranche' (*The Story of an African Farm*)."

JOSEPH HENRY SHORTHOUSE

Parody-burlesque of *Jean Inglesant, a Romance* (1880):
James Fribblesaint. By H. F. Lester. Published in *Ben D'Ymion and Other Parodies*, 1887, as "by the author of 'The Undersized Pedagogue Matthew, a Metaphysical Spiritualistico-sensational Romance' (*The Little Schoolmaster Mark, a Spiritual Romance*)."

HAWLEY SMART

Parody-burlesque of *Long Odds* (1889):
What's the Odds? or, the Dumb Jockey of Jeddington. Published in "Our Novel Shilling Series" as "by Major Jawley Sharp."

HENRY STANLEY

Parody-burlesque of *In Darkest Africa* (1872):
Across the keep-it-dark Continent; or, How I found Stanley. By Sir F. C. Burnand. Published in *Some Old Friends*, 1892, having previously appeared in *Punch*.

HENRIETTA ELIZA VAUGHAN STANNARD (pseud. John Strange Winter)

General burlesque of Mrs. Stannard's novels:
Mignon's Mess-Room. By R. C. Lehman. Published in "*Mr. Punch's*" *Prize Novels*, 1892, as "by Tom Rum Summer, author of 'Mignon's Ma' (*Mignon's Secret*), 'Mignon's Hub' (*Mignon's Husband*), 'Footle's Father' (*Bootle's Baby*), 'Tottle's Tootsie, 'Ugly Tom' (*Beautiful Jim*), 'Your Rich Richard' (*My Poor Dick*), 'A Baby in Barracks' (*Siege Baby*), 'Stuck' (*Pluck*), 'Horp-Love' (*Houp-la*), 'Went for that Policeman' (*He Went for a Soldier*)."

ROBERT LOUIS STEVENSON

Parody-burlesques of *Treasure Island* (1883):
A Buccaneer's Blood-bath. By R. C. Lehman. Published in "*Mr. Punch's* "*Prize Novels*, 1892, as "by L. S. Deevenson, author of 'Toldon Dryland' (*Across the Plains*[?]), 'The White Heron' (*The Black Arrow*), 'Wentnap' (*Kidnapped*), 'Amiss with a Candletray' (*The Master of Ballantrae*), 'An Outlandish Trip' (*An Inland Voyage*), 'The Old Persian Baronets' (*The New Arabian Nights*)."
The Pirate's Hand. A Romance of Heredity. Anonymous. Published in *Judy*, 1888, as "by the author of 'The Strange Case of Doctor Shuffle and Mr. Glyde.'"

EUGENE SUE

Parody-burlesque of *les Mystères de Paris* (1842):
Sir Brown: A Mystery of London. By Albert Smith.

Published in *The Shilling Book of Beauty*, 1856, as "by Mons. Dernier Sou, author of 'Mysteries of Everywhere.'"
Parody-burlesque of *le Juif errant* (1844–45):
    Parodie du Juif errant. By Charles Philipon and Louis Huart. Brussels, 1845. Translated into English in 1846, by E. Appleyard, as *The Parody of the Wandering Jew.*

WILLIAM MAKEPEACE THACKERAY

General burlesques of Thackeray's novels:
    The Coachman, The Cook, and Their Prodigy the Page. By the Rev. Edward Bradley (Cuthbert Bede). Published in *The Shilling Book of Beauty*, 1856, as "by Wm. Breakpeace Thwackaway." Burlesques Thackeray's satirico-facetious style in *The Yellowplush Papers*, etc.
    Mrs. Tippikens' Yellow Velvet Cape. Anonymous. Published in *The Puppet Showman's Album* (n.d.), as 'by W. M. Thwackaway.'"

ANTHONY TROLLOPE

General burlesques of Trollope's novels:
    The Beadle; or, The Latest Chronicle of Small-beerjester. By Sir F. C. Burnand. Serially in *Punch*, beginning July 10, 1880. Published as "by Anthony Dollop, author of 'Beerjester Brewers' (*Barchester Towers*), 'The Halfway House at Aleinton' (*The Small House at Allington*), 'Thorley Farm for Cattle' (*Orley Farm*), 'Family Parsonage' (*Framley Parsonage*), 'The Prying Minister' (*The Prime Minister*), 'Pearls before Swine; or, Who Used his Diamonds' (*The Eustace Diamonds*), 'Rub the Hair' (*Ralph the Heir*), 'The Way We Dye Now' (*The Way We Live Now*), 'Fishy Finn' (*Phineas Finn*), 'Fishas Wildux' (*Phineas Redux*), 'Dr. Thorne and David James' (*Dr. Thorne*), 'Star and Garter, Richmond' (*Castle Richmond*), 'Rachel Hooray' (*Rachel Ray*), 'The Jellies of Jelly' (*The Kellys and O'Kellys*), 'The Bertrams and

Roberts' (*The Bertrams*), 'Lady Pye-Anna' (*Lady Anna*), 'Tails of All Creatures' (*Tales of All Countries*), "'Arry 'Otspur' (*Sir Harry Hotspur of Humble Thwaite*), 'Mary Greasily' (*Mary Gresley*), 'Vicar of Pullbaker' (*Vicar of Bullhampton*), 'McDermott of Balladsingerun' (*Macdermots of Bally-cloran*), 'Can't You Forget Her?' (*Can You Forgive Her?*), 'He Knew He Could Write' (*He Knew He was Right*)." It is a parody-burlesque of *The Warden*, (1853), *The Last Chronicle of Barset*, (1867), and all the "Cathedral Novels." Republished in *Some Old Friends*, by F. C. Burnand. 1892.

Parody-burlesque without title. Anonymous. Published in *Tennis Cuts and Quips*, 1884. General burlesque of "Cathedral Novels"; speaks of "Ballchester Towers."

JULES VERNE

General burlesque of Verne's pseudo-scientific novels:
Through Space on a Formula. By R. C. Lehman. Published in "*Mr. Punch's*" *Prize Novels*, 1892, as "by Rules Spurn, author of 'Gowned and Curled in Eighty Stays' (*Around the World in Eighty Days*), 'Twenty Thousand Tweaks Sundered the Flea' (*Twenty Thousand Leagues under the Sea*), 'A Tea with Ice' (*A Winter amid the Ice*), 'A Doctor on Rocks and Peppermint' (*Dr. Ox's Experiment*), 'A Cab-fare from the Sun' (*From the Earth to the Moon and a Trip around It*), 'The Confidence of the Continent' (*The Secret of the Island*), 'Attorney to Dissenters up at Perth' (*A Journey to the Centre of the Earth*), 'Lieutenant Scattercash' (*Captain Hatteras*)."

IZAAK WALTON

Parody-burlesques of *The Compleat Angler*:
The Incompleat Angler. By Sir F. C. Burnand. 1876. This deservedly popular parody-burlesque went into several editions.

The Milkmaid's Song

"Come live with me and be my Spouse,
    We'll keep a Cottage, Pigs, and Cows;
    And I will dress in Lace and Silk,
    While you shall Pig, and Dig, and Milk.

"There you will Work and Hoe all day,
    While I enjoy myself, Away.
    If this you'll do, we'll have no Rows,
    Come live with me and be my Spouse!"

Walton's Angler Imitated. Anonymous. Published in several installments in *Punch and Judy*, 1869.

Mrs. Humphry Ward

Parody-burlesque of *Robert Elsmere*, (1888):
    Bob Sillimere. By R. C. Lehman. Published in "*Mr. Punch's*" *Prize Novels*, 1892, as "by Mrs. Humphry John Ward Preacher, author of 'Master Sisterson' (*Miss Bretherton*)."

Edward Noyes Westcott

Parody-burlesque of *David Harum*, (1898):
    Dan'l Borem. By Bret Harte. Published in *Condensed Novels: The Two Series Complete*, 1903.

Augusta Ann Evans Wilson

Parody-burlesque of *St. Elmo* (1866):
    St. Twel'mo; or, the Cuneiform Cyclopedist of Chattanooga. By Charles H. Webb. New York. 1867. A review in *The Nation* said: "How much 'St. Elmo' deserves ridicule and how hard it must have been to made an effective travesty of it sufficiently appear from this, that Mr. Webb has been able to incorporate with 'St. Twel'mo' whole pages of 'St. Elmo'. His premeditated absurdities are so exactly in keeping with

Miss Evans' unconscious silliness that only one who remembers 'St. Elmo' would ever suspect in 'St. Twel'mo' diversity of authorship; to use Mr. Webb's joke, 'a little Evans leaveneth the whole lump.'"

JOHN STRANGE WINTER

(See Henrietta Eliza Vaughan Stannard.)

MRS. HENRY WOOD

General burlesque of Mrs. Wood's novels:

Selina Sedalia. By Bret Harte. Published in *Sensation Novels Condensed*, 1871, as "by Miss M. E. B—dd-n and Mrs. H-n-y W—d."

EDMUND HODGSON YATES

Parody-burlesque of *Black Sheep* (1867):

Ba! Ba! Black Sheep. Anonymous. Published in *The Mask* for June, 1868. Yates's novel had been turned into a successful play; the parody-burlesque is supposed to be the play turned back into the novel.

GENERAL AND UNIDENTIFIED BURLESQUES

The Adventures of John Longbowe, Yeoman. By Bret Harte. Published in *Condensed Novels: The Two Series Complete*, 1903. This "Modern-antique Realistic Romance" is in general burlesque of historical romances, with special reference to A. Conan Doyle's, such as *The White Company*, 1890.

The Hoodlum Band; or, The Boy Chief, The Infant Politician, and the Pirate Prodigy. By Bret Harte. Published in *Condensed Novels: The Two Series Complete*, 1903.

The Lost Heiress, A Tale of the Oakland Bar. By Bret Harte. Published in *The Golden Era* (California), February 24, 1861, under the pseudonym "J. Keyser." It is a burlesque of the "fashionable" love romance. One of the earliest that he wrote, it is not included in *Condensed Novels*.

N. N. By Bret Harte. Published in *Sensation Novels Condensed*, 1871, as "a novel in the French paragraphic style." Parodies the style of Hugo and Dumas.

Stonybroke. By R. C. Lehman. Published in *"Mr. Punch's" Prize Novels*, 1892. The burlesquer allows the reader one guess at the authorship of this Boat-Race Novel. It tells of a boat race between Oxbridge and Camford. All the participants are noblemen. Oxbridge wins through the prowess of the hero, Lord Stonybroke.

Who'd Be a Sailor, A Story of Blood and Battle. By R. C. Lehman. Published in *"Mr. Punch's" Prize Novels*, 1892. It is a burlesque of novels which give "a prophetic but accurate account of the naval battle of the immediate future."

Crinoline. By W. M. Thackeray. Published in *Novels by Eminent Hands*, 1847, as "by Je-mes Pl-sh, Esq." It is a burlesque against the French authors of the time who undertook to write about England and the English without understanding the subject. The principal character is "Munseer Jools de Chacabac," who, prepared for the task by having read *The Vicar of Wakefield* in the original, comes to London to write a series of articles about British life for his Paris newspaper. He might stand for Dumas, Soulié, Roger de Beauvoir, or others whom Thackeray had laughed at for the same thing in his *Paris Sketches*. There is also some burlesque of G. P. R. James and Disraeli.

A Plan for a Prize Novel. By W. M. Thackeray. 1847. Suggestions for a fashionable novel in the French style; the author was to receive an additional rake-off from certain commercial firms whose products he would advertise in describing the dress of his fashionable characters.

Decourcy: A Fashionable Novel. By Albert Smith. Published in *A Bowl of Punch*, 1848. Burlesque of the "fashionable" novels, such as *De Clifford; or, The Constant Man*, 1841, by Robert Plumer Ward. Nearly all of the heroes of "fashionable" novels had the aristocratic *de* before their surnames.

The Bishop of Blackberry's Secret, A Sensation in Three Chapters. Anonymous. Published in *Funny Folks*, February 27, 1875.

The Desperado of the Wilderness. Anonymous. Published in *Gleanings from "The Blue,"* 1881. Burlesque of "Boys of England" type of story.

The London Fog; or, The Butcher of Grosvenor Square. Anonymous. Published in *Fraser's Magazine* for December, 1846, as "passages from an unpublished French novel." Like Thackeray's *Crinoline*, it burlesques the ignorance of French writers who write about England and the English; it is aimed at Eugene Sue, Paul de Kock, George Sand, and probably at Dumas and Hugo. The introduction to Sue's *le Juif errant* (1844–5), is directly parodied.

Young Harry; or, With the Haz Pirates from the Hebrides to the Havannas. Anonymous. Serially in *Punch*, beginning March 11, 1882, as the first of the series: "Our Boys Novelist, being Stories of Wild Sport and Stirring Adventure, for the Amusement and Instruction of the Youths of all Nations." It is represented as being "by the author of 'The Madcap Middies,' and 'The Menniaque Indians of the Strait West Coast.'"

Wet Bob; or, The Adventures of a Little Eton Boy amongst the Hot-whata Cannibals. Anonymous. Published in *Punch*, April 22, 1882, as the second and last of the series, "Our Boys Novelist." It is represented as being "by the author of 'The Three Young Benchers, and How they all Got the Woolsack,' and 'From Back Yard to Yard-Arm.'"

BIBLIOGRAPHY

BIBLIOGRAPHY

THE following is a selected list of books and articles dealing directly or indirectly with fictional parody and burlesque. Professor Richmond P. Bond's *English Burlésque Poetry, 1700–1750* has been listed here mainly because of its excellent bibliography, to which I refer the reader interested in the broader aspects of burlesque.

I wish to acknowledge my indebtedness to the following works, not mentioned in the footnotes or bibliography, which have been helpful in dealing with particular parts of my subject: *The Tale of Terror*, by Edith Birkhead, London, 1921; *The Early American Novel*, by Lillie Deming Losche, New York, 1930; *Dickens, Reade and Collins, Sensation Novelists*, by Walter C. Phillips, New York, 1919; and *The Haunted Castle: A Study of the Elements of English Romanticism*, by Eino Railo, London and New York, 1927. I also wish to thank Miss Winifred Husbands of The University of London for allowing me to use in manuscript form her Master's thesis containing a valuable descriptive list of English novels from 1780–1800; and Mr. Robert A. Lancaster, Jr., Secretary of the Virginia Historical Society, for allowing me to see and to use the manuscript reading list kept by his ancestress, Madame M. M. de Rieux, from 1806–1822.

Anonymous, Review of Delepierre's *La Parodie chez les Grecs*, etc., *The Athenaeum*, July 1, 1871.

——, Leader on parody, *The Daily News*, December 3, 1888.

——, Leader on parody, *The Family Herald*, July 28, 1888.

——, Leader on parody, *The Globe*, November 17, 1880.

——, Leader on Parody, *The Saturday Review*, February 14, 1885.

284   BIBLIOGRAPHY

Bennett, H. R., *Literary Parody and Burlesque in the Seventeenth and Eighteenth Centuries*, M.A. thesis, University of London, 1914.*

Bond, Richmond P., *English Burlesque Poetry, 1700–1750*, Cambridge (Mass.), 1932.

Delepierre, Octave, *La Parodie chez les Grecs, chez les Romains, et chez les modernes*, London, 1870.

D'Israeli, Isaac, *Curiosities of Literature*, Article on parody, London, 1791–1834.

Hamilton, Walter, ed., *Parodies of the Works of English and American Authors*, London, 6 vols., 1885–1889.

Jerrold, W. and Leonard, R. M., *A Century of Parody and Imitation*, London, 1913.

Kitchin, George, *A Survey of Burlesque and Parody in English*, London and Edinburgh, 1931.

Leonard, R. M. and Jerrold, W., *A Century of Parody and Imitation*, London, 1913.

L'Estrange, A. G., *A History of English Humour*, London, 2 vols, 1878.

Martin, A. S., *On Parody*, New York, 1896.

Matthews, Brander, Article on parody, *The Galaxy*, May, 1874.

Millevoye, Charles H., *Satire des romans du jour*, Paris, 1802.

Montespin, M. le Père de, *Traité des belles-lettres sur la poésie française*, Avignon, 1747.

Morillot, P., *Scarron et la genre burlesque*, Paris, 1888.*

Moss, Mary, "The Last of the Burlesquers," *The Bookman*, February, 1903.

Reives, Blanche, *Is Burlesque Art?* London, 1880.

* Quoted from the bibliography of *English Burlesque Poetry, 1700–1750*, by Richmond P. Bond.

Rogers, Winfield H., "The Reaction against Melodramatic Sentimentality in the English Novel, 1796–1830," *Publications of the Modern Language Association*, March, 1934.

Russell, Frances Theresa, *Satire in the Victorian Novel*, New York, 1920.

Russell, Percy, *A Guide to British and American Novels*, London, 1894, pp. 106–107.

Stone, C. R., *Parody*, London, [1915].

Walker, Hugh, *English Satire and Satirists*, London, 1925.

Watkins, M. G., Article on Charles Cotton, *The Gentleman's Magazine*, February, 1884.

Wright, Thomas, *A History of Caricature and Grotesque in Literature and Art*, London, 1865.

INDEX

INDEX